William McKendree Gwin,
whose name is almost unknown to Americans today, was ~ ̣ ̣ ̣ ̣ ̣ ̣ ̣ ̣go.

BETWEEN TWO EMPIRES

The Life Story of California's First Senator

WILLIAM McKENDREE GWIN

Also by Lately Thomas

A Debonair Scoundrel

*The Vanishing Evangelist:
The Aimee Semple McPherson
Kidnaping Affair*

Sam Ward: "King of the Lobby"

Delmonico's: A Century of Splendor

*The First President Johnson:
The Three Lives of the Seventeenth
President of the United States*

BETWEEN

TWO EMPIRES

The Life Story of California's First Senator

WILLIAM McKENDREE GWIN

BY

LATELY THOMAS

HOUGHTON MIFFLIN COMPANY BOSTON

1969

A portion of
this book originally appeared
in American Heritage
in April 1964.

E
415
.9
.G9358

TO
NEMESIS

"Gwin . . . the almighty providence of California."

Hubert Howe Bancroft

Contents

Illustrations

Introduction

AN ATTEMPT TO write the life of William McKendree Gwin presents unusual hazards for several reasons.

First, because of the dearth of significant original sources — letters and personal records, which can reveal the springs of character, clarify motives, and explain actions. Gwin was a public man who preserved his papers, only to suffer the double calamity of having them burned twice — once by the army of General Grant during the Civil War, and again in the destruction of the family home in the 1906 San Francisco earthquake and fire.

Second, because of the extraordinary confusion that marks the many allusions to Gwin to be found in accepted works of history. These follow a singularly repetitive pattern, at one moment describing him as a politician of great ability and untiring zeal, a senator who served California brilliantly during its critical formative years and accomplished much of lasting value; and then, perhaps in the same passage, depicting him as morally mean, a crafty, sly schemer, prompted by sordid motives and impelled by greed, without a shred of statesmanship.

The two halves of this picture do not fit together to make up the semblance of a man. Somewhere along the line, it appears, Gwin was judged erratically, it may be misjudged, and successive historians accepted the first appraisal without corroborative investigation.

To arrive at a more convincing portrait of the man, good or bad, was the purpose of this study. Gradually, as information was acquired, the outlines of a remarkable personality emerged, projected across a broad band of time and territory. Primitive Texas, plantation life in Tennessee, turbulent early Mississippi, the California gold rush, the United States Senate during momentous debates, Paris in the glittering Second Empire, the dreamlike, visionary empire of Maximilian in Mexico — Gwin moved amid these, and not inconspicuously.

Inducted into politics by Andrew Jackson, he remained politically active until his death in the administration of President Grover Cleveland. An opportunist in the healthy, adventurous sense of the word — quick to detect and seize a legitimate chance to advance himself or the people whose advocate he became — he gave all his talents to the service of California and laid that state under a debt to him that was simply enormous. In the maelstrom of wartime passions his fame suffered, he was politically cut adrift, and today his name is hardly recalled except by specialists and historians. Yet for that very reason, because of the long obscurity, his story contains elements of novelty, of discovery and surprise seldom to be met in the biography of a public man.

Further research may sharpen the features of the portrait presented here. Meanwhile, this narrative may serve to acquaint our time with a man of consequence in his own era, whose life was a romance of achievement and frustration, and whose services to his nation are still visible and fruitful, although his name has been dimmed by the mists of time.

ENTER: lawyer, doctor, senator, state-builder, and interrogator of emperors — William McKendree Gwin.

PART ONE

An Empire Gained

Chapter I

THE DAY WAS gray and cold. Scudding clouds spat down flurries of sleet and snow. But the mood of the throngs lining the avenue was boisterous and lighthearted. The date was Monday, March 5, 1849, the place the city of Washington, and the event the inauguration of a new President of the United States — Zachary Taylor, "Old Rough and Ready," hero of Buena Vista and Monterrey in the late war with Mexico and victorious standard-bearer of the Whig party. March 4, the day prescribed for the inauguration, falling upon Sunday, the formalities and festivities had been postponed, inasmuch as the merrymaking (three inaugural balls were planned) would hardly become the decorum due the Sabbath.

Crowds milled through the streets. Spectators waved flags and streamers from windows and housetops as the Presidential parade moved slowly toward the White House. Seated in an open carriage drawn by four white horses, the new President lifted his hat repeatedly in acknowledgment of the cheers. Sunk in a corner was the retiring President, James Knox Polk of Tennessee. He did not lift his hat in response to the cheers. Four arduous years in the office which he had not coveted, had accepted with reluctance, had filled with fidelity, and was laying down with relief, had drained Polk's vitality; he would survive this day by only three months.

On the steps of Willard's Hotel two men stood watching the noisy procession. In appearance they offered a striking contrast: one tall and erect, with aquiline features and a mane of

silver-gray hair; the other short, with a massive head on a
stocky body, and dark, brooding eyes. Neither man smiled as
the bands blared past. Both were Democrats, and for their
party the rejoicings heralded the beginning of four barren
years out of power. All around them patronage-parched Whigs
were gloating in anticipation of dividing the spoils of victory.

Eying the parade morosely, the short man wondered aloud
what might be his companion's plans now. Without hesitation, the tall man responded that he was heading for California.

California? The stocky man — who was Stephen A. Douglas, United States senator from Illinois — seemed startled, and
his friend explained. The Congress that had just adjourned,
he said, had imitated its predecessor in failing to provide a
government for California, an area that was filling up with
gold hunters and immigrants. Thousands of Americans were
pouring into the region, but the protection of a territorial government had been denied them. Conditions there were
chaotic, intolerable, and the people would not endure them
much longer. Since Congress had shirked its responsibility,
the Californians would be forced to organize their own government as a state and seek admission to the Union. That policy,
the tall man concluded, he was going to California to advocate
and "to advocate with success." Within twelve months from
that day, he predicted, he would hand Senator Douglas his
commission as a United States senator from the new state of
California, for transmittal to the clerk of the Senate.

Douglas pondered this extraordinary prediction. None knew
better than he the obstacles that lay in the path of an aspirant
to the United States Senate, and the audacity of the proposal
was obvious. Nevertheless, after a moment's reflection, he
turned to his companion and said that he believed the latter
would carry it through, and heartily wished him success.

The tall man lifted his hat in salute and strode into the hotel.

Eleven months later — having traveled to California and back and carried out his program to the letter — the tall man handed Senator Douglas his credentials as United States senator from the fledgling state of California.

The name of this personification of self-confidence was William McKendree Gwin. A familiar figure in Washington, he was known popularly, there and elsewhere, as Dr. Gwin.

2

A man who could plan such a program of action and carry it to completion with so little bravado was not of ordinary stature. On what basis of reason was that prediction of March 5, 1849, made? And what caused Stephen A. Douglas, who was as canny a politician as Washington contained, to conclude that Dr. Gwin would do what he said?

Two factors, two forces, had been at work to produce that seemingly offhand announcement — brilliant imagination, that gave an insight into things to come, and the ability to see things as they are. His heritage helped. By blood he was Welsh, and the Welsh are a nimble-witted, subtle people. As a race they are endowed with poetic imagination and an acuity of calculation which baffled Englishmen sometimes have called cunning, although significantly never "low cunning." The craftiness of the Welsh is that of Merlin the magician, not the lumpish knavery of Caliban.

William McKendree Gwin had this free-ranging imagination and power of calculation conjoined. In addition, he was a product of the American frontier, and possessed the alertness and readiness for swift action that characterizes the pioneer who dwells amid constant peril and is inured to taking risks. In Gwin, natural sharpness had been whetted to a fine edge of efficiency by years of fruitful practice.

His family's history was solid but not spectacular. His fa-

ther, James Gwin, came from Wales shortly after the Revolutionary War and settled at Charleston, South Carolina. But
soon he moved into the hill country along the western border
of the state. In the autumn of 1791, attracted by reports of
fertile lands to be obtained beyond the mountains, he joined a
wagon train of twenty families heading for Tennessee. The
passage through the Cumberland Gap and along Boone's Trail
was accomplished safely, although Gwin stated laconically
that at times the Indians were "troublesome."

James Gwin took up a holding near Fountain Bend, in the
northern part of Sumner County, northeast of Nashville in
Middle Tennessee. There he prospered. Occasionally he
fought Indians in Kentucky and Tennessee, acquiring a reputation as a marksman, and he formed a close friendship with
his neighbor, Andrew Jackson.

The plantation society of Middle Tennessee followed the
pattern prevailing in tidewater Virginia and the Carolinas.
The settlers were patrician in spirit, Southern in customs and
sympathies, and in addition had a special sturdiness imparted
by frontier conditions. Growing wealthy from the cotton and
tobacco they cultivated, the Tennessee aristocrats built spacious, airy homes designed for hospitality, and the pride
they took in these handsome country seats was evidenced by
the names they gave them — Cragfont, Clifton Place, Fair-
view, the Hermitage, Carnton, Rattle and Snap. When Methodist Bishop Francis Asbury visited Nashville in 1800, he was
surprised by its already populous, settled appearance. The
bishop preached (he noted in his journal) to "not less than a
thousand people in and around the stone church; which, if
floored, ceiled, and glazed, could be a grand house." These
improvements were soon added as the town burgeoned into
"a center of refinement and culture."

One of the first Methodist missionaries in Tennessee was
William McKendree, a Virginian who had fought in the Con-

tinental army during the Revolutionary War, and in 1787 entered the ministry. He preached through the western settlements and became the first presiding elder in that area. In 1808 he was elected the first American-born bishop of his church.

James Gwin, a thorough Welshman, was deeply religious, and in 1803 he entered the Methodist ministry, in part inspired by the example of his intimate friend, McKendree. Parson Gwin rapidly became noted in the region for his energetic piety and powerful exhortations to repentance. Intensely patriotic, in the War of 1812 he enlisted as chaplain of the Tennessee Volunteers, going with them to New Orleans; and in the battle General Jackson rated his neighbor's fighting qualities so highly he placed the parson in command of fourteen hundred sharpshooters in the second line of defense. The appointment carried the rank and title of colonel, but Gwin preferred to be known simply as a clergyman. A story long cherished in Tennessee illustrated his independence and pugnacity. When a quartermaster sneered at the chaplain's black coat, Gwin took it off and thrashed the scoffer into a respectful mood. Then pulling on his coat, he knelt and prayed just as vigorously for the quartermaster's salvation.

Such a man was bound to be popular in a frontier community, and Parson Gwin was known and loved far and wide. A contemporary expressed the general estimate of him as "a sturdy pioneer of religion and patriotism . . . a man of pronounced ability and great decision of character, an evangelist in the pulpit, a soldier when the frontier had to be defended, and enjoying, through life, the confidence and respect of Andrew Jackson." No higher commendation could be bestowed in Tennessee.

*

3

James Gwin had several sons. The first he named Samuel, for the biblical connotation; the second he baptized William McKendree, in honor of his good friend. William McKendree Gwin was born in the family home on October 9, 1805. To place the date of the boy's birth in its historical perspective: in October, 1805, Thomas Jefferson had just begun his second term in the White House; Robert Fulton would not launch the *Clermont* as the first successful steamboat for two years to come; and only a year had passed since Aaron Burr had killed Alexander Hamilton in the most famous duel, up to that time, in American political annals. Five other children would be born to James Gwin, but of these, only William McKendree would attain national prominence.

The family's circumstances being easy, young William received the best education the region could provide. In the Southern style, he studied with tutors until ready to read law in nearby Gallatin, where he was admitted to the bar at the age of twenty-one.

Immediately he gave evidence of that independence of decision which later would characterize his actions. The Tennessee bar at that time was renowned for brilliance. Young Gwin appraised the situation, and concluded that it would be hopeless for a newcomer to compete against so much established talent; he had no confidence in his ability to sway a jury, or to make a public speech of any kind. Consultation with his father resulted in William's deciding on a medical career, and he was enrolled in Transylvania College, at Lexington, Kentucky. This was the most progressive college west of the Alleghenies, and Gwin was forced to work hard at his studies. In March, 1828, he submitted his thesis (twenty-three closely written pages on the subject "Syphilis") and received his medical degree.

The next question was where to practice. Gwin was ambitious and energetic. He had the pride of his class, but did not shrink from striking out for himself. Mississippi, recently made a state, was attracting settlers from Tennessee, and Gwin reasoned that opportunities would be greater in a new, growing community. So he joined the movement and hung out his shingle in Vicksburg. Shortly, however — again with a shrewd eye to the future — he moved to Clinton, a town west of Jackson which seemed likely to become the capital of the state. There Dr. Gwin practiced medicine successfully for six years.

The principal interest and recreation throughout rural and small-town America at that period was the discussion of political questions. Men of talent and ambition entered politics because it offered the most direct road to power and social eminence. In the South especially, political leadership was honorable, resting in the hands of the wealthy planter class. Commerce was considered beneath the dignity of gentlemen, whereas public office was their perquisite, and statecraft theirs by inheritance. In Mississippi this attitude was somewhat modified by the frontier conditions, and men of good family were able to pursue wealth without losing caste; but politics was the preferred occupation for those who considered themselves born to rule, and the favorite topic among all classes, high and low.

The politics of Mississippi were turbulent, like those of any yeasty new state. Its population was made up of three diverse elements whose interests mutually clashed. Around Natchez was a nucleus of large landowners, proprietors of plantations worked by gangs of slaves. Many of these were English by birth or education, and they despised the small farmers, mechanics, and tradesmen who swarmed in the "pine woods" counties in the northern end of the state. Along the Gulf was an overflow of French-Spanish creoles from Louisiana, who were looked down upon by Americans of all factions. The Natchez patricians controlled the banks, voted the Whig ticket, and at the time of Jackson's elevation to the Presidency in 1828 they ruled the state. The "pine woods" element generally was Democratic, egalitarian in its views, and Protestant in its religion. The creoles along the coast were Catholics, and they fished as they could in the troubled waters.

This was the situation when Gwin arrived in Mississippi, and almost at once he was asked by President Jackson to undertake the task of building up the Democratic following in the state. From earliest boyhood Gwin had been taught to revere and serve Andrew Jackson, his father's closest friend. Jackson's principles — his fierce patriotism, democratic beliefs, Southern sympathies, devotion to the national welfare, and unalterable fidelity to party and friends — were Gwin's own; they had been bred into him. For Gwin, Jackson's wishes were commands. At the same time, the confidence reposed in him by the President opened the door of political opportunity at what was, in Gwin's case, a precociously early age. As a preliminary, Jackson summoned the doctor to Washington to deputize for several months as a confidential secretary, the President's regular secretary, Colonel Andrew Jackson Donelson, having been called back to Tennessee by his wife's illness. For six months Gwin lived in the White House (occupying the room in which President Garfield one day would lie dying), and under Jackson's tutelage he became acquainted with the foremost men in government.

Returning to Mississippi, Gwin resumed his practice, but in 1833 Jackson drafted him again for active political service by appointing him United States marshal for the southern district of Mississippi. This was one of the richest gifts in the executive power. The marshal's fees were large, the total income of the office being about $150,000 annually, half of which went to the marshal. The position also carried political prestige, and offered exceptional opportunities for speculations in land at a time when all America was on a spree of gambling in the new lands opening in the Southwest.

Gwin's appointment struck a snag in the Senate. George Poindexter was the erratic and vindictive senior senator from Mississippi. A Whig, he was fanatically opposed to Jackson, and to thwart the President he invoked senatorial privilege and succeeded in having the Senate reject Gwin's nomination. But a friend of the doctor's went to John C. Calhoun, to whom he was related by marriage, and convinced him that an injustice had been perpetrated. Calhoun did not know Gwin and had no personal interest in the appointment, but he moved for a reconsideration, obtained it, changed his vote, and secured the confirmation. All this took months, however, and Gwin was not inducted as marshal until June, 1834. To accept the position he relinquished medical practice permanently.

Poindexter, by his action, had earned a place at the very top of the list of Jackson's personal enemies, and "Old Hickory" waited for a chance to pay back the grudge. But the Mississippian found new means to express his loathing, when Jackson appointed Samuel Gwin, the doctor's brother, to the office of land register at Mount Salus, in Mississippi. Samuel Gwin was a veteran of 1812 and the President was always watchful of the welfare of his former comrades in arms. Moving slyly, Poindexter persuaded the Senate to adopt a statement of policy condemning the appointment of residents of one state to government positions in another. Samuel Gwin was a resident of Tennessee, and the Senate, acting under this policy, rejected his Mount Salus nomination.

This second act of defiance by the egregious "Poins" aroused the President's easily kindled wrath, and he resubmitted Samuel Gwin's name. Again the Senate declined to confirm the appointment. Thereupon Jackson refused to name anybody to the Mount Salus office. This threw all land transac-

tions in that area into confusion, and brought odium upon
Poindexter, who was blamed for the stalemate. At length,
faced with an ultimatum from the White House, the Senate re-
scinded its resolution. Jackson then submitted Samuel Gwin's
nomination a third time, and it was confirmed. From then on
Poindexter walked in danger of losing his political scalp, for
Jackson was unforgiving.   ·

The sequel of this unedifying quarrel was tragic, and Samuel
Gwin was the victim. Outraged by Poindexter's opposition,
he hissed the senator during a political rally, and was challenged by a former law partner of "Poins," Judge Isaac Caldwell. The antagonists met under savage conditions: armed
with six-shooters, at the word they advanced toward each other
firing. Caldwell was killed on the spot. Gwin was agoniz-
ingly wounded, and suffered for months before dying. That
duel went down in Mississippi history as the bloodiest ever
fought in the state.

4

The term of Senator Poindexter was due to expire in 1836,
and Jackson sent out the order to expunge him. Dr. Gwin
plunged into this fight with zest. Already he was a leader in
Democratic affairs in Mississippi, and his intimacy with the
President gave him great prestige in the party. The Democrats'
chances seemed slim, for Poindexter was popular, was a hard
campaigner, and was backed by the dominant political element. Casting about for a candidate, the Democrats hit upon
a Natchez lawyer named Robert John Walker.

Coming to Mississippi from Pennsylvania, where his father
was a federal judge, Walker had built up a reputation for what
his biographer has called a remarkable ability to "corrupt the
law without breaking it." The demand for his professional serv-

ices was brisk. Walker craved two of the good things of life with equal fervor — wealth and power. He felt that he could outdo Poindexter in scurrility and lung power, if necessary, and he was eager to run. But unfortunately his record as a Democrat was clouded by a single act of apostacy. This had occurred when Jackson, in his war upon the Bank of the United States, withdrew the government deposits and precipitated a crisis that was to culminate in the great panic of 1837. Walker had involved himself recklessly with the Natchez banks, was heavily in debt, tangled in a mass of get-rich-quick schemes, and in a fit of demoralization he had written a letter to a Whig politician denouncing the President's action. Hardly had the letter left his hands when he recanted; but the record was there, and it was sure to be used by the Whigs against him.

"Old Hickory" never forgave a turncoat or deserter, and in Mississippi no Democrat could hope to be elected against White House disapproval. Yet the party could find no other candidate who, in their judgment, stood a chance against the active, agile, and argumentative "Poins." None could suggest how the backslider might be restored to Presidential favor, and Gwin recalled that Walker "wept like a baby" when he realized that his one lapse had apparently cost him a political career.

Gwin solved the problem with the finesse that usually marked his tactics. He did not take the party's predicament to Jackson directly, for he knew the old man's hatred of traitors; instead, he explained the situation to Donelson, whom the President trusted. The secretary discovered, apparently, that Jackson had not heard about Walker's temporary aberration, but was aware that Walker had spoken out against the "vile" Poindexter. Soon a letter reached Gwin from the White House, putting the seal of approval on Walker, calling him, among all the candidates for the Senate, "the first in point of talents, attainments, and personal integrity."

The letter was used in the red-hot campaign, and in January, 1836, Walker was elected to the Senate as "Old Hickory's" man. It was the death stroke for "Poins"; he went into permanent eclipse, while the jubilant Walker posted to Washington with a haste that seemed almost indecent. By this feat of political jugglery Gwin cemented his influence as party boss in Mississippi. Walker would prove grateful ("within practical limits," Gwin would sometimes smile), and their political association would endure for many years.

5

Dr. Gwin and Robert Walker were associated in other than political ventures. Both were deeply involved in the speculation in public lands which came to a peak in the thirties. Walker's brother had gone to Texas, and had become enthusiastic over that region. Texas was about to achieve independence from Mexico, and on his brother's advice Walker invested recklessly in Texas lands. His assets already were mortgaged several times over, and he was operating on the flimsy credit extended by the Mississippi banks. The magnitude of Walker's involvement may be gauged by the notes he endorsed almost indiscriminately. It was common practice for friends to endorse each other's notes rather carelessly, and Walker signed one for $150,000, although at the time his only wealth consisted of his income from legal fees. Gwin also became interested in Texas, but did not invest immediately, his interests being engaged elsewhere.

Between them, Gwin and Walker floated a scheme to acquire some million acres of Indian lands — the Cocchuma tract, ceded under the Treaty of Dancing Rabbit Creek. The partners formed a syndicate with Henry S. Foote, John A. Quitman, and Joseph Davis, elder brother of Jefferson Davis; and this syndicate induced some hundred and fifty investors in Tennessee, Mississippi, and Arkansas to buy shares. Gradually control was secured of nearly 70 percent of the tract. Political pressure was used to loosen the purse strings of Natchez bankers, and for a while the syndicate racked up formidable profits. When in 1837-38 the financial bubble burst, the Cocchuma lands affair came under the scrutiny of a committee of Congress, and while charges of fraud were plentiful, little was proved. Nevertheless, Gwin and Walker suffered severe losses and acquired a name as speculators.

With youthful disregard for caution, Gwin had taken other financial risks, and he was hit hard. Nominally he held title to thousands of acres of wild lands in Mississippi and Arkansas, and he owned well-developed plantations in the first state; but his position as marshal complicated his liabilities, for he was responsible for large sums of money which he had accepted on the strength of notes that were either repudiated, or paid off in ruinously depreciated bank scrip, when all land values plummeted. Plantations purchased a few years previously for thirty dollars an acre were sold for as little as sixty-five cents an acre, and the disaster was general.

In the midst of this, Gwin was accused of misappropriating funds allotted to pay Indian claims, and it was only after a hard tussle that he was able to disprove the charge. Then the courts added to his embarrassments by ordering him, in some instances, to accept almost worthless notes in return for escrow deposits which he had made as marshal, but compelled him to remit to the claimants in gold. Wearily the doctor confided to a friend that he considered himself lucky to have got $18,000 out of one bank which owed him $50,000 and was trying to cheat him out of the whole sum. The state's financial reputation went on the rubbish heap when it repudiated its bonds to the amount of several million dollars. But the crash did have one good effect upon Gwin: it taught him caution in making investments, and, as he said afterward, from the experience he learned "a great deal about human nature."

Walker was ruined by the collapse, and for years to come would be harried by creditors. He was dunned in the corridors of the Capitol, and at one time his Congressional salary was attached; only by practicing law before the Supreme Court could he support his family. His Senate position did provide a measure of sanctuary, it is true, because certain creditors were reluctant to risk invoking political reprisals. Nor did this circumstance go unnoticed by Dr. Gwin as he wrestled with his own difficulties.

6

The year 1834 had been important for Gwin for a number of reasons. Not only had his appointment as United States marshal been confirmed in that year; in 1834 he had paid his first visit to Texas.

In Clinton he had married Caroline Simpson, and two children had been born to them, neither of these attaining maturity. In 1834 his wife had died, and partly to escape from melancholy reminders, and partly to wait out the action of the Senate on his appointment he had accepted the invitation of a family friend from Tennessee, Sam Houston, to visit Texas. Houston was soon to become president of the Texas Republic, and Gwin stayed with him at Nacogdoches. The visitor from Mississippi fell under the spell of Houston's enthusiasm for the region, as well as that of his close associate, Thomas Jefferson Rusk, the future Chief Justice of Texas. Gwin explored the district on foot and on horseback, and his active imagination enabled him to foresee the country Texas could become. Before returning home he made his first investment in Texas lands, and he would add to this purchase over the years until he owned immense tracts; one comprised six hundred thousand acres "at and around" (as the lawyers say) the three forks of the Trinity.

In Houston's circle was a Kentucky couple, William and Mary Logan, with whom Dr. Gwin became friendly. Logan was a surveyor and had been drawn to Texas because of the professional opportunities it offered. His wife, the former Mary Elizabeth Hampton Bell, was the daughter of a well-known tavern keeper in Kentucky, the landlord of the inn at Mammoth Cave. In those days taverns were centers of news and politics, and a popular tavern keeper was a man of consequence in his county. Mary Bell, a high-spirited brunette, had married Logan at fifteen, and Gwin noticed approvingly that in business and political matters she seemed to display a keenness of judgment beyond her years.

This 1834 visit to Houston had a sequel. In 1835 William Logan died, and the next year Gwin returned to Texas and wooed and won the young widow. The pair were married at Vicksburg in 1837, with Houston's blessing; Gwin was then thirty-two, and his bride twenty-one. They would prove ideally matched, for their tastes and interests coincided and they were mutually ambitious. Four children would be born to them (three of whom would outlive their father); their domestic life would be affectionate, and the family tightly knit.

Up to now Gwin had demonstrated ability as a political manager and party leader in the state, but he had declined to seek elective office. His business, and his duties as marshal, engrossed him, and after the 1837 collapse the struggle to pull clear of a maze of obligations became all-absorbing. These very difficulties may have influenced him to accept his party's nomination for Congress in 1840. Robert Walker contended that Gwin looked longingly at the partial relief from creditors afforded by a seat in Congress; and, indeed, it may have been a contributing cause, although undoubtedly Gwin's motives were mixed. In any event, he ran as the Democratic candi-

date, and in so doing discovered capabilities of which he had
not been aware. At the start he was, in his own words, "as
timid as a woman" before an audience, and Mississippi audiences could be rough; but by dint of determination and practice he overcame his shyness and developed into an effective
public speaker. Wisely he made no attempt to imitate the
spread-eagle oratory of his friend Walker, but excelled in setting forth an argument logically and sticking to the facts. He
won the election, and at the opening of the 1841 session took
his place in the Twenty-seventh Congress at Washington.

As a member of the House of Representatives, Gwin made
no pronounced impression upon his colleagues; he would be
remembered mainly for having been assiduous in watching
over the interests of his district. A fellow member deemed him
"a good businessman." He did not attempt to participate prom-
inently in debate, especially on national issues, but was regular
in committee work. The few speeches he did make showed an
awareness of national needs that was unusual in a Southerner, and a concern for the national welfare as well as the
good of his state; but in matters of general policy he was content to follow his party, the national leadership of which was
almost exclusively Southern.

Neither at this time nor later could Gwin be called backward
in claiming what he thought was due to him, or in collecting
a fee for services rendered. One instance of this businesslike
attitude occurred in connection with the so-called Chicksaw
Indian claims. When the Chicksaws ceded their tribal lands,
the federal government undertook to invest their funds in
"safe and valuable" securities. Gwin found out that some of
the funds had been placed in stocks of dubious value, on which
no dividends had been paid; and also that, by error, payments
amounting to $112,042.99 had been charged against the Chick-
saws' account instead of against the Treasury. Gwin offered to
obtain rectification of this mistake, and received the warrant

of the chiefs to act as their agent, in a strictly private capacity. He presented their claim and pressed the grievance until the accounting error was corrected, and the dubious stocks were replaced by others of solid worth.

His task completed to the satisfaction of the Chicksaws, Gwin presented a bill for his services. This was in the form of an assignment signed by the chiefs transferring $56,021.49, or exactly half, of the recovered funds, to his personal account. This requisition was approved by a Treasury auditor, but the Comptroller referred it to the Indian Office for examination, and the Chicksaws thereupon protested that the fee was excessive. This was a matter of opinion, for there was no doubt that Gwin had carried out his part of the bargain. The claim became snarled in charges and countercharges, and would lie in the Indian Office until 1850, when it was paid in full. It may be to the point that in 1850 Gwin was a United States senator. The episode, however, does throw some light upon the varied sources of Gwin's income at successive periods in his career.

Mary Gwin did not accompany her husband to Washington, for she was awaiting the birth of a child. The doctor put up at a lodging house — one of the communal "messes" patronized by Congressmen during the sessions — where another lodger was John C. Calhoun. As a Jacksonian, Gwin had been reared to detest Andrew Jackson's *bête noir*, the chief exponent of the "damnable doctrine of Nullification." However, Gwin was sensible of his obligation to the South Carolina senator for getting his appointment as marshal confirmed, and across the dinner table he expressed his gratitude. The talk drifted along, and Gwin found himself agreeing with some of the old man's opinions, especially his fervent belief in the expanding role of the United States on the North American continent. Gwin was convinced, as was Calhoun, that the nation must reach westward to the Pacific Ocean, and southward into Texas and northern Mexico. As a result of these conversations, Gwin found his attitude toward the man who was the ogre of "Old Hickory's" world radically changing, and he conceived a genuine admiration for Calhoun. His devotion to Jackson was not lessened, but his political sympathies were widened to take in Calhoun's viewpoint on some issues. Nullification Gwin never approved; he was solidly with Jackson against that heresy; and it was his tact that enabled him to retain the esteem of both the great rivals. On several occasions he even acted as an intermediary between them without giving offense, although a reconciliation was impossible.

7

Gwin's financial embarrassments, meanwhile, had not been solved, and halfway through his term he was on the point of resigning in order to devote full attention to extricating himself from the morass of debt. For the sake of the party, however, he consented to complete his term in the House, but in 1842 he refused to accept renomination.

Returning to Mississippi, he threw himself into business, and in this sphere displayed conspicuous ability. Among other activities, he helped to set up commission houses which financed and supplied planters and marketed their crops; one such firm, Halsey & Gwin, of Vicksburg, was capitalized at a million dollars, and he had an interest in others almost as large. Compelled to revisit Washington periodically on personal or party errands, he kept up his connections with Congressional and other government leaders. Politics was still his avocation, although sidetracked for the time being.

On one of these visits to the capital, Gwin called on Calhoun and took part in a conversation that he never forgot. Calhoun had become Secretary of State under President Tyler, and was working for the annexation of Texas. As a large investor in Texas property, Gwin favored this step, and as an expansionist he believed it was inevitable.

During the discussion, Calhoun pulled out a map of the continent, and placing a bony finger on the Bay of San Francisco, prophesied with visionary fervor that before many years a city would arise at that point which would command the trade with the Orient and dominate the entire Pacific littoral — an American city, surpassing New York as a port. Gwin was thrilled by the rapt old man, by the cadaverous face, the burning eyes, and the quavering finger tapping the map at a spot which to most Americans was as remote and misty as Zanzibar.

That year the Democrats nominated the "dark horse," James Knox Polk, of Tennessee, as their candidate for the Presidency. The Polks came from Gwin's country, and he swung actively into the campaign. Polk was elected, and there was expectation that Dr. Gwin might be taken into the cabinet. However, the claims of Senator Walker were given preference, and Gwin lent his aid in obtaining for Walker the Treasury position, instead of the relatively minor Attorney Generalship. The matter required jockeying and diplomacy, for George Bancroft, the New England historian, already had been named to the Treasury; however, conflicting interests were resolved, in part through Gwin's adroit intercession, and Bancroft agreed to accept the Navy Department instead.

Walker, who throughout the negotiations had despaired of getting his wish, was effusively grateful, and he tried to persuade the governor of Mississippi to appoint Gwin to fill out his unexpired Senate term. But the governor grumbled that Dr. Gwin was not popular with all segments of the party in the state; and besides, he was too noticeably surrounded by "broke speculators." Gwin's frenzied financing had earned him a reputation which he would never entirely shake off.

In 1845, the doctor's name was again mentioned for the Democratic nomination to the House of Representatives, but he discouraged the move. The choice then fell upon Jefferson Davis. To friends, Gwin had confided that the only capacity in which he would be interested in returning to Congress would be as a United States senator, and there was little prospect of his attaining that goal, considering the political situation. His friend Walker did procure Gwin's appointment as commissioner of public works at New Orleans, in charge of construction of the great customshouse there. Under ordinary conditions the position would have been a sinecure (his two fellow commissioners accepted it in that spirit), but Gwin devoted much time to acquiring the site, approving plans, negotiating contracts, and generally getting the project under way.

He had unofficial responsibilities at New Orleans, also, for he was expected to advise the administration confidentially on political developments in the Southwest. Secretary Walker took frequent counsel with the doctor on public and private business, and Gwin became one of the most efficient gatherers of the economic data on which the secretary based his sweeping tariff reforms of 1846.

Upon the outbreak of the war with Mexico that year, New Orleans became a shipping point for men and supplies being sent to the front. The port hummed, business boomed, and the value of Gwin's Texas holdings rose as the armies of Generals Zachary Taylor and Winfield Scott scored victory after victory. Commission houses handling consignments of war materials reaped a harvest, and Gwin shared in this. His debts were paid, his bank balance moved pleasantly over to the credit side of the ledger, and soon friends were estimating the doctor's income at $30,000 to $40,000 a year. This included the profits from the plantation which he maintained in Mississippi as a permanent base of operations.

Wealth gave Mary Gwin the means to realize her social ambitions, which were of the first order, and her entertainments in New Orleans became notable. Life in the creole city could be delightful for the patrician class, and the Gwins entered into its pleasures with zest. Not ambitious socially himself, the doctor enjoyed seeing his wife shine, and the Gwin home was a center of hospitality. There the most influential citizens of New Orleans were seen, attracted by the lively atmosphere, the irreproachable fare, the friendliness of the hostess, and the tact and geniality of the doctor, who was known to be privy to secrets of state.

Elimination of his money worries gave Gwin leisure to look over the political field once more. The United States Senate was still his goal, but there were no senatorships available in either Mississippi or Louisiana, and none likely to become available in the near future, the custom in the South being to retain public men in office if they gave satisfaction. The principle of rotation, to give every aspirant a chance, was more generally accepted in the North.

In 1848 the war with Mexico ended. In the autumn of that year, Zachary Taylor, the hope of the Whigs, rode into the Presidency on the strength of his battlefield exploits. Gwin accepted the result of the election realistically, and foresaw the lean years in store for his party. He would be deprived of his commissionership, of course, although he cared little for that; his thoughts were reaching out westward, toward the new territories gained from Mexico. Frontier-bred, he could respond to the prospect of limitless opportunity which a new country offered. Then, in the interval between Taylor's election in November, 1848, and his inauguration in March, 1849, history took a turn that changed Gwin's life and the lives of thousands of Americans. The great gold rush to California began.

Word of the gold discoveries had reached the East months previously, and had aroused mild interest tempered by skepticism. There were rumors that men were scooping gold out of the ground with common shovels, but sensible people dismissed such fantasies as palpably absurd. In December, however, in his message to Congress, President Polk officially, though cautiously, confirmed the richness of the discoveries. To prove his point, he placed on display at the Treasury several thousand dollars' worth of "dust" that had actually been washed out of the beds of Sierra streams.

The response was the start of a stampede to reach this El Dorado. Thousands of men forsook their occupations, said good-bye to homes, families, friends, and obligations, raked together what capital they could, sold or abandoned going businesses and steady employment, and headed for the Pacific coast. Some went by the months-long voyage around Cape Horn; others took the steamships that plied to the Isthmus of Panama, crossed to the Pacific side, and continued north from there by whatever means they could find. In the Midwest, wagon trains set out to traverse two thousand miles of prairie, desert, marshes, and the loftiest mountains on the continent. The urge was to get to the golden strand as fast as possible — for who could tell how long the mines would hold out?

In New Orleans the newspapers published sensational accounts of California doings, with maps showing the best routes for getting to the "diggings." Dr. Gwin recalled his conversations with Calhoun about the destiny of the Pacific West. Throngs of immigrants were hastening toward the spot on San Francisco Bay where the old Nullifier's skinny finger had tapped the map. Lawyers, mechanics, clergymen, clerks, farmers, tradesmen, seamen, teachers, bankers — every class and kind of men — were bent on one mission, a quick cleanup at the mines and return home.

But the enormous expanse of California embraced other resources besides gold. Before '49, immigrants had been drawn there by the region's agricultural possibilities, and Gwin had read glowing reports of California's fertility. A new country appealed to his imagination, and he was quick to realize that such a setting was wide open to political ambition. In a new country there are no political parties to help or hinder, no cliques, no vested interests to placate or combat. Opportunity is open to all comers, and the most capable and energetic carry off the prizes. Gwin had an honest ambition to play a part on the national stage; he felt himself equipped for it; he belonged to the ruling class; and as a political leader he had given proof of enterprise and skill. He was wealthy and would be under no necessity to scramble for gold. The more he thought of the political vacuum in California, the more he was tempted to fill it.

Having great confidence in his wife's judgment, he put the question up to her. Should he join the westward rush, he asked, in search not of more wealth, but of political honors? As soon as the state could be organized, a United States senatorship would be available, and why should he not have it?

Mary Gwin was eager to play a social role in Washington, and as the wife of a senator she would be able to vie with the best. The prestige of the Senate was exceeded only by that attaching to the White House, and in some sections of the country, notably the South, it stood even higher in popular esteem. Mrs. Gwin thought the matter over; she could see that nationally the Democrats were in eclipse; but might not they take over the unorganized West? Her decision was that the doctor should lose no time in heading for San Francisco and the gold regions.

Confirmed in his own calculations and backed by the enthusiasm of his wife, Gwin moved swiftly. In February he traveled to Washington, and arrived in the capital at the end of the month. On March 4 Congress adjourned without having provided any governmental status for the harassed Californians. The doctor settled his accounts at the Treasury and bade good-bye to friends. He had just come from a final call at the Treasury Department on March 5 when he encountered Senator Douglas in front of Willard's Hotel; and it was there, while watching President Taylor's inaugural parade, that he disclosed his intentions to Douglas, a friend of long standing.

That same day the doctor left Washington for New Orleans, and after a hurried leave-taking of his family boarded a ship for the Isthmus. Within a year, he assured Mary Gwin, he would be back, a member of the United States Senate.

Chapter II

IN THIS RACE to snatch a brilliant prize, time seemed against the doctor. The steamship from New Orleans landed him at Chagres, on the Atlantic side of the Isthmus of Panama, and from there naked Indians poled him in a *pongo* boat up the Chagres River. He camped in the jungle, transferred to mule-back, and on the Pacific side descended to the port of Panama, ancient stronghold of Spanish power, reaching Panama City on the last day of March. There it appeared that his journey might end, for there was no transportation obtainable northward to San Francisco Bay. Why the recently instituted steamship service had been suspended, or perhaps had failed entirely, nobody knew. Weeks had passed since the last ship had taken several hundred immigrants north, and no vessel had appeared since then. Meanwhile, the pestilential town was overrun by California-bound gold hunters, and more swarmed in every day. Some fourteen hundred immigrants were cooped in the dismal place, fretting away health, energy, and money. Food was wretched and shelter inadequate. Fever and cholera were endemic, and many of the Argonauts left their bones at that spot. In desperation a few risked pushing off in coasting vessels of dubious seaworthiness, and some even in rowboats, trusting to luck to be able to pick their way along the dangerous coast. Of these many perished by thirst or shipwreck.

Gwin waited with the rest, making himself agreeable to the authorities in the meanwhile; but it was mid-May before the steamship *Panama* hove in sight, coming up from the Horn on her maiden passage from New York. In the stampede that developed to get aboard, even to secure sleeping space on the bare deck, tickets changed hands for as much as a thousand dollars; and when the ship weighed anchor again on May 10 every inch was crammed with two hundred and ninety passengers, triple her normal capacity. Gwin was among the fortunates to get aboard.

He was not the only distinguished passenger. Thomas Butler King, a Whig Congressman from Georgia, proprietor of one of the showplace plantations of the South, on St. Simon's Island, was accorded the luxury of a stateroom by virtue of his prestige as White House emissary. King was traveling to California as President Taylor's personal representative, to observe conditions and make recommendations as to state government. Other passengers included army officers whose names would become famous in a few years' time ("Fighting Joe" Hooker, the Civil War general, then a captain, was among these) and a score of men who would bulk largely in state and national affairs during the next two decades.

During the tedious voyage along the uncharted, rocky coast, every moment fraught with risk of shipwreck, Gwin made no secret of his expectations in regard to the Senate. More than once, in desultory conversation or over a leisurely card game, he remarked that he probably would be retracing that route in a few months, on his way back to Washington as senator-elect from the state yet to be formed, and his air of distinction, his unruffled self-confidence, and the rumors of his exalted connections in the political world convinced those within hearing that he would succeed.

His appearance was striking — six feet two inches tall, erect and powerfully framed, with features which an unfriendly critic once described as "in every respect except hue those of a Mohawk chief." The comparison was intended to be insulting, but it was apt, for Gwin's countenance and bearing did suggest something of the dignity and fierceness of an Indian warrior. The vigorous nose, firm-set lips, and strong jaw denoted determination, while the searching gray eyes could turn wary and calculating in an instant. His high forehead gave an impression of intellectual strength, and this effect was heightened by a mane of prematurely gray hair that was swept back imperiously. His personality was magnetic and his manner polished, his courtesy inbred, that of a Southern aristocrat; but underneath the patrician and cultured exterior was a core of resiliency and predatory ruthlessness appropriate to the frontier.

Gwin surmised that Butler King also had political aspirations in California, and it required little adroitness on his part to draw out the toplofty Georgian, who was as vain as he was complacent. Yes, King admitted, he was going to work for the formation of a state government, and with White House backing was rather confident that he would be returned as the new state's first senator. Gwin, a seasoned tactician, was not unduly perturbed by King's competition.

2

Dense fog lay upon the water of the Golden Gate when the *Panama* finally nosed into San Francisco Bay on the morning of June 4, 1849. The great paddle wheels of the ship churned sluggishly, for the coal supply had been exhausted and the captain had been reduced to ripping out woodwork to keep up steam. After her four-month voyage the steamer's sides were streaked with salt and her paint was peeling. The throng on her deck was tense, their hearts beating with hope and excitement as they neared the end of their travels. Bit by bit the sun burned through the fog, disclosing on either hand only sand dunes and bare, burned-out, lifeless hills, and hope gave way

to foreboding that perhaps the mines had given out, and the
gold seekers had departed. Then the *Panama* rounded into
Yerba Buena cove and the settlement came into view — an un-
tidy agglomeration of shacks and tents that belied its imposing
designation as San Francisco City.

Among the first passengers rowed ashore was Dr. Gwin. He
was impatient to set foot on land, for three months of the year
he had allotted himself to achieve his goal already had been
spent. His first action was to inform his wife of his safe
arrival; and weeks later, when Mary Gwin read this letter in
New Orleans, she announced that from then on her birthday
would be June 4, the date of the doctor's landing. She had
been born on June 24, but June 4, she was certain, marked the
beginning of a splendid career for herself and her husband.

Gwin had brought credentials with him, including letters
from James Buchanan, President Polk's Secretary of State.
These were addressed to Thomas O. Larkin, United States naval agent and former consul at Monterey, and to the postmaster at San Francisco, William V. Voorhiss. It was indicative of
California's remoteness that Buchanan had regretted he
could not furnish the doctor with any letter to a representative
of the State Department in California, because there was none;
in fact, the only place in the United States statutes where the
name "California" appeared was in the act authorizing the appointment of a postal agent there.

Buchanan's introduction procured Gwin a lodging in the
house occupied by Voorhiss — a rough frame dwelling off the
Plaza, or Portsmouth Square as it is called today. The post office was a low adobe building in the Plaza, and was the focal
point of the settlement. Upon the arrival of a ship bringing
mail, long lines of men would form, waiting to collect precious letters from home.

Gwin's quarters were luxurious compared to the improvised
shelters that made up most of the so-called city. The popula-

tion was continually changing, men setting out for the mines, others drifting in, either loaded with gold or crushed by disillusion and failure. The only commodities that were cheap and abundant were gold and silver. Food prices were fantastically high (a plate of beans eaten off an upturned barrel cost eight dollars) and newcomers often ran out of money. To relieve the distress of some of his fellow passengers, Gwin stood an open sack of Mexican dollars in his room and invited any in need to help themselves. Men who otherwise would have fared badly gratefully took advantage of this gesture of generosity. It may be added that a sack of silver dollars was worth less than a sack of flour or rice at that time of topsy-turvy values.

Within a few days, thanks to such public-spirited actions and to his striking appearance, Dr. Gwin was recognized as one of the leading citizens of the place, where anybody who had been on hand longer than a month was regarded as an "old settler." His name was included with those of other "prominent citizens" who signed a broadside summoning the people to a meeting in the Plaza on June 17, to consider the failure of Congress to provide a government for California.

At this rally, which brought out the entire population, both Gwin and Butler King spoke in favor of forming a state government and seeking immediate admission to the Union. Resolutions were adopted declaring the right of the people, for their own protection, to elect delegates to a constitutional convention which would set up such a government, in order that "the great and growing interests of California may be represented in the next Congress of the United States."

This action, for which there was no lawful precedent, evoked a protest from General Persifer F. Smith, commanding the Department of the Pacific, and a warning that it would be his duty to suppress such an election. The reaction of the *Alta California*, the town's leading newspaper (already issued three

times a week and soon to become a daily) demonstrated how
little respected by the community was the military regime
which technically governed California. Reminding the general that he was "simply a military officer," the *Alta* asserted
that "any action of his interfering with the inherent right of
the people . . . to enact laws for themselves is an act of
usurpation, or unauthorized despotism, and should be re-
sisted to the death!"

Since the general had only a corporal's guard to back him
up, he wisely subsided.

3

California's condition in 1849 was without a counterpart in
history. It is necessary to cast a backward glance over
the events of the preceding years of tumult in order to understand how the way had been prepared for the step which
Gwin and others contemplated. The demand for a state government was the culmination of a process that had been going
on for many months.

Before the influx of immigrants from the States, California
had been a sleepy outpost of the Spanish — and later the Mexican — empire. Its inhabitants generally were of a purer ra-
cial stock than most Mexicans, for many of them had come
directly from Spain. They were a sunny, likable people, easygoing and generous, who lived by raising cattle on vast
ranches. They loved their land.

Immigrants from the United States had started to filter in
during the early forties. The farseeing among these believed
the United States would soon encompass everything to the
Pacific Ocean, if only to forestall annexation of the region by
France or Great Britain, both of which powers were suspected
of having designs upon the territory. The native Californians
welcomed the newcomers at first; but as more and more

pushed in, among them adventurers and fugitives from either failure or the law, friction developed, and the Californians began to realize that their land was coveted by the Yankees, just as Texas had been coveted, and eventually would be annexed in the same way.

In June, 1846, the suspicions of the Californians had been confirmed by the "uprising" of a band of confused, irresponsible Americans, who hoisted the Bear Flag of independence at Sonoma and proclaimed the Republic of California. These self-deluded *insurrectos* proceeded to seize property, imprison inoffensive citizens, and generally to carry on like the freebooters they were. The Californians believed that this group was acting with the secret cooperation of the United States. And when Captain John Charles Frémont, a topographical engineer of the United States Army, came to the assistance of the rebels with a few soldiers, the Californians were sure that Washington had instigated the "uprising" for a sinister purpose. War with Mexico broke out just then, and American military and naval forces completed the conquest of California just as the residents had feared.

During the turbulence of 1846, there had been a large influx of immigrants from the States, and during the next two years this kept up. As long as the war lasted, the conquered province remained under martial law, and that setup was continued nominally after the conclusion of peace. But the American settlers were not disposed to live under martial law: after all, hadn't they won the war, and wasn't California American territory now? They clamored for the civil rights to which they had been accustomed in their home states.

By the Treaty of Guadalupe Hidalgo, which terminated the war, the laws which had been in force in California under Mexican rule were continued in force until a permanent government should be established by Congress. These laws were primitive, vague, and totally incompatible with the changed conditions. Their enforcement was in the hands of local officials called alcaldes, whose functions roughly combined those of judge, justice of the peace, sheriff, land register, and licensing agent. The alcaldes had maintained order in their localities by applying the rules of common sense, rather than the book of statutes, for no written code existed in California at the time of the conquest.

Property rights were a fertile source of disputes between the immigrants and the native ranchers. The immense land grants bestowed by Spain and Mexico had never been properly surveyed; their boundaries often were mere guesswork, so that sometimes nobody could be sure just who held title to what. Disagreements would have been inevitable even with goodwill, and there was not much goodwill. Americans who had purchased land from the ostensible owners sometimes found that they had bought a succession of lawsuits.

But property rights was only one of the exacerbations stemming from the conquest and the dislocation of the original social pattern. Civil affairs were thrown into confusion, and the military authority was all but helpless. The military governor tried to fill the gap by appointing the best qualified men he could find as alcaldes and leaving law enforcement to their discretion. The result was chaos. Many of the alcaldes were Americans, and while those who had lived in California for several years understood local customs well enough to deal out rough justice, others were ignorant of traditional ways and intolerant of everything Spanish. There was no uniformity in their rulings, and often their decisions were arbitrary and despotic.

As early as January, 1847, well before the gold rush, the *California Star*, a newspaper published at San Francisco, had voiced the popular disgust with the system and had called for somebody to find and publish "the written laws of the territory . . . without regard to the statements of A, B, or C, in rela-

tion to certain clauses which probably never existed. . . .
We heard a few days since that the *alcalde* of Sonoma had
adopted the whole volume of Missouri statutes as the law for
the government of the people in his jurisdiction. If this is allowed, we will have as many legislators in California as we
have *alcaldes* or justices of the peace, and the country will be
thrown into more confusion in a short time than ever existed
in any part of the world inhabited by civilized men."

Despite all such appeals, the legal anarchy prevailed, and
the shocks it produced were intensified by the gold rush. The
commonest domestic concerns were affected. An example, by
no means unique, was the experience of an American woman
who had been deserted by her husband. She wished to marry
again, and applied for a divorce to her alcalde, a former lieutenant of volunteers. The native Californians, as Catholics,
had had no divorce law, and the alcalde could find nothing in
the Articles of War that empowered him to dissolve the marriage bond. The woman was thus left without recourse, there
being no civil courts to appeal to.

According to one theory openly propounded, there was no
law at all in California. Martial law, it was argued, automatically terminated upon the conclusion of peace, and Congress had put nothing in its place. The extreme to which this
theory could be carried was illustrated by a conversation
which an immigrant from Maryland heard among a group of
drovers sitting around a campfire at Sutter's Fort. The question was whether murder could be considered a crime in California, since there was no statute forbidding it. The young
man who overheard this discussion, carried on with much
gravity and earnestness, was James King of William, and he
never found the answer to the conundrum. He was murdered.

By the summer of 1849 the population of California had
jumped to an estimated one hundred thousand, and the influx
had only started. Something had to be done to organize these

new inhabitants sensibly, and before Gwin's arrival there had
been several abortive attempts to form a state government.
When the *Panama* brought mail showing that, once more, Congress had made no provision for a government in California,
the call for the Plaza rally of June 17 was the result. The people would wait no longer.

Actually, the military governor of California, General Bennet Riley, who had headquarters at Monterey, had issued a
proclamation calling for election of delegates to a constitutional convention before the San Francisco rally was announced. There was no legal ground for Riley's action, and so
indifferently was it regarded that the agitation continued in
San Francisco. But the governor's proclamation did give an
appearance of legality to the election, and August 1 was set
as the day when the people would vote.

4

Gwin and Butler King both set out to canvass the interior
camps and beat the drums for statehood. They went separately. Gwin traveled lightly, but King made his progress official by requisitioning an escort that included both the military and naval commanders at San Francisco, with their staffs.
Accompanied by this pompous entourage, the Georgian made
himself ridiculous. Scorning the advice of men who knew how
hot California's valleys can get in July, he ordered regular
marches through the heat of the day, and in a short time fell
a victim to sunstroke. For a while it was thought that he
would die, but he rallied. His popularity did not. Even Gwin
could not resist the mild jibe that though the Presidential envoy could command the resources of the Army, Navy, and
Treasury Departments, he apparently didn't have the sense
to come in out of the sun.

In the mining communities of the Mother Lode country Gwin preached the gospel of state government with success. He addressed a Fourth of July gathering at Sacramento, the supply depot for the northern mines, and then moved south to Stockton, which supplied the southern mines. Everywhere he was given an enthusiastic welcome. His reputation as a friend of the great men of his party had preceded him (he had seen to that), and his manner was imposing. Even his gray hair was an asset among the predominantly young men who peopled the "diggings." Gray hair seemed to the youthful and inexperienced crowds he faced to be a guarantee of maturity and ripe judgment, and although Gwin was only forty-four, he looked considerably older. Above all, his call for statehood was popular.

Upon his return to San Francisco, he encountered a excited crowd in the Plaza, and learned that a public trial of the leaders of a gang of rowdies calling themselves the Hounds, or Regulators, was being organized, and that members of the gang were being rounded up. The Hounds had perpetrated many outrages, including robberies and assaults, and the night before had climaxed their depredations by an organized raid on the camp of some Chilean miners, at the foot of Telegraph Hill. The camp had been looted and wrecked, and many of the miners beaten viciously. The attack stirred public indignation, and the ringleaders were seized, to undergo trial and punishment.

On the spot, Gwin was chosen by the crowd as one of two judges to preside with the alcalde over the trial. Counsel for prosecution and defense were appointed, witnesses were called and testimony was taken, while the crowd stood by. The prisoners were convicted and banished from San Francisco. There was some doubt as to how the sentence would be carried out, until the captain of a United States warship in the harbor volunteered to transport the offenders to parts unknown. The offer was accepted, and for a while violence was sharply curbed in the sprawling community.

Gwin's participation in this alfresco rehearsal for the Vigilance Committees of the fifties increased his prominence and popularity, and on August 1 he was easily elected a delegate from San Francisco to the constitutional convention due to meet at Monterey on September 1.

Chapter III

THE CALIFORNIA CONSTITUTIONAL convention of 1849 has been likened to the Philadelphia constitutional convention of 1787, as another striking example of the capacity of Americans for self-government. In both instances, it is true, Americans amply demonstrated that they possessed the knack; but to view the achievements of these conventions as an overnight "political miracle" is to ignore the historical sequence that led up to those exhibitions of political maturity. European scholars have never ceased to marvel that "a wilderness" should produce so much political sophistication, failing to realize that the men who composed these conventions had benefited by a long process of training in political affairs. Generations of fending for themselves had taught them the pitfalls to avoid and the aims upon which to concentrate.

In California, the men assembled at Monterey in 1849 had been seasoned by the kaleidoscopic events of the immediately preceding years, especially by what had occurred since the American conquest. They came together fully understanding the realities of their situation and needs, unencumbered by theories. Their land was new, different, and tumultuous, and they drew up a constitution that would foster an orderly growth for thirty years to come; nor, when it would come to be supplanted, would the change be entirely for the better.

Chief credit for the success of this 1849 convention is given by all authorities to William McKendree Gwin. More than any other one man, it is agreed, Gwin was the political architect of California. He dominated the 1849 convention, and the organic law there spelled out bore his impress in many important ways. Both friend and foe praised the doctor for his services at Monterey, although differences of opinion arose as to his motives.

Here we encounter an anomaly of Gwin's career. The senator-to-be was destined to pass through every phase of political fortune and misfortune; he would be adulated and reviled, trusted and suspected, loathed and honored, until the truth about his character and his actions became difficult to determine. Historically, Gwin was to be "written up" by a generation of historians who had come to oppose him and his party with a virulence distilled from wartime hatreds; he was to suffer from a "bad press."

During the fifties, this emergent negative attitude toward him would be reflected in the "explaining away" of his undeniably notable contributions to the 1849 convention; his benevolent accomplishments would be viewed as a mask for malignant self-seeking, and his good works ascribed to bad motives. His pronounced and useful talents as a conciliator, a compromiser, who gained ends by indirection rather than by frontal assault, would be put down as ingrained duplicity and craftiness. His parliamentary suppleness would be construed as want of principle. The epithet that would be applied to him again and again is "the great schemer," and in one way or another all his "schemes" were assumed to be sinister. The means by which his true motives were determined have never been explained; nor how those who denounced the reasons for his actions, while praising the results of those actions, were able to penetrate behind his plain spoken words. How far such hindsight assumptions by his critics were soundly based must be examined; for here, perhaps, lies the key to Gwin's character and to his vicissitudes later on.

❋

2

The convention was scheduled to meet at Monterey on September 1, 1849. Some delegates arrived by that date, and met, but in default of a quorum adjourned pending the arrival of the San Francisco delegation. This group made the hundred-mile trip to Monterey in a sailing vessel chartered by the army quartermaster at San Francisco. They were lost in the fog four days, skirting one of the most dangerous coasts in the world, expecting every moment to strike a rock and founder, and subsisting on meager rations. The only provisions for the party of thirty were a forequarter of beef, a little salt pork, a little rice, and "execrable hard tack." On September 3 the party stumbled ashore at Monterey, half-famished and wholly disgruntled, and they got down to business at once.

Monterey was a village of adobe houses and shacks, located on its own bay, and under Mexican rule it had been the seat of government for Northern California. The place was ill-equipped to house and feed a gathering as large as the convention and the many hangers-on who thronged there for one purpose or another. Some of the delegates had had the foresight to bring blankets and sleeping rolls, and they camped where they could. Shelter of a sort, amidst the fleas and chickens, was found for others, but food was scarce. Thomas O. Larkin, the Yankee trader who had served as United States consul at Monterey before the conquest, was a delegate, and every day he punctiliously invited one of the other delegates to lunch, and another to dinner, although at times his larder was strained by this hospitality.

The physical discomforts, however, were taken in stride and the convention was soon organized. There were no precedents to serve as guides, and in the general unfamiliarity with legislative processes Gwin's experience moved him at once into the forefront. Long afterward survivors of the convention were to say that he wanted to be chosen president of the assemblage, but if so, there is no evidence that he exerted himself seriously to obtain that position; and when Dr. Semple, an American who had lived in California several years, was elected president, Gwin expressed himself as entirely satisfied. The truth was that he enjoyed the greater freedom of the floor, and he was made chairman of the key committee, assigned to frame a constitution. He also served actively on other committees.

The forty-eight delegates formed a heterogeneous group in respect to origins, interests, and prepossessions. There were seven Spanish-speaking Californians, representing mainly the southern end of the territory. Thirty-five of the delegates had been in California longer than one year, and these greatly outnumbered the thirteen who, like Gwin, had arrived within the last year. Five of the delegates had been born in Europe; all the others, except the Californians, were natives of the United States. Twenty-two had come from free states (New York, Pennsylvania, New Jersey, Ohio, and the New England area), while fourteen were from slaveholding states (Virginia, Maryland, Kentucky, Tennessee, Missouri, and Florida). There were fourteen lawyers, eight merchants, eleven farmers, and fifteen engaged in other occupations. Youth predominated: nine of the delegates were under thirty years old; twenty-three were between thirty and forty; and twelve were between forty and fifty; while ripe age was represented by four men who were over fifty.

The aspirations, property interests, and sectional prejudices of the delegates were widely diversified. To reach agreement on a constitution that would satisfy the basic needs of each faction, in a manner that would inure to the benefit of all, they would have to rely on their own good sense, patriotism, and feeling for order, for their situation was unique and their divisions ran deep. Besides the barriers of language and national character which separated the Americans from the Spanish Californians, there was the cleavage between the Americans who had taken root in the country before the gold discovery, and the newcomers whose main interest was mining. Northern and Southern delegates were certain to disagree over the ever present issue of slavery. And there were jealousies between the delegates from the northern part of the territory, where most of the gold mines were located, and those who represented the southern region, which was agricultural, long settled, and conservative.

It was in this motley assemblage of men, well intentioned but handicapped by inexperience in the sort of work they were undertaking, that Gwin's abilities stood out to advantage. He was by far the best informed and the most politically seasoned delegate, and by general agreement he was the ablest. His Eastern connections gave him prestige: presumably he could command a hearing for California in national councils. As a modern essayist has phrased it, he possessed "the talent, courage, firmness, and fidelity to friends to qualify him as a leader." And in addition his methods were diplomatic. Josiah Royce, a California-born historian who followed the lead of Hubert Howe Bancroft in attributing to Gwin a thoroughly bad character, conceded that in the convention's debates the doctor was "conciliatory, thoughtful, learned, and reasonable. He avoided above all directly broaching sectional topics, or matters that could arouse jealousy between classes of people." He displayed (said Royce) "marvelous skill" in the means by which, "although unable to carry his point, still in minor matters [he] directed the course of the proceedings." Gradually, this same authority continued, the doctor attracted about him "such a following that . . . he made himself a power in the convention and assured for himself a prominent position in the future political life of the State." It was Royce's considered opinion that a detailed study of the convention debates "would read in large part like a chapter from [Gwin's] political biography." And then Royce put Gwin upon a pedestal of dubious fame by terming him "intellectually the most admirable of all the unprincipled political intriguers in the history of California."

3

Since this moral disapproval, expressed long after the event, goes to the heart of the controversies that were to rage around Gwin in the fifties and sixties, it is necessary to examine a little the validity of the charges that were raised against him. These boil down to the contention that Gwin was politically unprincipled; that he veiled rapacity with a show of generosity; that he was selfish, sordid in motives, insincere, and interested only in acquiring and retaining personal power.

As instances of his supposed duplicity and deviousness the action he took on two important issues confronting the 1849 convention is sometimes cited. The issues in question were the proposal to permit slavery in the state, and the delineation of the state's boundaries. Slavery was an issue from which no region or section of the nation was exempt. The slave states and the free states at that time were even in number, fifteen of each. Their representation in the Senate thus was evenly balanced. The addition of another state in either category would upset the balance, and it was over this question that Congress had repeatedly deadlocked and failed to provide a government for California.

The constitution drafted at Monterey included a clause prohibiting slavery in California forever. This clause was adopted unanimously. Gwin voted for it, though he came from a slaveholding section, owned slaves, and by his superior abilities and experience it would have been natural for him to have assumed the leadership of the pro-slavery Southern delegation in the con-

vention. Later his vote to exclude slavery from California
would be construed by men hostile to him as an act of deception, a mere yielding to political circumstances, since the Southern delegates were outnumbered by free-staters almost two to
one. It was claimed that even while he was voting for the antislavery clause, he was bringing to the brink of success a cunning scheme to create a separate slave state out of a portion of
California's territory at some future date.

This "plot," as it was termed, was intimately connected with
the question of the boundaries to be assigned to California.
Gwin wanted to include all the territory ceded by Mexico. This
was a vast domain, largely uninhabited, that had gone under
the designation of Alta California. It embraced not only modern
California, but Nevada, Utah, Arizona, and parts of Wyoming,
Colorado, and New Mexico.

Opponents of this plan objected that California, itself in the
throes of birth, could never exercise effective authority over so
immense an area, and that as fast as settlers moved in, the territory would be bound to split up into several states. These opponents wanted to set the boundaries about as they stand now,
taking in the ocean front from Mexico to Oregon.

In urging the larger area, Gwin's secret objective, his critics
later averred, was to pave the way for the creation of one or
more slave states out of the unwieldy range of territory. This
was not his purpose as he stated it in debate. He conceded that
it was doubtful that Congress would admit a state as large as he
proposed, but would insist upon a division; and in that event,
he went on, each of the states so formed would demand access
to the sea. The Atlantic coast was not monopolized by a single
state, he pointed out, but was shared among fifteen, and he desired to see a similar distribution in the West; the reason being
that it would give the Pacific area a greater voice in setting
national policies. He stated his motive, for the clear understanding of the other delegates, as follows:

I have not the remotest idea that the Congress of the United States would give us this great extent of boundary if it was expected that it would remain one State. And when gentlemen say that they will never give up one inch of the Pacific coast, they say what they cannot carry out. So far as I am concerned, I should like to see six States fronting on the Pacific in California. I want the additional power in the Congress of the United States of twelve senators . . . for it is notorious, sir, that the State of Delaware, smaller than our smallest district, has as much power in the Senate as the great State of New York. . . .

In this expectation of an eventual division of the state, Gwin's critics maintained that he and his Southern associates plotted to add one or more slave states by stealth, since they could not openly, and that Gwin cynically enlisted support for his scheme among the suspicious native Californians by appealing to their fear of being swallowed up by the invading horde of Americans. These Californians would gladly have been independent of the northern portion. The fact is that the two sections were and still are so antipathetic and dissimilar in their needs that sentiment for separation has persisted to this day.

Gwin carried his boundary plan through two committees, but the convention voted it down and set the state's borders approximately as they exist today. And no person, either then or later, ever produced proof, or claimed that he had received the slightest intimation from Gwin himself, that he acted at Monterey from motives other than those he avowed.

4

Dr. Gwin was a Southerner born and bred; his family, his home, his property, his friendships were in the South; he had been nourished by its institutions, he loved its customs, and every issue affecting the South was of concern to him. However, his was not a parochial mind. His mind instinctively ranged out toward new horizons and new lands and new conditions; he never was and never became a narrowly sectional politician on questions that involved the national welfare. As a Congressman in 1842, his speeches showed an awareness, at least, of the needs of the nation as a whole. His diligence in promoting the interests of the burgeoning Southwest (Mississippi itself was scarcely out of the frontier stage) was based in part upon his conviction that opening up that area would contribute to the well-being of the entire nation. He believed in the expansionist role of the United States. His wholehearted enlistment in the cause of California was rooted in a commitment to that policy. The United States, in his view, required a strong establishment on the Western shore for its own safety and the realization of its full greatness. There is no passage in any of his speeches, made at Monterey or elsewhere, which indicates that his interest in California was derived from devotion to either the slave states or the free states. He held slavery to be incompatible with the soil, climate, and topography of California. In his words, later appropriated by Daniel Webster, the question of slavery in California had been settled by nature. And obviously a society where free men willingly bent their backs to perform the roughest sort of manual labor, as the miners did, offered no congenial ground for a master-slave relationship.

Gwin's private views on slavery were those entertained by many enlightened and well-meaning men of the South. He owned slaves, and he would not go so far as his associate, Robert Walker, who manumitted his slaves just before the Civil War. Gwin detested what he felt to be the ignorance and bigotry of the abolitionists, who would gladly have sacrificed the nation in order to achieve their end. In the Senate he would maintain that the "peculiar institution" was benevolent in fact, that mutual affection subsisted between the slaves and their masters. This was not mere rhetorical license; it was a belief held, however fallaciously, by many good men in the South. Regarding the economic value of slavery, Gwin, as an astute businessman, had reservations. If we may accept his statement made years afterward, he went to California in part "for the express purpose of withdrawing [myself] and [my] posterity from that part of the country where slavery existed, believing . . . that the institution of slavery would be a curse to the white inhabitants where it prevailed." This may be discounted but the fact is that Gwin did leave the South; he did come to California; he did settle his family there; and he would round out his days as a Californian, in the state he had helped to vote free.

One may take into account the interesting testimony of one observer of the Monterey convention, William Tecumseh Sherman, then a lieutenant of dragoons stationed in California. Sherman had been detailed by General Persifer Smith to report on the Monterey proceedings; and he recorded that although slavery was an important issue, the debates on the subject seemed to him perfunctory and he saw no excitement at any time. This surprised him, because of the extreme views held by some of the Southern delegates, who admittedly would have liked to form at least one slave state out of the ceded territory. Sherman recalled nothing to indicate that Gwin had favored or abetted the aspirations of these extremists. And in the debates Gwin had exerted all his influence to dispose of the issue of slavery decisively and permanently, so that there could be no future agitation of the question. To the North, he cautioned the delegates, slavery was "a sentiment; to the South, a point of honor. A point of honor which may dissolve our confederacy. . . . Leave no room to bring it up, in the consideration of your constitution."

That the man who uttered this warning — which he would repeat many times in his career — should, by sly scheming, have attempted to make possible a future revival of the issue, is hardly to be credited, and in the absence of corroborative evidence such an assumption must be put down as conforming to neither the probabilities nor the facts.

5

Gwin's contributions to the drafting of the Monterey constitution were practical as well as theoretical. When the delegates assembled, the only model they had to work from was a copy of the Iowa state constitution which he had brought along, and which had the merit of brevity. This he had reproduced for use as a guide. Later a copy of the New York state constitution was procured, and these two served to help shape the Monterey document.

Gwin's influence was discernible in the drafting of numerous clauses. He inserted provisions for public schools, a step in advance of the time. He strove hard to impose an absolute ban on dueling, putting it on a legal par with murderous assault and murder, but the delegates watered this down to forfeiture of civil rights. As it turned out, even this would not be enforced. He led the fight to prohibit state banks, of which he had had sorry experience in Mississippi. He opposed a large state debt, and urged the delegates to move with caution in "infringing the rights of the people by legalizing the association of capital to war on labor." Aristocratic in his tastes, his policies were in the main Jacksonian and democratic.

Both in debate and in committee he displayed great strategic ingenuity. If a resolution threatened to cause friction, he would withdraw it, and attain his objective by the clever use of amendments. Always open to compromise, he was never mandatory or dictatorial. He proved adept at drawing discussion to a close, and was able to meet objections without wounding sensibilities. Quick to spot the essential point or flaw in an argument, he could state it clearly. No other delegate rivaled him in effectiveness, and it was due in large part to his address, his statesmanlike and long-range views, and his tireless application that the convention produced a workable constitution and wound up its labors on October 31.

General Riley, the military governor, honored this stride toward the addition of a thirty-first state by a thirty-one-gun salute and a grand ball. The dancing was mainly by men with men, for there were few women in Monterey, but the delegates celebrated heartily, having reason to be satisfied.

Ratification of their work by popular vote came on November 13. The voting was perfunctory and the constitution was approved almost unanimously. At the same time, the voters elected a governor, lieutenant governor, legislature, and two Representatives to Congress. Election of the state's two senators was left to the legislature.

6

This first legislature of California met in San Jose one month after its election. The weather was dismal; that winter was one of phenomenal rains, and the town and countryside resembled a continuous quagmire. Primitive accommodations added to the misery, and the members hastened to dispatch their business and escape from the "wind, rain, and cold wittels."

The contest for the senatorships was spirited but good-natured. John Charles Frémont was riding a wave of popularity for his part in bringing California under the Stars and Stripes, and he was elected on the first ballot. Gwin was the runner-up, trailed by Thomas Butler King (fully recovered from his sunstroke) and Captain Henry Wager Halleck, the army engineer and lawyer who had been serving as Secretary of State.

On the second ballot Gwin led, but failed to secure a majority. The third cast was conclusive, Gwin receiving twenty-four of the forty-seven votes. The date was December 31, 1849.

Leaving San Jose in haste, the senator-elect plowed through the mud back to San Francisco, and the next day, January 1, 1850, steamed out of the Golden Gate aboard the mail steamer *Oregon,* bound for the Isthmus and Washington. At Monterey the *Oregon* paused to let Frémont come aboard in a driving rain, carrying his tiny, ailing wife, Jessie Benton Frémont, in his arms. The run down the coast thereafter proved uneventful. Stops were made at Acapulco and Mazatlán to take on fuel and fresh fruits, and then Gwin saw Panama come into view again. Frémont had become so alarmed by Jessie's illness that he decided to wait at Panama until the next month's ship up the Atlantic side, but Gwin pushed on. He recrossed the Isthmus by the same primitive, laborious means he had used nine months previously, and at Chagres was rowed out through the surf to the steamer *Empire City,* bound for New Orleans.

The day Gwin left Chagres was January 24, 1850, and that day, unknown to him, saw the entrance upon the political scene of California of his great adversary, David Colbrith Broderick. On January 24, 1850, Broderick took his seat in the senate of the California legislature, and thereby rang up the curtain upon a drama that for intensity, duration, violence, and tragic consequences has few counterparts in American political history.

Chapter IV

OF THE THOUSANDS attracted to the new land of California, relatively few came with any intention of remaining. Most of the gold rush immigrants hoped to make a quick cleanup at the mines, take their "pile," and return home. But there were some among the newcomers who had no desire to return to the conditions of life which they had formerly known. California for them was a refuge and "a new chance." David Colbrith Broderick was one of these.

It would be hard to find two men more dissimilar, in their origins, education, social background, previous attainments, temperament, or character, than Broderick and Gwin. In their forcefulness, political talent, and readiness to risk much to attain success, they were equal; and they shared one fixed ambition. Since by chance they had chosen the same place and time to realize that ambition, it was inevitable that they should clash and in time mutually destroy each other.

William McKendree Gwin had been born to a life of comfort and esteem; David Broderick had been born to obscurity and sordid surroundings. Gwin had been educated for two learned professions, law and medicine; Broderick acquired his fragmentary education through grim application long after his youth. For Gwin the road to political preferment had been an easy highway, along which he had been helped by the most powerful influences in the land; Broderick was forced to batter down the door to political opportunity. Gwin's patrons were men of renown; Broderick's were the spawn of the slums.

Gwin was blessed by an affectionate family relationship; Broderick was a solitary. Gwin's nature was social and buoyant; Broderick's was repellent and gloomy. While Gwin moved amidst a society noted for grace, elegance, and charm, to Broderick that society existed only to be displaced. In short, Gwin was rich and favored; Broderick was poor and, in the modern phrase, mightily underprivileged. But their ambition was the same.

2

The "short and simple annals of the poor" describes the story of Broderick's early life. His father was a stonemason who came from Ireland early in the century and found employment on the Capitol Building in Washington; the capitals of the columns along the east front, standing before which Zachary Taylor, on March 5, 1849, took the oath of office, were his handiwork.

David was born in Washington on February 4, 1820, the older of two sons, his brother, Richard, being born in 1822. In 1834, when David was fourteen, the family moved to New York City, where David was apprenticed to a stonecutter who maintained a yard at the corner of Washington and Barrow streets. Already the lad was tall and muscular, and he soon developed into a competent journeyman. In 1837 his father died, and the support of his mother and brother fell to him. His devotion to the family was intense; he worked hard; and since they were inured to poverty and familiar with the shifts by which the poor live, they managed to make ends meet.

But David was not content with a workingman's life. Around him, in the swiftly growing city, he saw wealth and comfort and social elevation, and these he coveted for himself and those dependent upon him. He was ambitious to rise in the world; and as a first step he joined a volunteer fire com-

pany, Number 34. It speaks well for his sharp wits and aggressiveness that in a short while the company chose him their
foreman. This was a position of high honor in his world. Some
of the fire companies enjoyed close links with the city's political
organization embodied in Tammany Hall, and in the rivalry
for favors the volunteers fought each other about as much as
they fought fires. In that sort of bare-knuckle brawling Broderick proved a formidable prop for company Number 34.

From running fires to running errands for Tammany was a
natural step, and before he was twenty Broderick was representing the Ninth Ward in the Democratic party's city and
county conventions. The Ninth Ward extended to the Hudson River west of Washington Square, in the area later known
as Greenwich Village; sparsely settled, it was considered of
little importance at the Hall, and Broderick's position was
among the lowliest on the Tammany ladder.

New York's Democrats were ruled then by an old-line, "respectable" element, which took its cues from the courtly Albany
Regency, headed by Martin Van Buren, a very wily and cultured gentleman. Tammany's grand sachem, Elijah J. Purdy,
was of Knickerbocker stock, and he showed his breeding when
rewards were handed out after an election victory: the well-
paying jobs, the ones that carried profit and prestige, fell to
representatives of the "best families," while the rank and file,
as typified by Broderick, were assigned the places that involved
much labor and little pay — such as lamplighters, watchmen,
or petty clerks. This unequal distribution of favors grated on
Broderick, as it grated on others in the organization.

Two mavericks of Tammany who spoke out boldly against
the prevailing favoritism were Mike Walsh and George Wilkes.
They were two of a kind, half-genius and half-charlatan, and
Wilkes, in addition, was thoroughly corrupt. Walsh was a rab-
ble-rouser who respected no man when he felt called upon to
lash the oppressors of the poor. The worst of these harpies, he

maintained, were venal politicians who worked hand in glove with the predatory rich. Walsh's tirades enraged his Tammany superiors, but he was so idolized by the crowd that they were compelled to swallow his impudence. He could be silenced by no ordinary tactics. Once when hecklers yelled, "Throw him out!" he bellowed back:

"Come up, come up here, you cravenly, cowardly scoundrels! You that are hallooing, I mean, and pull me off the stand yourselves! Isn't this a pretty scene, there now — a parcel of hirelings, menials, police officers, and their companions — the very stool pigeons and thieves I've been describing! Abject, willing slaves! Yes, slaves by choice, while you flatter yourselves that you are Democrats!"

This contempt for servility struck a responsive chord in young Broderick, and he became a warm admirer of Mike Walsh and an avid reader of Walsh's incendiary newspaper, *The Subterranean.*

The time finally came when Walsh's indiscriminate outbursts led to his arrest for criminal libel, and he was sentenced to a term in the city prison. Broderick was outraged by this demonstration of injustice, and in the heat of his anger he urged Mike to seize the crown of martyrdom in the cause of free speech, and hurl himself into the East River from the police boat as it took him to prison on Blackwell's Island. Walsh perceived the dramatic possibilities in such a gesture, and consented; and Broderick came to the dock to bid the hero an eternal good-bye. In a voice that must have startled the attending policemen he called out, as the boat pushed off:

"Hero! Martyr! Farewell forever! I shall remain behind to see that posterity does you justice!"

By the time Walsh reached midstream he had decided to live and vindicate himself. Broderick never forgave him.

*

3

Associated with Walsh in editing *The Subterranean* was Wilkes, a man of many sides, most of them seamy. A chameleon of the sewers, he was as versatile as he was dissolute. But Wilkes was educated and he had the gift of words. When it came his turn to languish in jail for uttering libels, he used the time to write a book entitled *Secrets of the Tombs.* In a racy style, spiced with salacious anecdotes, he exposed the blackmail that was practiced by the courts and police against prostitutes and petty crooks. Since Wilkes had participated in the practice, his account rang true, and the book became a best seller.

Wilkes's character may be judged by the result of a suit for slander which he brought against one John Chamberlain, who had stated publicly that Wilkes "acted like the son of a prostitute, and lived like one brought up in a brothel, and had been supported by the wages of prostitution." Chamberlain pleaded the truth of his statement, and in an affidavit amplified it, asserting "that the said George Wilkes, plaintiff herein, filled that role [pimp] with the said Kate, and as her 'fancy man' frequented her house, took her money, gratified her lusts, eating the bread that had been won and wearing the clothes that had been bought by the wages of prostitutes."

The jury agreed with Chamberlain and Wilkes lost the case.

This man — gifted, erratic, unprincipled — became the political mentor of young David Broderick. Wilkes saw possibilities in the ignorant stonecutter, and set out to help him fulfill them. Lack of education was Broderick's biggest handicap, and Wilkes laid out a course of reading. At the same time he took his protégé behind the scenes of the city's political setup, laying bare its innermost secrets. There was not a trick of politics, no matter how base or corrupt, that George Wilkes did not know and on occasion practice, and Broderick was introduced to them all. He proved an apt pupil. But for book learning he had no taste, and this side of the education Wilkes offered him he neglected.

It was not by choice that Broderick accepted the tutelage of a man like George Wilkes. At his social level, such men were looked up to, envied, and imitated, for they had risen to the top of their class. Broderick would never be ashamed of his beginnings, though he would never be so weak as to glory in them, and he would candidly admit that he would have liked to have been born into better surroundings. But he never apologized for having grasped a hand held out to him in helpfulness, whether it was clean or dirty.

4

In 1842 (when Dr. Gwin was winding up his term in the House of Representatives) Broderick's mother died, and his affection became centered upon his brother, Richard. Through Tammany influence he had acquired two saloons — one of which he had named The Subterranean in honor of Walsh and Wilkes. The profits from these he began to set aside to provide Richard with a good start in life.

Thanks to his political tutoring, he had learned that Tammany Hall, which seemed to control the city by vote-rigging, bribery, patronage, and perjury, was really a front for the genteel moneyed interests, who held the real power. To that all-powerful upper class, Broderick was painfully aware, he and his sort were distasteful; sunk in a slum, he probably would stay there. But his resentment against the injustice smoldered.

Then in 1844 he suffered a traumatic shock when his brother was killed in a horrifying accident. Richard, rummaging with pals in a foundry scrap heap, found an apparently "dud" bomb, and tried to bore into it with a red-hot poker. The bomb exploded and Richard was blown to bits.

Broderick's grief was harrowing. For months he brooded, his thoughts turned inward, shunning company. Where before he had been noisy and pugnacious, he grew morose and taciturn. Richard's death left him without an outlet for his stormy affections; society seemed to have repulsed him at every point. He felt capable of great actions, but first the world had thrust him out, and now fate had ground him down with a terrible affliction. He yearned to be respected, yet respect, he saw, was a tribute that only power could exact. Very well: he would meet the world with the world's weapons.

The sort of power he understood best was political, and gradually his grief-saturated reveries became focused. What position commanded more respect, or exercised greater power, than that of a United States senator? Should he sit in the chamber on whose ornamentation his father had worked, that would be compensation for the injustices life had heaped upon him! The thought became a fixation and a personal challenge.

He started by running for Congress from his district in 1846. Although he was on the Tammany ticket, he was defeated, for which he blamed Tammany's behind-the-scenes masters, the city's rich and powerful. He was convinced that they had refused to admit him to their privileged circle, and that his uncouth appearance and boorish manners would always be unacceptable to them.

During this campaign, Broderick acquired a friend to whom he managed to reveal glimpses of his inner feelings. This was Daniel Sickles, a roistering young Tammany lawyer with fine manners and razor-sharp brains, but not a scruple to his name. Sickles was made free of the city's respectable society, but was perhaps more at home in the carousing underworld of politics and dissipation. As bold as Broderick, he had the advantage of a sound education and social polish. Sickles was struck by Broderick's deadly earnestness; like George Wilkes, he sensed a strength in the man to which he responded but which he could not explain. With his customary careless generosity, Sickles had pitched in and campaigned for Broderick, and he was disappointed by the defeat.

The depth and intensity of Broderick's gratitude for this help, so good-naturedly extended, startled Sickles. "If you ever need me," Broderick told him with grim fervor, "call me, and I will be your slave." Sickles took no promises, least of all his own, very seriously, but he believed in this one.

Two years later Sickles was given another glimpse into his friend's mind, when, in a burst of confidence, Broderick told him that there was no future for himself in New York, where he would always be an outsider, and that he was pulling up stakes and joining the rush to California. Nothing held him in the East, he said; he was alone in the world; and if he should fail, nobody would be hurt except himself, while if he succeeded it would be without favor from anybody. Furthermore, he knew exactly the goal he was aiming at. "If I ever return," he said, "it will be as a United States senator."

Sickles saw not the slightest chance of such an ambition being realized, but he wished his strange, remote friend good luck.

Broderick disposed of his saloons. There is a story, which may be apocryphal but is certainly true in spirit, that he emptied the barrels of whiskey into the gutter, vowing never to take another drink, smoke tobacco, or touch a playing card. Whether the story is true or not, the fact is that thenceforth he lived in Spartan austerity, without any of the normal distractions and satisfactions of life. Nothing — and David Broderick meant *nothing* — should be permitted to stand in his way or deflect him from his course.

When Zachary Taylor entered the White House, Broderick was at sea, on his way to the Isthmus. From Chagres, he, like Gwin, crossed to Panama City by canoe and muleback, and like Gwin he found himself marooned on the Pacific side with no ship to carry him farther. The two men were in Panama at the same time, among the hundreds stranded there. It is possible that Broderick may have heard Gwin's name, but it is certain that the doctor had never heard of the insignificant Tammany hack.

The cost of living at Panama was extravagantly high, and many of the immigrants exhausted their money there. Broderick may have suffered financially, for he did not take a mail steamer to San Francisco, the passage rates being high, and when he landed he was virtually broke. Just how he did make his way north from Panama is uncertain. It is recorded that he landed at San Francisco on June 13, 1849 — nine days after Gwin — from the bark *Stella,* although no vessel by that name is listed as arriving during June.

5

Broderick was said to have been weak from the aftereffects of fever contracted at Panama when he touched shore at Yerba Buena cove. But he met with a ready welcome from the numerous New Yorkers already on hand. One of these was Colonel Jonathan D. Stevenson, a former Tammany associate, who had led a regiment of volunteers to California during the late war with Mexico. Stevenson was a rich and influential man in San Francisco, and he put Broderick in touch with another New Yorker, Frederick C. Kohler, an assayer. Kohler had been a volunteer fireman in New York, and perhaps had known Broderick there.

With Stevenson's financial help, the two ex-firemen formed a partnership to manufacture the gold "slugs" that were used as a substitute for currency in local trade. These "slugs" were little wedges of gold stamped "$5" and "$10," although they contained only four dollars and eight dollars worth of gold. Since only the last person to hold them stood to lose, they were accepted everywhere at face value, and Kohler and Broderick found their product in brisk demand. Kohler contributed his assayer's skill and Broderick provided the brawn to cast and file the "slugs." By December, the two had amassed a capital of several thousand dollars.

Meanwhile, Broderick had kept an eye on the political developments leading up to adoption of the state constitution, although he took no part in them. In December, however, a vacancy occurred in the senate of the new legislature, and he declared himself a candidate. There was no party organization; he simply announced that he was in the running. Once the state government had been set up, few men cared to bog themselves down in public office, the salary paid to a legislator being a pittance compared with what a man could earn otherwise. At the mines, for instance, one could wash out twenty to fifty dollars a day in gold, if he had the least luck, and there was always the chance of uncovering nuggets worth much more. And merchants, during those early months of the gold rush, simply could not supply the demand for supplies of all sorts, from baking powder and fancy vests to shovels and mule harness. Politics, however, was Broderick's vocation, and with a little canvassing he succeeded in winning election to the state senate. The contest aroused scarcely a flicker of interest.

Liquidating his partnership with Kohler, Broderick went to San Jose and took his seat in the senate on January 24, 1850. Ironically, it was on that date that Dr. Gwin left Chagres on the last leg of his journey to assume his place in the more illustrious Senate at Washington.

Chapter V

THE ARRIVAL AT New York of Senator-elect Gwin caused a sensation. Word had come through that the Californians had adopted a state constitution, but it was not known that a Congressional delegation had been chosen, and there was immediate speculation that the admission of this new state might bring about the long-mooted dissolution of the Union.

With Gwin were California's first members of the House of Representatives, Edward Gilbert and George W. Wright. They excited curiosity because they seemed living examples of the swiftness with which the whole trend of a life could be altered in the West. A few years previously, Gilbert had been a journeyman printer in the shop of the Albany, New York, *Argus*; now, although he had barely turned thirty, he owned San Francisco's leading newspaper, the *Alta California,* and was rich. Wright, who had been poor and obscure when he reached California, had started in business with capital provided by a small loan from a miner who had struck it rich, and had quickly become affluent himself.

But Gwin overshadowed his associates, and in the absence of Frémont, who was still at Panama, public attention focused on him. Without pausing, he pushed ahead to Washington, and had the satisfaction of fulfilling the prediction he had made to Senator Douglas eleven months before. Until his state should be recognized by Congress, he must remain a senator-elect, but he had no doubt that he would be seated shortly.

The violence of the political storm that arose quite surprised

him. At issue was the question of the extension of slavery into
the territory taken from Merico. The general controversy between North and South had been fought over for a generation.
With the balance between the slaveholding and non-slaveholding states even, the admission of California would upset this
equilibrium, and neither side wished to give up the status quo.
The fact that the Californians themselves had written a ban on
slavery into their constitution only made the situation worse,
for the slave states denied their right to do this, and the action
was construed in those quarters as a violation of the federal
constitution.

Gwin found Washington much agitated over the matter, and
some of his Southern friends mourned his apostacy in having
voted to keep California free. Calhoun sent for him and re-
proached him for having betrayed the interests of the South.
The old man would not be mollified by Gwin's explanation of
the political realities, but warned that the Union was doomed
if Congress should admit California on the proposed basis.

Not a few members of Congress, particularly Southern hotheads, resented Gwin's presence in Washington while the issue
was being debated, and after making the necessary preliminary
calls, Gwin and his colleagues tactfully withdrew to New York.
From there he kept in touch with the struggle which continued throughout the spring and the abnormally hot and oppres-
sive summer. In the Senate the debate brought together for
the last time the three giants, Clay, Webster, and Calhoun. Before the session ended Calhoun was dead, and Webster and
Clay would follow shortly.

Calhoun's estrangement grieved Gwin; he was moved by the
old senator's reproaches in their last interview. He could not
but contrast that scene with the last communication he had
received from General Jackson. This had been in 1845, at a
time when Gwin was under fire regarding the Chicksaw claim.
A rumor was circulated that "Old Hickory" had repudiated

his friend, and in the last letter penned with his own hand, written a few days before his death at The Hermitage, Jackson had urged Gwin to take heart, saying:

> It is the day of vituperation and slander, and you, like all other public men, must expect your share. I trust my character is too well known to believe that I would abandon a friend who once had my confidence and esteem without positive proof that he had done some act sufficient to forfeit it. I have been your friend. I am still so, as I was your venerated father's and brother's, whose memories I cherish with the liveliest recollections. I have full confidence in your patriotism and democratic principles, and you possess too much honesty and personal worth, and those high, lofty, and honorable feelings, ever to permit you to do an act dishonorable, or that would tarnish the good, moral character which you have brought into life with you and have sustained to this present day. I am, as I have ever been, your friend, and my best wishes for your prosperity and happiness, and that of your family, will attend you through life; and if we should not meet again here below, I hope to meet you in blissful immortality. My whole household salute you and yours.

A new era was starting, which aligned men in new ways — a time of fierce squalls before the hurricane. From first to last, Gwin would be in the very eye of the storm.

2

The first action of the California delegation upon reaching Washington had been to call upon influential members of Congress to solicit their support, and among these leaders was perhaps the most influential of all, Henry Clay. After careful consideration, according to Gwin, Clay "expressed his desire that the State should be instantly admitted, and said he would exert himself for its instant admission."

President Taylor also assured the Californians that he was

for admitting the state at once, and said he would submit the constitution to Congress with a recommendation that it be approved. The President had almost boxed the compass in his views on California since taking office. On the day of his inauguration, as he rode back from the Capitol with ex-President Polk, he had expressed his opinion that California was too remote to be identified successfully with the national interest, and that the best course for the people there would be to declare their independence and establish their own republic. With what heart-sinking Polk had heard this airy dismissal of a task he had devoted his life to accomplish can only be conjectured, for he made no audible reply. But a year later the President had become convinced that California must be attached to the Union speedily to protect American sovereignty in the Far West.

Trusting to these pledges, Gwin had withdrawn to New York. But word soon reached him that Senator Clay had shifted his position. Filled with alarm, Gwin hurried back to Washington, where Clay explained that certain members of the House of Representatives had called on him and "had pledged their honor" that they would prevent the admission of California until the whole question of slavery in the territories was decided to their satisfaction. Clay said they controlled enough votes to carry out their design, and they had assured him that they were prepared "to prosecute their determination even to the destruction of the government." Faced with this adamant opposition, the senator said he was elaborating a many-phased compromise which he hoped would bridge the crisis and preserve the Union.

Under the circumstances, Gwin agreed that it would be unwise to risk an immediate vote. As a Southerner, he saw the Union as a confederacy of sovereign states, but the destruction of that Union he believed would be catastrophic for all concerned. As one day he would tell his fellow senators:

I acquiesced in the view of the senator from Kentucky. I did not want the admission of California to cause the destruction of the Union itself; and hence I was willing to have her just right delayed, and the privileges to which she was entitled, as a portion of the confederacy, overlooked, for a time, rather than that her admission should result in the destruction of the very confederacy of which she sought to be a member.

While Clay was drafting his great compromise of 1850 — the crowning achievement of his life, the aged statesman believed — Gwin frequently was called into consultation; he was both an authority on California, and one who knew intimately the South's temper and the extent to which it could make concessions. Daniel Webster also leaned on Gwin's knowledge of the Pacific area, and it was Gwin who helped to shape those portions of the Massachusetts leader's Seventh of March speech devoted to showing that climate itself had settled the question of slavery in California.

One senator who favored California's admission unconditionally was the new Whig member from New York, William Henry Seward. A former governor of New York State, a free-soiler and outspoken opponent of the extension of slavery, Seward, like Gwin, was aware of the national scene, and he was ready to vote California into the Union with or without slavery, so important did it seem to him that the nation should build up its outpost on the Western coast. Gwin welcomed Seward's support, and their similarity of views on Western issues led to a close understanding between them, although they subscribed to basically different political theories.

Clay's impassioned defense of his compromise measure, which offered something to everybody, but everything to nobody; Webster's momentous speech, in which he placed the welfare of the Union above that of any of its parts; the dying Calhoun's stubborn refusal to surrender one iota of the South's claims — these are written into the record of that debate over California. Threats of dissolution were freely uttered, and fear that the taunts portended action alternated with hope that they would prove to be merely bluster. Gwin, whose sympathy and association with the Southern spokesmen gave him a sound basis for judging realistically, was persuaded that the threats were serious; and his apprehension increased when President Taylor applied pressure to compel California's admission, irrespective of the slavery question.

Summoning the California delegation to the White House, the President asked them to draw up a memorial to both houses of Congress, setting forth why California should be bound to the Union without further delay. Taylor opposed Clay's compromise, and told the Californians that if they would consent to divorce the slavery issue from that of simple admission, he "pledged himself . . . that California would be admitted in a week."

The memorial was prepared and forwarded to Congress. But the battle grew hotter. A band of Southerners, led by the fiery Robert Toombs of Georgia, called at the White House and demanded that Taylor veto the Clay compromise, should it reach his desk; if not, the South knew where its interests lay. "Old Rough and Ready" retorted with a promise of "hangings" if the South tried to wreck the Union.

In a major speech, on July 2, Seward dwelt upon the ludicrous spectacle of rich California, begging to incorporate its magnificent resources into the Union and being spurned:

> If an alien in our land should chance to enter here during this high debate [cried Seward], he would ask whether California was a stranger and an enemy; or an unbidden and unwelcome intruder; or a fugitive, powerless and portionless, and therefore importunate; or an oppressor and scourge of mankind, and therefore hateful and dangerous. We should be obliged to answer, No! California . . . has brought us to the banks of streams which flow over

precious sands. . . . She delivers into our hand the key that
unlocks the long coveted treasures of the Eastern world. California refuses only to let us buy and sell each other within her
domain. . . .

Then suddenly, in July, President Taylor died and was succeeded by the smooth-speaking Vice-President, Millard Fillmore. The nation's shock diverted attention from the California debate long enough to ease the tension; but Gwin always
remained convinced that had Taylor lived, the issue would
have been forced to a point that would have precipitated the
Civil War ten years sooner.

3

Shortly after Fillmore's accession, Mary Gwin arrived in
Washington with her family to lend support to the lobbying
on behalf of California. The doctor stayed prudently at New
York. From her hotel in the capital Mrs. Gwin campaigned
assiduously, as did also Jessie Benton Frémont, who had
reached Washington with her husband at the peak of the agitation.

Through the summer the suspense held. Although Clay's
grand compromise was rejected, most of its provisions were
embodied in separate bills, which were passed one by one, and
in September, California's statehood was ratified. President
Fillmore signed the act of admission on September 9, 1850, and
two days later Gwin and Frémont took their seats in the Senate.

The news was received at San Francisco with jubilation. All
business ceased while the city gave itself up to parades, fireworks, feasting, and oratory. As far away as Europe California's emergence was greeted with astonishment. *The Times*
of London made no effort to conceal its amazement, saying:

Here was a community of some hundreds of thousands of souls, collected from all quarters of the known world — Polynesians and Peruvians, Englishmen and Mexicans, Germans and New Englanders, Spaniards and Chinese — all organized under old Saxon institutions, and actually marching under the command of a mayor and aldermen. The extemporized State had demanded and obtained its admission into the most powerful federation in the world. A third of the time that had been consumed in erecting our house of Parliament has sufficed to create a State with a territory as large as Great Britain, a population difficult to number, and destinies which none can foretell.

For Gwin the triumph was complete. Eighteen months after President Zachary Taylor's inauguration and the national rout of the Democrats, a brilliant victory had been plucked from the rubble of his party's defeat. Not only had he been elected to the Senate, but he had also contributed powerfully to adding another Democratic state to the Union. True, his success was not unalloyed. Twelve Democratic senators had voted against seating him, including Jefferson Davis and others of Gwin's Southern friends. Davis had stressed that his vote implied no mistrust of Gwin, whom he praised, but was meant to register a doubt of the constitutionality of his election. This somewhat effusive demonstration of personal regard and political skepticism, made by the South's most rigid theorist, seemed to hint at special difficulties in Gwin's position which in time might become severe. Gwin was a Southerner and a slaveholder. Although his more ardent Southern party intimates approved him personally, politically they viewed him somewhat askance. What sort of spokesman would he prove to be for a state composed of free men, nominally Democratic in its party allegiance, yet neither wholly Southern nor wholly Northern in its sympathies and outlook? California was admitted but it was still considered a remote and inaccessible region, of uncertain loyalty. The note of doubt was barely audible, but it would grow louder.

Chapter VI

CALIFORNIA NEEDED EVERY facility and amenity of civilized life, and needed them in a hurry. Roads, bridges, docks, harbors, schools, courts, lighthouses, currency, laws, postal service, transportation, a governmental establishment — the list was endless. The Eastern states, long since settled, had acquired these adjuncts of government progressively, through years of growth; California required them all at once, and on a scale that grew by the hour. The infant state had no means of providing for itself, for it was without industries, its unstable population had not shaken down into regular social or economic patterns, and it had no revenues to spend. As a result, the federal government was called upon to assist the state during the most critical period of its growth. For this assistance it would reimburse the nation many times over in its principal product — gold.

Gwin quickly learned that the representative of a new state occupies a position of infinite delicacy at Washington. When, in his old age, he reviewed his first months in the Senate, he described with feeling the drawbacks and obstacles that beset him at the very time when the demands made upon him were the greatest, and admitting of the least delay. Speaking of a Congressional delegation so placed, he said:

> They, if any members of Congress, are entitled to have extended to them the generous confidence of their associates. Forced by the necessities of their State to bring forward many and important

measures, the passage of which is essential to the prosperity of their constituents, and subjected to be assailed at home by jealous rivals and persons whose private interests may clash with the legislation for the benefit of the State at large; charged with doing too little by some, and too much by others, and, no matter how pure their motives, falsely assailed by base and unscrupulous calumniators, and accused of legislating for their own benefit; a member of Congress from a State just admitted unto the Union has to pass through an ordeal that no man can appreciate until he tries it.

As he would remind impatient constituents, a new state must transact more business with the executive departments than half a dozen old states, and the discharge of this particular and pressing business involved much toil and often unpleasantness.

The new senator worked energetically in the few remaining days of the session. Between Gwin and Frémont there was no rivalry for preeminence, because both were familiar figures in the capital, and both possessed powerful friends. Frémont, however, was handicapped by the anomaly of his position in Washington. A few years before, after a humiliating court-martial for actions growing out of a conflict of command in California during the war, he had resigned from the army in disgust. The basic fault had lain with Polk and his cabinet, who had issued contradictory orders; but Frémont's cause had been harmed by an injudicious defense raised by his redoubtable father-in-law, Senator Thomas Hart Benton of Missouri. The indignity of his situation had rankled, and his return to the capital as a senator was both a vindication and a reminder of injuries under which he still smarted.

In addition, Frémont was preoccupied with anxieties over both his political prospects and his business concerns. At the time of their election to the Senate, Gwin and Frémont had drawn lots to decide which of them would serve the full term of six years, and which the short term that would expire in

March, 1851. Frémont had drawn the short term (to Jessie Frémont's disgust; this evidence of "injustice" convinced her that Gwin was an opportunist and untrustworthy), and his reelection would be up to the California legislature due to meet in January, only a few months ahead. At the same time he was involved in business negotiations in connection with the Mariposa grant, a tract in California which he had acquired before the discovery of gold. Now it gave promise of including the richest mineral deposits in the world owned by a single individual, and Frémont's time and attention were to a large extent taken up by the search for capital to develop it. Although he introduced eighteen bills affecting California (none of which was passed then), his Senate appearances proved to be little more than ornamental.

At the same time, the state's Representatives, Wright and Gilbert, were content to yield precedence to Senator Gwin. He possessed legislative experience and political influence which they did not; and they fell in readily with his counsel that measures vital to the state should originate in the Senate, which, being a more compact body, might be brought to act more swiftly than the unwieldly House.

The Congressional session had three weeks to run. In that brief time, Senator Gwin introduced a long list of bills to benefit California, and pushed to final passage three of them — for the construction of lighthouses along the Pacific coast from Oregon to Mexico; for extending the federal judiciary to California; and for appointing Indian agents. His other bills included provisions for opening a road across the Sierra Nevada; for setting aside land grants for schools and a university; for appointment of a recorder of land titles; for a survey of the public lands; for establishing a land office; and a code for regulating the working of the mines.

✿

2

When Congress adjourned on September 30, Frémont, acting on Gwin's advice, set out immediately for California to begin campaigning for reelection. This left Gwin the sole spokesman for California in the Senate during the second session of the Thirty-first Congress. That session opened in December, and produced a series of acts that laid a solid foundation for California's orderly growth for years to come. The credit for these measures was justly due to Senator Gwin.

They embraced a wide range of activities and projects. Bills were passed to establish a branch mint and customshouse at San Francisco; to construct a naval shipyard and dry dock at Mare Island; to provide a marine hospital; to conduct a hydrographic survey of the two-thousand-mile coast; to create machinery for adjusting the welter of land claims that was plaguing the state; to give California one million six hundred thousand acres of the public lands for internal improvements; and there were numerous other acts of fundamental importance. Since Gwin was a member of the Finance Committee of the Senate, as well as chairman of the Naval Affairs Committee, he was well placed to procure appropriations for these projects.

His most consistent opposition came from his friends of the slaveholding states. These men were averse to spending national funds for public improvements; under their doctrine of state sovereignty they considered such expenditures unconstitutional, and they could hardly grasp the extraordinary conditions that prevailed on the West Coast. In their own communities, customs, habits, and the social structure had become crystallized; but in California, where everything was in flux, the simplest conveniences had to be improvised without reference to traditions. The obstacles to be surmounted were as formidable as the problems were unique. Raw materials, for example, had to be transported enormous distances at immense cost

— around Cape Horn, for the most part — and labor of any
kind was either painfully scarce or totally unprocurable in a
country where able-bodied men were better employed in the
gold mines. Ranches that before 1848 had produced annual
revenues in the hundreds of thousands of dollars were reverting to wilderness for lack of labor to cultivate them. Hundreds
of ships lay rotting in San Francisco Bay, abandoned by their
crews, who had run off to the mines. Soldiers deserted by
squads and companies, scorning their pay of eight dollars a
month, when a common laborer could command twenty dollars
a day. Such wage-work was always available to a man who
failed to strike it rich. To frugal Eastern legislators, reports of
such conditions sounded like fantasy, if not the delusions of
delirium.

Over and over again, Senator Gwin was forced to explain to
his colleagues the unprecedented nature of life in California.
The sums he sought exceeded anything dreamed of for comparable enterprises in the East, and the Southern bloc repeatedly protested that his estimates were monstrously inflated.
But Gwin was supple and tenacious, skilled in maneuvering,
tireless in committee consultations, and effective in floor debate. California, his theme ran, must be made strong, not only
as a bulwark against possible foreign aggression, but as an
asset to the entire nation. This was the aim of his strategy, although his tactics were constantly changing and never were
arbitrary. If the Senate turned down a request for a large appropriation, he would split the sum into several portions and
by means of amendments to other bills obtain the money piece-
meal. His dexterity in this respect aroused the professional admiration of his fellow senators. Dr. Gwin (as he still liked to
be called) was acknowledged to be without a superior in the
practice of legislative sleight of hand.

Sometimes the arguments he had to answer were naïve to
the point of being ludicrous. When he proposed an appropri-

ation of $100,000 for a blacksmith shop at the Mare Island
Navy Yard, Senator Mason of Virginia exclaimed in tones of
outrage that in the entire Old Dominion there was not a smithy
that had cost one hundred dollars, let alone one hundred thousand! The blacksmith shop which Gwin had in mind, of course,
would have two hundred forges and spread over acres of
ground. Gwin wryly joined in the laughter raised by his Virginia associate's anguish, and saw the bill die. But after some
cloakroom missionary work, he revived the request in a different form and got the appropriation. The incident illustrated
the play of Gwin's imagination and the boldness of his proposals, for he was bent upon providing an installation that
would serve the maritime needs of the whole Pacific coast for a
century to come, and this he accomplished.

A politician dealing with politicians, Senator Gwin was
never dogmatic or obstinate or unyielding. He believed pro-
foundly in the saying that the art of government is the art of
evolving workable compromises, and he would bargain to attain his ends. His strength lay in adaptability and willingness
to consider reasonable objections, and in his readiness to meet
opponents halfway. He was aware that inflexible principle
sometimes can best be applied flexibly; his concern was to get
results, and he got them. No state was ever served by a more
conscientious, capable, and energetic advocate of its interests.
Yet his concern for California was neither sectional nor parochial. He believed that California's gains were synonymous
with the nation's, and he was ever mindful of the welfare of the
United States. For the next century, certainly, California
would send to the Senate no man comparable to Gwin in intellectual capacity and parliamentary address, or in any respect as valuable to the state. Despite Frémont's slight priority
in point of election, Gwin was what he came to be called —
"California's first senator, and the architect of the State."

＊

3

In his work to build up the West, Gwin occasionally received assistance from his nominal political adversaries. Free-soilers voted for some of his California measures because they mistrusted the Democrats who opposed them. Between Seward and Gwin there was a partial community of views that led to a cordial relationship, although on the basic issues that divided the North and South they disagreed. Seward, like Gwin, felt that a strong California was imperative, and he cooperated in securing passage of many of Gwin's proposals.

Seward was an enigma to his contemporaries, especially to strict constructionists. His intelligence was bewilderingly eclectic, and by temperament he seemed to prefer to move toward an objective by indirection rather than along the open path. He was known to use the most positive declarations to cloak the vaguest intentions, and was adept at obfuscation when he seemed to be most transparently candid. Loyal to principles, he would often appear disloyal because he declined to petrify his principles into dogmas. In this respect he resembled Gwin, and this trait or tendency engendered a bond of understanding between them.

In the debates on California, Seward would remind the senators that for every dollar of federal funds they voted, that state was returning thousands of dollars in tangible wealth, in addition to creating an expanding market for the products of the East. The frequency with which Seward came to the support of Gwin's measures, and the personal cordiality between the two, led to comment upon the California senator's flair for maintaining a foot in opposite camps, without offense to either.

This reputation for social and political amphibiousness was enhanced by Mary Gwin's success as a hostess. Washington society was predominently Southern in tone, but the Gwins did not limit their hospitality to Southerners. Mrs. Gwin saw to it

that their house, at the corner of Third and C streets, drew
visitors of different political hues. The politician-journalist
John W. Forney, who observed the Washington scene for a
quarter of a century, deemed Mary Gwin "exactly the mate"
for such a man as Senator Gwin: "fashionable, liberal, dashing,
generous." Although Forney, later a Radical Republican,
found that she was "full of Southern partialities," he conceded
that the Gwin home was "as hospitable as plenty of money
and pleasant people could make it."

Gwin himself Forney sketched with a touch of malice as he
appeared upon his entrance into the Senate:

> [He] had grown to be a veteran in the bitter conflicts of the
> South, where he had held any number of places, emigrated to
> California, like the rest, to better himself. . . . He was then just
> forty-five, full of vigor, resources, busy, continuous, resolute, not
> over-scrupulous, and intensely ambitious.

One might expect among politicians like Forney (himself far from overscrupulous) a professional craftsman of
Gwin's ability would inspire wariness as well as admiration,
and the California senator's flexibility did arouse some misgivings. For any public man who could not, or would not, take
a clear-cut stand one way or the other, upon the basic issues,
the coming years were bound to be stormy. In times of ex-
tremes, the middle-of-the-roader is suspect. In 1850 and 1851,
however, the nation was entering upon a brief period of relative
calm and harmony. Passage of the compromise acts had quieted the slavery agitation except in isolated pockets, and the
nation breathed with relief that disruption had been averted.
The outlook seemed favorable for indefinite extension of the
truce between North and South, and at the capital this easing
of sectional tensions was reflected socially.

To this prevailing mood the Gwins readily conformed; it
matched their own tastes. Senator Gwin, though a Democrat,

maintained an easy relationship with the Whig President Fillmore, and was often at the White House. In the Senate he refrained from opposing Fillmore's appointments, and this courtesy was returned in the form of a few crumbs dropped from
the feast of federal patronage for Senator Gwin to distribute.
This, in turn, produced a good effect at home, and did no harm
at Washington.

In March, 1851, at the close of the session, Gwin bade his
family good-bye and sailed for Panama on the way back to
California. He intended to report on his stewardship, inspect
the situation there, and solidify his support in the state. His
journey coincided with the meeting of California's second
legislature; and from that body Gwin would gather the first
inklings of the changes that were recasting political roles in
California with startling rapidity.

Chapter VII

THE LEGISLATURE THAT convened in San Jose on January 2, 1851, was different in spirit, if not in makeup, from the one that had elected Gwin and Frémont a year before. California's first legislature had been notably upright and efficient. The members had transacted the state's business expeditiously and gone home. True, some observers averred that this was because there had been nothing to steal: the state had collected no taxes, no sinecures had been created, the public cupboard was bare.

By 1851 the situation had changed. Now there was money in the till, and many hands were itching to dip into it. There was no guile in the members' greed; they simply reached in and grabbed. Again the weather was wet and dismal, and the prevailing liquidity extended to the legislators themselves. As sordid and sodden as any legislature in California's history, they demonstrated why a judicious writer termed the state's early history not one "for babes and sentimentalists," and why that legislature has come down as "The Legislature of a Thousand Drinks."

In part the epithet grew out of the electioneering hospitality of the several aspirants to Frémont's seat in the United States Senate. Frémont hoped to succeed himself, but Thomas Butler King was running strong, and there were other claimants. All the candidates, or their managers, held open house for lawmakers thirsty for guidance or rye, and the supply of both was unlimited. Copiously combined, they produced a befuddlement that prevented the legislature from electing anybody.

Over a period of four months, one hundred and forty-two ballots were taken, without either electing a new senator or slackening the flow of free liquor. Frémont had made himself unpopular in various ways, including his espousal of the cause of the native Californians, a political minority that was weak and steadily growing weaker. Butler King's pomposity had set people against him permanently; besides, having been named collector of the port of San Francisco, he was thought to be lining his pockets to the tune of $100,000 a year by kickbacks on exorbitant rents charged for government office space, and the legislators argued that since he had "got his," he deserved no more.

No candidate securing a majority, the legislature left Frémont's seat vacant for a year. This was not a unique occurrence: in other states wrangling legislatures had left Senate vacancies temporarily unfilled.

2

Abraham Lincoln once defined politicians as "a set of men who have interests aside from the interests of the people, and who, to say the most of them, are, taken as a class, at least one long step removed from honest men." Since Lincoln hastened to classify himself as a politician, he was singling out nobody in particular.

This description, doubled and tripled in forcefulness, would fit the politicians of California's first decade, taking them as a group. The average Western politician of that time considered the state a pocket to be picked, and himself the man to pick it. One positive good did accrue to the community from the preoccupation of most of its elected representatives with peculation: the young state was spared the affiliation of visionary schemes of government. The politicians abstained from tinkering with the machinery of the government that ground out the profit they enjoyed. Thus the solid foundation laid at Monterey and buttressed by the actions of Congress was not undermined.

The caliber of California's local politicians in this period might be judged by the second epithet applied to the legislature of 1851 — the "Water-Lots Legislature." This appellation commemorated the swindle that transferred some $11,000,000 worth of San Francisco waterfront property from the state to the city, and from the city to private speculators.

The waterfront of San Francisco was steadily being extended into the bay by filling in the mud flats of Yerba Buena cove. Abandoned hulks were dragged close to shore and used as foundations for buildings, the space around them being filled in by the earth scraped off the nearby hills. In this way block after block of valuable real estate was added as the city's population increased.

In recognition of this process of continuous growth, the city authorities marked off streets and building lots that were still completely submerged, some a quarter of a mile offshore. These were the "water-lots," and trading in them was a source of much profit.

The entire waterfront had belonged to the state, but the 1851 legislature, by a sleight of hand, transferred the property to the city, with the practical result that the "water-lots" were turned over to the ring of predatory politicians who were managing municipal affairs. The steal was worked out systematically. As the first step, claims were filed against the city on various grounds, and judgments for large sums were obtained from obliging judges. The city authorities then sanctioned the auctioning off of property owned by the community in order to pay these judgments. At this point, David Broderick introduced in the senate a bill transferring title to the waterfront from the state to San Francisco. The bill was passed, and the "water-lots" were auctioned off. Strangely, David Broderick was able to bid in some of the most valuable lots at bargain prices; and the property he acquired in this way was the only real wealth he would ever possess.

Broderick occupied a position of strategic strength in the legislature of 1851, standing head and shoulders above the other members in ability and firmness of purpose. At the start of the session, the governor, Peter H. Burnett, resigned, and John McDougal, the lieutenant governor, took his place. Broderick was elected president *pro tempore* of the senate and thus became acting lieutenant governor, and in this position he made his weight felt. McDougal was described by one of his less censorious successors: "Well, when you say he was a drunkard, you pretty much state the whole case; there was not much in him outside of whiskey." As governor, McDougal indulged his "predilection for promulgating proclamations" so liberally as to become known as "I, John McDougal." Such a governor was quite in tune with the "Legislature of a Thousand Drinks."

As senate leader, Broderick gave satisfaction. His rulings from the chair were prompt, clear-cut, and impartial, and he was attentive to business. Half the senate might be in a state of fuddlement, but as an abstainer Broderick kept his head and kept the legislature on its course. At the close of the session he had made many friends and had earned a name for incisiveness.

3

On April 23, when the legislature was reeling toward adjournment, Senator Gwin reached San Francisco aboard the steamer *California,* after another tedious three-week voyage from Panama. The budget of news brought by the ship was eagerly devoured by the news-hungry town. As samplings of what was going on in the East and the South: in New York State, the legislature had elected a United States senator — former Governor Hamilton Fish — and the *Alta California* remarked severely that the mode of election in New York appeared to be "by hocus-pocus," and in its opinion New York politicians were "a queer lot." New York City's Roman Catholic Archbishop Hughes was erroneously reported to have been made a cardinal. And a paragraph sufficed to relate an incident in Mississippi:

A Negro in Paulding, Mississippi, having committed an outrage upon the person of a white lady, and afterwards murdered her son, the citizens turned out *en masse,* arrested the Negro, and burned him alive.

As a variant from this news, Senator Gwin published an "address to the people of California," giving a report of his exertions on their behalf in Washington. This was a political custom of the time, and the list of accomplishments that Gwin presented was impressive. In recognition of his services the legislature voted a resolution of thanks — which, because it failed to mention the state's two Representatives, Gilbert and Wright, later critics would aver to have been managed by Gwin so as to appropriate all the glory for himself. If there was any such management, neither Wright nor Gilbert raised any objections, and Gwin's influence over the legislature was hardly that great.

Shortly after the senator's arrival, the session adjourned. The occasion was celebrated by a grand banquet for three hundred guests, at which Senator Gwin presided. In a grateful speech, he alluded to the unhappy situation of all present, separated from their wives and families, and struck so responsive a chord that a dozen other speakers took up the theme. One of the unsuccessful candidates for Frémont's seat, John B. Weller, rolled out Wolsey's speech from *Henry VIII:*

> Cromwell, I charge thee, fling away ambition:
> By that sin fell the angels . . .
> Corruption wins not more than honesty. . . .

And not a legislator blinked.

After this outpouring, Gwin embarked upon a tour of the state, and was received everywhere with flattering attentions. As Hubert Howe Bancroft would superciliously put it, "Patronage was sought of the great man — and the great man did not despise the help of the meanest." Gwin's objective was to consolidate the Democratic organization in the state, where numerically the Democrats led their old rivals, the Whigs. Southerners were firmly in control of the Democratic party machinery. This had come about naturally, by virtue of the Southerners' greater political experience and the imposing airs of the "Chivalry," which, in the West as in Washington, overawed most of their competitors from the Northern states. Southerners swaggered and domineered, they were arrogant in manner, and not a few of them held all Yankees in contempt. The Democratic "Chivalry" rallied to Gwin as the state leader, for although he did not share all their peculiarities and prejudices, he was one of them.

The opposition faction began to cluster around David Broderick, who was not daunted by Southern pretensions. Northern workingmen, mainly Irish and German, turned to Broderick as a counterpoise against Gwin and his faction, and Broderick found a use for them. This element the "Chivalry" decried, dubbing them scornfully the "Shovelry." Between these factions the struggle for control of the party would be carried on with growing intensity.

Gwin apparently was not alarmed by the developments he saw during his 1851 visit to the state, although he noted changes. The party organization he set up followed the pattern prevalent in the South, the keystone being control of the federal patronage, by means of which the party's nominating conventions — city, county, and state — could be kept in line. With the 1852 national election at hand, and all signs pointing to a Democratic victory, Gwin was prospectively the chief dispenser of executive favors, and he was therefore much courted.

His grip on the state party appearing firm, he headed back to Washington. Much legislation on California's behalf was to be introduced in the new Congress, and as the state's only senator, he would be forced to carry a heavy load.

4

The changes that had taken place in California by 1851 in reality were profound. In many respects the conditions prevailing in 1849 and 1850 were already far in the past. The first arrivals in the gold rush had been often men of substance, above average in education, wealth, and aggressiveness. Many of them not only had personal ability, but they enjoyed influential business, social, and political connections in the East.

Behind this first wave of immigrants, who came by sea, there had been a less distinguished group, who came by land. The covered wagons that lumbered across the plains from the farmlands of the Midwest did not began to converge upon California in large numbers until late in 1850. Besides farmers, they brought the so-called "mechanics," or workingmen, small tradesmen, and others of little means. More democratic in their habits than their immediate predecessors, these newcomers would form the solid substratum of California's permanent population.

Behind these, in turn, swarmed a third element that was neither desirable nor helpful in building up the state. They included the ne'er-do-wells and the unscrupulous and the criminals, including not a few thieves, bullies, and confidence men who had been driven out of Eastern cities. Mixed with the outright criminals was a breed of corrupt political hangers-on who had been trained in the ways of Tammany and its counterparts, and were eager to put their talents to profitable use.

Broderick knew some of the New Yorkers arriving in this hodgepodge, and he enlisted their help in setting up an organization in San Francisco modeled upon Tamany Hall — a political machine staffed by disciplined workers at the precinct level. His first step was to form a volunteer fire company. This he used as a nucleus, and since the great majority of San Franciscans were fully occupied with "getting ahead" and gave little heed to politics, his success was rapid. He turned to account every trick he had learned in New York — stuffing ballot boxes, the use of "repeaters" who voted as often as they were told to, "shoulder strikers" who roughed up citizens venturing to protest, and the employment of thugs and bullies to intimidate, coerce, and destroy ballots when necessary. By the summer of 1851 Broderick was emerging as the political boss of San Francisco, where for all practical purposes he *was* the Democratic party. Nothing could be done there without his consent, and his consent was for sale.

Some of the henchmen he employed were graduates of Eastern prisons. Such was Billy Mulligan, a quarrelsome dipsomaniac whom the warden of the Tombs in New York City had termed "as desperate a character as could be found." Broderick put Mulligan in charge of the city jail, under Broderick's handpicked sheriff, David S. Scannel, a former dive-keeper in New York. Mulligan also served as tax collector.

Another notorious rowdy was "Dutch Charley" (his real name was Charles P. Duane), whom Broderick made chief engineer of the fire department. "Dutch" bragged that he could deliver a thousand "ringers" on election day, marching them from precinct to precinct in military formation. How tightly the system worked was observed by E. D. Keyes, an army officer stationed in San Francisco in the fifties. A friend of his wished to vote for a certain candidate, and did so; he then had qualms about his legal right to vote in that precinct. Keyes advised him not to worry, for he had noticed that the

judge of elections was "Yankee Sullivan," a prizefighter with
an unwholesome reputation, in the pay of Broderick. When
the returns were published the next day, the name of the man
for whom Keys's friend had voted did not appear in the list; all
votes cast for that candidate Sullivan had "counted out."

Broderick's method of financing his machine was simple.
He made no secret of it: he put the public offices up for sale.
A man who expressed a desire to become district attorney, a
judge, an alderman, or an assessor, would be invited to discuss
the matter with the boss. The proposition would be put bluntly
and squarely to the prospective candidate. Broderick would
say:

"The job you want is worth so many thousand dollars a year
in 'perquisites.' Give me half, and I will see that you are nominated and elected. I need the money to grease the wheels of
the machine that will put you in office and keep you there."

If one prospect balked, there was always another, because
Broderick delivered on his promises. With the sums thus hi-
jacked, he maintained his organization, placing as many of his
henchmen as he could on the public payroll, and subsidizing
the others out of his private funds. He was no hypocrite in
this, but quite outspoken, and claimed that he would prefer
to have the support of the honest element of the city, but the
respectable citizens held back. "You won't go down and face
those shoulder-strikers," he told them. As a result, he worked
with men who would carry out his orders. Although his grip
on the city was absolute, his power did not extend into the
state; there the "Chivalry" held sway.

The rise of this "lone, strange, extraordinary" man puzzled
people who had not met him, for everything about him seemed
harsh and repellent, even to the reddish ruff of whiskers under
his chin. But to people who had felt his magnetism, his leadership was no mystery at all. Men were drawn to him irresisti-
bly, or were violently repelled; it was impossible to feel neutral

about him. He neither cajoled nor flattered, but was peremptory, irascible, and given to coarse invective when opposed. He demanded complete obedience, but rewarded loyalty. Although he permitted himself no indulgences and lived austerely, caring nothing for society and ignoring women, he countenanced the most flagrant licentiousness among his followers. He had no personal greed, but was grasping in his official capacity as head of the machine.

A first-rate boxer, since coming to California he had made himself a crack pistol shot, a fact which his henchmen advertised. His followers were fanatically devoted to him, and acted, it was said, "more like lovers than friends." Upright men were drawn to him. His usual mood was saturnine, and he could make the erring cringe. He seldom smiled and was never gay, confided in few, and spurned more proffers of friendship than he accepted. He was never free from a sense of loneliness; he brooded on the loss of his family. Having belatedly become aware of the gaps in his education, he now read voraciously, mostly history and literature, and admired the poetry of Shelley particularly. Honest in his personal dealings, he probably never associated the word "scruple" with politics. The goal he had set for himself — a seat in the United States Senate — was always before him; nothing else mattered; setbacks merely hardened his will to succeed.

5

The corruption fostered and protected by Broderick was bound to boomerang; the backlash occurred in June, 1851. Crime had become so prevalent that, in the words of a contemporary, "no decent man was in safety to walk the streets after dark, while at all hours, both of night and day, his property was jeopardized by incendiarism and burglary." The law-enforcement agencies, controlled by Broderick, were in league with the criminals; no jail could hold a Broderick stalwart for long.

In June, 1851, two hundred law-abiding citizens banded together in a secret Committee of Vigilance with the avowed intention of purging the city of the worst of its undesirables. Four miscreants were hanged, more were exiled or fled, and the courts were frightened into assuming the virtue they did not possess. During the commotion Broderick remained out of sight, although some of his men were dealt with severely. "Dutch Charley" was seized for stabbing a theater manager who suggested that he buy a ticket if he wished to see the show, but was bailed out by Broderick at a cost, it was gossiped, of $50,000. The money was used to induce witnesses to disappear, and "Dutch" was freed for a while longer.

When it considered its task finished, this first Vigilance Committee of San Francisco published the names of its members and became dormant. Senator Gwin had taken no part in the upheaval; he had not been called upon either to sanction or to reprehend the temporary overthrow of authority. Broderick reappeared and found his power not vitally affected. He still controlled the ballot boxes.

Chapter VIII

THE NEWSPAPERS OF San Francisco had denounced the 1851 legislature as "infamous," "arrogant," "rowdy," "drunken," "perjured," and "traitorous." The *Alta California* had hoped that the next legislature would "rescue the State from the labyrinth of imbecility, vagueness, and iniquity into which it has strayed." But when the 1852 session opened, the *Alta* reported that it detected the same "combinations, arrangements, pledges, promises, log-rolling, and swapping of votes." In Bancroft's judgment, California had entered upon a "moral, political, and financial night," in which "gold-drunkenness" would infect all public activities.

One of the first actions of the 1852 legislature was to fill the Senate seat left vacant by Frémont. Butler King had dropped out of the race, and the winner was John B. Weller: he had the backing of Gwin's "Chivalry," and they controlled the legislature. Broderick offered himself as a candidate, and while never seriously threatening Weller, he did receive enough votes to underline his emerging prominence in the party.

One year had been clipped from Weller's term, and at Washington he would prove to be a shadow of Gwin, who had, meanwhile, been increasing the state's indebtedness to him by fresh legislative successes. One measure he pushed through at this time was the appropriation to build a United States branch mint at San Francisco. This facility was direly needed, for gold mining was the cornerstone of California's economy, and the miners required a means of disposing of their "dust" cheaply and conveniently. Between the authorization of funds for the mint, and its actual construction, years were to elapse, and this delay would create much trouble for Gwin later on.

In 1852 Gwin introduced his first bill to connect the East and West coasts by a railroad, a project of the highest importance and one which he would continue to advocate year after year. The chief obstacle the proposal encountered was the choice of a route. Northerners wanted the railroad to pass through the free states; Southerners wanted it to run through the slave states; and there was also a central route. Gwin favored any practical route, although he deemed the southern route the least difficult from an engineering viewpoint. Speeding up of communication between the coasts was what he sought, and any method that would accomplish that received his support. Not less than four weeks was required to send a letter from New York to San Francisco, and frequently the delay would be nearer two months. The postage on a letter was forty cents, and Gwin was instrumental in cutting this down to six cents, as a minor contribution toward facilitating communication.

In August, 1852, the Gwins suffered a private grief in the loss of their daughter, Mary Bell, named for her mother. The child was only eleven, and she died suddenly, probably a victim of the malarial fevers exhaled by the mud flats that festered along the Potomac. The funeral was in keeping with the family's wealth and prominence. The chaplain of the Senate pronounced the eulogy, and Gwin's Congressional colleagues served as pallbearers. Mary's classmates from the Catholic seminary at Georgetown attended in a group, and mourning souvenirs were distributed — large squares of white satin printed with the eulogy. The bereavement curtailed Mrs. Gwin's social activity for the rest of the session, and in the autumn the senator returned to California to campaign in the Presidential election.

❂

2

Gwin reached San Francisco aboard the *California* on October 7. He stumped the state for the Democratic ticket headed by Franklin Pierce of New Hampshire, and Pierce was elected, the Whigs also losing control of Congress. With the Democrats back in power, Gwin's stock rose, and there was speculation that he would be taken into the cabinet; but again he preferred to remain outside, the Senate being more congenial to him. He was looked upon as the probable dispenser of virtually all the federal patronage that would reward the faithful, and this took in hundreds of jobs, large and small.

Normally Senator Weller and the two Representatives — Joseph McCorkle and Milton S. Latham — would participate in handing out the plums; but against Gwin they were overmatched, as they soon realized. Broderick, too, received a shock when he was left out in the cold, although he and his machine had worked as loyally for Pierce's success as had Gwin and his "Chivalry"; nevertheless, the jobs seemed to be going to the "Chivalry" or their friends exclusively. The customshouse became so staffed with needy "Chivs" that it was referred to contemptuously as the "Virginia poorhouse." But Broderick had no influence at the White House, and he was unknown to the party's national leaders. His attempts to gain recognition fell flat, and the few trifling jobs that were tossed to him failed to allay his anger. To him the situation seemed to be that of New York all over again; no matter how he might struggle, the aristocrats would continue to shut him out. Since the senator was the leader and embodiment of his toplofty antagonists, Broderick singled out Gwin as the special target of his smoldering hatred. From this time on, the elimination of Gwin became the settled aim of his rival.

Actually, the situation was more complicated than Broderick's hunger for office allowed him to perceive. President Pierce was extremely partial to his comrades in the Mexican War, and their claims took precedence over all others, even Gwin's recommendations. Since that war had been fought principally by troops recruited in the Southern states (the war being highly unpopular in some sections of the North), the lists of veterans were made up mainly of Southern men, and these had first call on the nominations. This was one factor that Broderick overlooked, but there were others. Class prejudice distorted his view; he hated the "silk-socked aristocrats."

Just at this time his rancor was fanned by an old associate from New York, the irrepressible George Wilkes. Politically Broderick had justified all his former teacher's hopes, and Wilkes attached himself to the boss as an intimate and valuable adviser. It may be that he persuaded Broderick to take on a more conventional and "respectable" appearance about this time. Instead of the miner's shirt and high boots that he had worn since coming to California, Broderick blossomed out in broadcloth, took on the tone and demeanor of a conservative businessman; dignified but tight-lipped, he was presentable in any company. His grammar improved, and toward men whom he deemed his equals he could be courteous and pleasant. But his aggressiveness was not lessened; he was little given to tact; and politically he was still ruthless.

3

In Washington, Gwin was being made to feel the effects of Broderick's rising enmity. Newspapers subsidized by Broderick opened a campaign of deliberate belittlement of the senator, centered upon amorphous imputations of venality. The innuendoes were the more poisonous because they remained vague. Gwin's great services to the state, which were being increased steadily, were acknowledged, but the motives behind these were somehow traced to selfish aims. Senator Gwin,

it was implied, was incapable of generous sentiment; under a
mask of benevolence he was avaricious, and his renowned
legislative finesse was just the talent needed for promoting sinister designs.

The delay in building the mint was seized upon, and here a
genuine grievance existed. The miners were incensed. It
was brought out that Gwin, after securing the original authorization and a $300,000 appropriation, had, by an extremely
devious *démarche,* succeeded in turning the appropriation
over to the Secretary of the Treasury, for use in underwriting
an assay office at San Francisco pending construction of the
mint. This was entirely proper, and a contract had been given
to the firm of Moffat & Company. Now the complaint was
made that the mint had not been built, and meanwhile Moffat
& Company charged the miners 2½ percent for assaying their
gold, whereas the normal charge was 1 percent. This gouge,
it was said, was costing the miners $21,000,000 in extra assay
fees, and Moffat, it was further charged, was splitting its profits with Senator Gwin. Hence the delay in constructing the
mint.

Proof of Gwin's improper involvement was not offered. On
the other hand, there was no doubt that the original appropriation had been detoured, for what reason was never satisfacto-
rily explained. The hardship to the miners was real, and the
unanswered allegations did Gwin's political fortunes no good.
By 1854, when at last the mint was opened, he had lost the support of the mining element permanently.

Another method resorted to, in the campaign to undercut
his reputation as a "wonder man," was systematic ridicule. No
matter what the senator did, Broderick's hired press mocked it.
Loss of dignity can be fatal to a public servant, and that was
the purpose of the campaign.

A duel developed between Gwin and Congressman McCorkle, who was already a figure of fun, because of his election

with the man he detested most — Milton S. Latham. The loathing was both personal and political, for Latham had stolen McCorkle's sweetheart and married her, and then had tried to "ditch him" in the party, as he believed. To be sent to Washington virtually hand in hand with Latham was humiliating; but when he found that he was being sidetracked in reaching for patronage favors by the mighty Senator Gwin, McCorkle's fury overflowed.

After both he and the senator had returned to California, they chanced to meet at the racetrack, and McCorkle heaped insults upon Gwin which the latter, with his Southern notions of honor, could not overlook. He sent a challenge which McCorkle accepted, and it was arranged that the antagonists, armed with rifles, should meet outside of San Francisco and exchange fire.

A Broderick-subsidized newspaper subsequently reported the affair in broad burlesque. According to this account, a crowd of spectators was on hand, liberally provided with picnic lunches and beer, and the first laugh came when it was discovered that nobody had brought the ammunition. This necessitated a delay while the neighborhood was scoured for powder and shot. These being procured, the opponents took their places at thirty paces, with their backs to each other. At the word, they were to turn and fire. The word was given, they turned and fired, and missed. They tried a second time, and missed again, and according to the reporter they stood up once more ("full of wrath, sausages, and cole slaw") and fired a third round, without hitting each other. Gwin was said to have winged a crow flapping overhead, and McCorkle was understood to have narrowly missed one of the seconds. Thereupon, the account read, a meaningless "arrangement" was written out (and strangely published in the newspaper) and the adversaries came riding back to town on mules. This treatment of what was never intended to be a laughing matter was de-

structive to Gwin, and the senator's "marvellous shooting" provided meat for jokes that are still occasionally revived.

By contrast, Broderick had fought his duel, and the newspapers had not ridiculed him. The provocation in his case, too,
had been political, and his life was saved only by his opponent's bullet hitting his watch; he kept the smashed timepiece
as a talisman. Broderick seldom carried a weapon, and scorned
the "Chivalry's" recourse to firearms. He carried a scar across
one cheek where he had been slashed in a barroom scuffle,
but he was seldom molested, for he looked dangerous and he
was.

4

While Gwin was occupied at Washington, Broderick
reached out for control of the state legislature by capturing
the party's nominating conventions and caucuses. The large
San Francisco delegation in the legislature he already controlled, but in other areas his influence was spotty. Gwin's
term was to expire on March 4, 1855, and the legislature
meeting in January of that year would either reelect him, or
replace him in the Senate. This legislature was chosen in the
autumn of 1853, but in spite of Broderick's efforts, the returns
showed that he had lost ground, rather than gained it.

The incumbent legislature would meet in one more session,
in January, 1854, before yielding to the incoming group.
Rather than wait and take his chances with the new legislature, Broderick decided upon a bold move. This, while unscrupulous, technically seemed legal — George Wilkes said it
was — and it had the advantage of action.

The plan was this: when the outgoing legislature should
meet in a few weeks' time, Broderick would try to change the
law regarding the election of United States senators, and have
the election moved ahead one year. This would place the re-

sponsibility upon the current legislature; their successors would be bypassed; and Broderick believed that by hook or crook he could obtain his election over Gwin. In this way he would gain his grand objective — a seat in the Senate — and would score a double humiliation and rout upon Gwin and the "Chivalry." The senator would be left to serve out the last year of his term as a "lame duck," shorn of power, repudiated by his state. Broderick would not take office for another year; but meanwhile he would have become the kingpin of the Democratic party in California. He would have California in his pocket.

PART TWO

Triumph and Disaster

Chapter I

THE CONFLICT BETWEEN Broderick and Gwin from 1849 to 1854 was not a conflict of principles or policies; it was a struggle between two irreconcilable personalities. Principles and the public welfare had little to do with it. Although from time to time the great issues that were agitating the nation would be invoked, they were remote from California. The plain fact was that the state was too small to contain the ambitions of two such rivals; one or the other would have to go. And since neither would yield, they were forced inexorably toward disaster. In one case, the disaster would be physical; in the other, it would be spiritual. Both men would pay the penalty for wanting what they wanted too much.

Gwin's adherents had gobbled up most of the federal patronage, but Broderick was not without resources to sustain his followers: he had considerable control over distributing the state patronage, which already was a scandal. At the close of the term of "I, John McDougal," John Bigler had been elected to governor of California. Bigler was rated by an associate who knew him well as "a good, fairly average sort of man"; but he was not so charitably viewed by his political opponents. One arraignment of the era of "Biglerism" summed up the achievements of his administration as follows:

> The State became bankrupt. Public credit was ruined. An unconstitutional debt was contracted. Ten million dollars was squandered. Offices were created for the sole benefit of those who filled them. Enormous salaries were attached to some offices, to

be divided among partisans. The worst men filled the highest places. Bullies, shoulder-strikers, and ballot box stuffers [produced] a reign of ruffianism.

Upon arriving in California without money or friends, Bigler had supported himself by menial labor, chopping wood and unloading cargo. Like Broderick, he resented the "Chivalry," and as a member of the 1849 legislature he had voted against Gwin. He and Broderick were compatible, and while the latter had been president *pro tempore* of the state senate they had worked together well. In 1853 Broderick helped materially in electing Bigler to a second term as governor, and in return Bigler swung much of the executive patronage Broderick's way. This enabled the San Francisco boss to keep his machine intact.

When Broderick decided to try to jounce Gwin out of the senate by a risky maneuver, he knew that he could count upon the benevolent cooperation of Governor Bigler. He also knew that the legislature would not be antagonistic to his scheme, if he bluffed and bribed liberally enough.

2

The outgoing legislature convened on January 2, 1854, at Benecia, the temporary state capital, on upper San Francisco Bay. Broderick's bullies were conspicuous in the bars of the hotels where the lawmakers bedded down. Billy Mulligan, a bantam in size but a terror when drunk, paraded the streets arm in arm with a desperado named Parker H. French, who had headed a band of cutthroats on the plains in the early days of the gold rush that robbed and murdered lone parties of immigrants. Another Broderick henchman was a "fixer" known as "Snaggle-tooth Billy" Williamson, and he was partnered by a gunman whose ferocity had been demonstrated

when he offered to fight a duel standing toe to toe with his opponent, each man with his pistol pressed against the other's
temple, to fire at the word. This results-guaranteed arrangement had been vetoed by the other party. Circulating through
the hangers-on was a graduate of New York's Sing Sing
prison, James P. Casey, now a San Francisco alderman and
editor of a newspaper subsidized by Broderick. And of course
there was "Dutch Charley" Duane. These men had been mus-
tered for the express purpose of putting over Broderick's plan.

Gwin did not lack support; he had a strong block among the
Democrats, and was popular with the minority Whigs. But
Broderick sprang a surprise when, without warning, he jammed
through the Assembly the bill moving up the election date
one year. In the senate the vote promised to be close, and the
opposition to Broderick braced itself for a fight.

The leader of the opposition group was a Whig who detested
Broderick and admired Gwin, and, by employing parliamentary ruses, he staved off an immediate decision. Broderick carried on a counteroffensive by bribes and intimidation. The
haggling was shameless, and some senators bragged about the
prices their votes had fetched, one asserting that he had been
paid $30,000 for his.

Not every member of the senate was purchasable; there were
a few who were too naïve, and a few who were too upright, to
succumb to the tempting offers made by Joseph C. Palmer,
Broderick's paymaster and cashier. Palmer was senior partner of San Francisco's largest banking house, Palmer, Cook &
Company, and on the steamboat coming to Benecia he offered
Senator Elisha T. Peck, a country storekeeper, $5,000 for his
vote on the election-date bill. Honest Peck was outraged; he
could hardly wait to tell his fellow senators about the insulting
suggestion. Arising solemnly in the senate, half of whose members already had been bought, he related the disgraceful incident.

The Gwin faction seized this diversion to press for an investigation, and one was voted. High-priced counsel suddenly appeared on behalf of the accused Palmer, but Senator Peck could retain only a recent arrival from Illinois named Edward Dickinson Baker. The latter saw that the investigation was not intended to bring out the truth, and in summing up for his client he ignored the facts and launched into a tirade against Broderick and his gang. His eloquence failed to help Peck, but Broderick was so impressed he engaged Baker as his principal legal mouthpiece thereafter. The investigators finally reported that Peck had "failed to prove his charge," but absolved him from lying in having made it.

But Broderick's gang was not through with the bribe-proof Peck. The legislature having chosen Sacramento as the state's permanent capital, the apparatus of government was transferred there — the lawmakers and their retinue of gamblers, whores, and bartenders.

The day before the senate was to vote on the change of the election date, Senator Peck was invited by a friend to take a buggy ride in the country and get away from the turmoil. Once they were outside the city, the friend whipped up the horse furiously and upset the buggy in a ditch. Peck was thrown out, escaping serious injury; but he felt that the "accident" had been a deliberate attempt either to kill him or to render him incapable of attending the senate the next day. Creeping back to the city, he related what had happened to the Gwin managers. They locked him in a room in the Magnolia Hotel with an armed guard overnight, while Billy Mulligan paraded the corridor outside uttering bloodcurdling threats.

The next day Peck was in his seat when the senate convened. The vote was taken, and Broderick's bill was rejected.

❖

4

This was a stunning defeat for Broderick; already he had been fancying himself a United States senator. His clique howled in fury, but the vote stood, and Broderick was forced to wait a year before he could try again. This meant that Gwin had gained that time to organize his resistance.

Broderick set to work grimly. His first move was aimed at capturing the party's forthcoming state convention. As chairman of the state central committee, he summoned the convention to meet at Sacramento in July. The first order of business would be to elect a permanent chairman and a credentials committee, which would decide which delegates would be seated. The faction capturing those key positions would control the convention and be in a position to name candidates and otherwise exert pressure on the legislature.

The only building in Sacramento large enough to accommodate such a crowd was a Baptist church, and it was rented. Broderick named as delegates his roughest strong-arm squad, and on the opening day he posted these men at the back door of the church, under instructions to rush in and occupy the front pews while the front door was being unlocked. In this way, the opposition delegates would be crowded into the rear of the hall, where they might be overlooked by the presiding officer.

But the "Chivalry" had spies in Broderick's camp, and his strategy became known. When Broderick's "crash squad," consisting of Billy Mulligan, Casey, "Dutch Charley," Rube Meloney, and a ferret-eyed Tennessean named William Walker, the future filibuster of Nicaragua, plunged through the back door, they collided with a squad of "Chivalry" delegates charging in the front door. A free-for-all developed around the pulpit platform, during which Broderick stalked in and as temporary chairman "called the convention to order."

It was calling on a whirlwind to cease and desist. The "Chivalry" was determined to elect "I, John McDougal" as permanent chairman, while Broderick had picked Edward McGowan. Two rival delegates jumped on the pews and yelled the nominations simultaneously. Indicating McGowan, Broderick ruled that "the chair recognizes the delegate from Santa Clara; the election of the other is contested."

This set off pandemonium. Supporters of the candidates hoisted them on their shoulders and bore them to the platform through brandished fists and pistols. A shot rang out, and three delegates dived through the windows. Rube Meloney screamed that he had been wounded, he could feel blood running down inside his trousers. Carried into the vestry, he was examined, but no wound was found; he had merely accidentally discharged the derringer he had tucked in his waistband.

During the fracas one excited delegate jumped on the platform and thrust a six-shooter in Broderick's face. The latter brushed the weapon aside, and acidly warned the man against being careless with loaded guns. The turmoil went on from three o'clock in the afternoon until eight that evening; as darkness fell lighted candles were stuck on chairs in front of the two rival chairmen. The pastor and his deacons begged the delegates to depart, only to be thrown out themselves. Calm came with exhaustion, and the opposing chairmen simultaneously declared the convention adjourned, linked arms, and marched down the aisle, followed by their surly but speechless adherents.

The next day each faction met separately and nominated its slate of candidates for state offices. The Democratic party in California had been torn wide open, and the breach would not be healed for half a century.

Gwin, in Washington, learned about the disgraceful uproar

after it was all over. The schism alarmed him and the party's national leaders, who were trying to unify the Democrats in anticipation of the next Presidential election. When the "Chivalry" ticket triumphed in the September voting, there was satisfaction at the capital, and the menace of Broderickism on the West Coast was believed to have been disposed of permanently.

Chapter II

DURING ALL THIS struggle for party control in California, Gwin was handicapped by being in Washington; direct retaliation was difficult against a cabal that seemed bent on destroying him. At times he grew so angry and disheartened that Charles Sumner, a freshman senator from Massachusetts, wrote to a friend that "Doctor Gwin despairs of remaining in the Senate." However, there were still loyal friends in the West, and the federal patronage remained a lever of power in Gwin's hands.

He continued to press forward legislation to benefit California. He voted for a homestead bill that followed the lines of the act eventually passed, in this being associated incongruously with another Tennessean, Andrew Johnson. As a Congressman, Johnson had begun his sustained fight to distribute the public lands among the "common people," a policy vigorously opposed by most Southern Democrats, and this became a main point of difference between Johnson and his party's leadership. When the Southerners finally voted for his bill, only to have it vetoed by President Buchanan, Johnson denounced what he believed had been a conspiracy to kill his measure under a show of supporting it. The frontier plebeian, Johnson, and Gwin, the frontier aristocrat, were about as incompatible as two men could be. They would encounter each other singularly again.

During this period, Gwin, aided by Weller, obtained appropriations for long-term projects in California amounting to more than $3,500,000, every dollar of which had to be wrung,

by ruse or sharp trading, from fellow Democrats who were reluctant to underwrite public works — "internal improvements"
was the phrase in use. Southern senators denied the constitutional right of the federal government to tax the people of one
state for the benefit of another, and it was only by Gwin's dexterity in matching *quid* for *quo* that new appropriations were
voted for the Mare Island Navy Yard, for fortifications, for the
marine hospital at San Francisco, for the land commission and
Indian subsistence, for appraisers' stores, for lighthouses and
the coast survey, for a comprehensive survey of public lands,
and for engineering studies looking to the determination of a
route for a Pacific railroad.

This last project commanded Gwin's unremitting attention.
He was named chairman of a select committee appointed by
the Senate to study and report on all feasible routes, while the
bickering went on. Missouri's potent Senator Benton insisted
upon the central route, along a line surveyed by his son-in-law,
Frémont; and Northern interests clung tenaciously to their demand that the line run from the Great Lakes to Oregon. After
all the studies were in, the southern route, running west from
New Orleans through Texas and along the Mexican border, still
seemed the most practical to Gwin, although he was prepared
to endorse any route that might be chosen.

The southern route, as drawn tentatively by the engineers,
dipped into Mexico at several points, and in order to bring it
entirely within the United States, a treaty (the Gadsden
Treaty) was negotiated to purchase from Mexico a strip of
land along the Arizona-Sonora line. Gwin wanted the treaty
to take in a much larger area — all the territory north of a line
running from a point thirty miles south of Mazatlán to the Gulf,
thirty miles below the mouth of the Rio Grande. This would
embrace the present Mexican states of Sonora, Chihuahua,
Coahuila, Durango, and Sinaloa, much of Nuevo Leon, and a
piece of Tamaulipas. For this great sweep of territory, much

of it desert and uninhabited, Gwin proposed that the United States pay Mexico $25,000,000, instead of the $10,000,000 that was being offered for the strip along the border. He fought hard to carry his plan, and when it was rejected he was so upset he refused to vote on ratification of the treaty at all.

This was not the only expansionist scheme which the California senator promoted in 1854. Learning that Russia, embroiled in the Crimean War, would be glad to divest itself of unprofitable Alaska for a nominal sum (a quarter of a million dollars was mentioned), he urged the United States to snap up the bargain. The suggestion was too forward-looking for the times, but Gwin kept the matter in mind and would return to it. Meanwhile, he interested his friend Seward in the subject.

Gwin was jealous of his dignity as California's representative and his sense of self-respect led to a serious difference with President Pierce's Secretary of the Treasury, James A. Guthrie, of Kentucky. Guthrie, who was of a churlish disposition, displayed what Gwin considered marked discourtesy during an official call, and the senator demanded an apology. This Guthrie refused to give, whereupon Gwin sent a challenge. In Southern circles this was a grave step, and the capital was agog over the prospect of an encounter between two administration stalwarts. But the cabinet intervened (some said the President himself took a hand) and an accommodation was reached by which Guthrie, without actually apologizing, disclaimed having intended to be rude, and Gwin accepted his explanation.

2

The senator was in Washington when the California legislature met at Sacramento in January, 1855, to reelect him or to choose his successor. Gwin felt that his interests were in trustworthy hands, and in the light of his record he was confident of reelection. It was the Southern custom to continue in office public servants of ability, and he could count on the largest block of votes in the legislature. While the Whigs were bound to present a candidate, they were too few to hope for success, and in a pinch, most of the Whig members would prefer Gwin to Broderick, Gwin's principal challenger. The latter had been perfecting his schemes, and again he sprang a surprise. From the start, the voting went against him, although neither he nor Gwin could amass a majority. Gwin led, but Broderick's mavericks refused to be corralled in sufficient numbers, and the "Chivalry" refused to desert Gwin. It became apparent that Broderick was keeping the legislature in deadlock: if he could not be elected, his strategy was to prevent the election of anyone, of Gwin above all. The upshot was that the legislature finally gave up the attempt and left Gwin with no successor; his term would expire in a few weeks, and his seat would lie vacant temporarily.

This outcome, although giving Broderick only partial satisfaction, was a shock to Gwin. He had been counting upon remaining in the Senate, and his wife upon remaining in Washington: thus the shabby return for his faithful and productive service to the state came as a blow. But as an old campaigner he swallowed the pill and set about in earnest to fight back. This meant digging in for a siege, and he moved his family to San Francisco, where Mary Gwin set up headquarters in a house on Jackson Street, and the work of rehabilitating the senators political fortunes began in earnest. Gwin's seat was destined to lie vacant for two years, during which time he assiduously cultivated the goodwill of party leaders in every county of California.

The autumn elections of 1855 took an unexpected turn when the Native American, or Know-Nothing, party swept into ascendancy, electing not only the governor but a majority of the legislature. The Democrats, divided in strength, were routed.

The Know-Nothings, so-called from their stock reply to questions about their policies ("I know nothing about that"), were opposed to foreigners and especially to Irish Catholics, but in California the party was oddly mixed, its membership even including numerous Irish, while its principles were indeterminate. Nobody could account for its mushroom growth, though many explanations were offered, and its success in California astonished nobody more than its own leaders. It was reliably reported that the party's nominee for governor, J. Neely Johnson, was the most startled man in the state when informed that he had been elected.

The crushing defeat of the Democrats changed the outlook for both Gwin and Broderick. As practical politicians, they realized that their best hope for survival lay in reconciling their differences temporarily. Broderick's predicament was more serious than Gwin's, because the 1854 struggle had left him personally almost bankrupt. He had spent money indiscriminately, mortgaging his properties and incurring debts. The initiative toward a common cause with his detested rival therefore came from him.

3

In April, 1856, Gwin's managers received the first intimation that Broderick was prepared to discuss a truce — "for the good of the party." For the moment, the hint was ignored, because as recently as 1854 Broderick had rejected a parallel offer from Gwin. During their knockdown battle over the senatorship, Gwin had sent his rival a note which read:

Dear Sir: If you will consent to withdraw your name for the U.S. Senate, I will use all my influence — and you know its value — to have you nominated for governor. The nomination is equivalent to an election. Your obedient servant, Wm. M. Gwin.

Broderick's reply was contemptuous:

D. C. Broderick presents his compliments to Senator Gwin, and begs to inform him that Broderick is in the habit of making the governors of California. To W. M. Gwin.

In the light of these letters (both marked "confidential"), the change of heart in 1856 seemed dubious to Gwin and his advisers. But Broderick had built his career upon a reputation for keeping his political pledges, even if they turned out to his disadvantage, and a conference finally was arranged.

The meeting was kept secret. The place was a real estate office behind an auction house on Merchant Street near Montgomery. Gwin was represented by a trusted friend. Broderick appeared for himself. Plain speaking was in order, and after much haggling a bargain was struck. Both men had a consuming ambition — to sit in the Senate — and the arrangement agreed upon would open the way for both to realize their desires simultaneously. The terms were these: in the coming (January) session of the legislature, Broderick would not enter into any contest with Gwin in the election to fill the existing vacancy; instead, he would try to succeed Senator Weller, whose term would expire in the coming spring. Gwin, under the agreement, was to aid him in this attempt. Thus, they hoped, by joining forces, in effect to elect each other.

The arrangement had both advantages and disadvantages for Gwin. He would have to accept a shortened term, contrasted with Broderick's full six-year tenure, but he would preserve his seniority, important for securing committee assignments. If both men cooperated sincerely, there seemed to be little doubt that they could both be elected.

During the conversation, Broderick exposed the intensity of his determination to become a senator, at one point springing up exclaiming:

"I tell you, sir — by God, for one hour's seat in the Senate

of the United States I would roast before a slow fire in
the Plaza!"

Time-serving pseudo-friends who had sponged on him and
deserted him in the crisis he cursed volubly.

"Talk of friends!" he burst out; "I have a few who are, but I
know others, damn them, for I have paid them and know the
quality of their friendship! In the session of '54 they cost me
a hundred and seventy-five thousand dollars! They nearly
beggared me! There was one fellow — " He spoke a name that
his listener recognized. "He was my friend! But to vote for me
that year he had to be paid twelve hundred dollars! Then he
wanted a gold watch, and after that was given to him he demanded a gold chain. I told Billy Graham to buy the dog a
slide and ribbon, and if he wasn't satisfied with that he could
go to hell! Ah! I know these friends!"

Striking the table with his fist, he shouted, "I am going to
that Senate! I shall go if I have to march over a thousand
corpses — and every corpse a friend!"

Gwin's readiness to sacrifice whatever might be required
for success had grown hardly less obsessive.

Chapter III

AT THIS POINT, all political planning went into the discard, for the second Vigilance Committee suddenly took over San Francisco, and its subsidiaries and imitators more or less took over the state. This upsurge of extralegal force broke the hold of Broderick's corrupt machine and imperiled Gwin and all the established political organizations.

The outburst came in May, 1856, one month after the two leaders had called off their feud. The dramatic story of the events of 1856 has been told many times, but a glance at its causes and consequences is necessary to appreciate how it affected the political situation.

The outbreak had two basic causes: criminal excesses, and a coincident business depression. Fraudulent bank failures and absconding financiers had been sharing headlines with accounts of assaults upon citizens. Life and property were felt to be insecure, and too often the agencies of the law were in league with the lawbreakers; trials were rigged, juries packed, and judges venal. A New York newspaper commented during 1856 that the news from California seemed to consist of "assassinations, murders, and hangings" — four hundred and eighty-nine murders during the previous twelve months, two-thirds of which had occurred in San Francisco. Six murderers had been hanged legally in the state, but in San Francisco not one had been strung up, legally or otherwise. Exploitation of the city by a corrupt political machine was held responsible for this record.

The machine was Broderick's. He was the master of San Francisco, and his henchmen were among the most flagrant lawbreakers. One word from him would have curbed the carnival of graft, robbery, and violence, but that word was not given. Desperadoes continued to abuse citizens until a crusading newspaper editor, James King of William, undertook to arouse the decent element to carry out a municipal housecleaning.

James King (he added "of William," his father's name, to distinguish himself from other James Kings) had come to California from Maryland in 1848, and after a spell at the mines had entered banking. His bank crashed in 1855, because of the dishonesty of men whom he had trusted. King turned publisher and dedicated himself to instructing San Franciscans in regard to the causes of the evils that were harrying them. He did not deal in generalities, but named names, times, and places. In the first issue of his paper, the *Bulletin*, published in October, 1855, he called for a purge of Broderick's hired bullies, promising:

> If we can only escape David C. Broderick's hired bullies a little longer, we will turn this city inside out, but that we will expose the corruption and malfeasance of its officiary.

Day after day he hammered home this theme, and the public responded; his paper was read everywhere.

2

A year-old murder of particular callousness provided King with a text to demonstrate cause and effect. Charles Cora, a gambler and pimp, had shot the United States marshal in cold blood because the latter had spoken insultingly of Cora's mistress, Belle Ryan, proprietress of a brothel. This slaying probably would have been passed over like many others, had not

King chosen it to illustrate how law enforcement had collapsed in the city.

Cora had been arrested and placed in the county jail — over which Billy Mulligan presided as the jailer. Belle Ryan, or as she styled herself, Belle Cora, retained a galaxy of high-priced legal talent to conduct her lover's defense, one of the lawyers being Edward D. Baker, the orator who had scalded Broderick in the Elisha Peck bribery investigation. Now Baker was on Broderick's payroll, and according to rumor the $30,000 fee that Belle handed him came from the boss's coffers.

When the *Bulletin* made the Cora case malodorous, Baker, it was said, tried to withdraw. But he had gambled away his fee, and Belle (or it may be Broderick) refused to release him; he was compelled to go through with the trial.

The *Bulletin* predicted, as the trial opened, that Cora would either mysteriously escape from Billy Mulligan's notoriously leaky jail, or would be freed by a packed jury. "Look well to the jury!" the *Bulletin* advised. "If the jury is packed, either hang the sheriff or drive him out of town and make him resign. If Billy Mulligan lets his friend Cora escape, hang Billy Mulligan!"

The scenario was played out exactly as the *Bulletin* had forecast, and Cora was saved by a hung jury. He was remanded back to jail to await a second trial, which the *Bulletin* said would never come off. And this case King held up as an example of the vicious misrule of Broderick's machine.

In May, 1856, James King was assassinated, and the man who shot him down on the street was James P. Casey, the ex-convict from New York. The shooting released the pent-up fury of the public, and two hours after the assault ten thousand men had collected outside the jail, where Casey had taken refuge. More than two thousand citizens, among them the town's leading citizens, thereupon revived the Vigilance Committee of 1851, took Casey and Cora from the jail, and tried them before a Vigilante court. They were sentenced to hang, and were executed publicly while King's funeral cortège was moving toward Lone Mountain cemetery.

For three months the committee enforced justice in its own way, while the legal authorities either acquiesced or looked on helplessly. Four men were hanged, a number were flogged, and scores were deported — Billy Mulligan and "Dutch Charley" Duane among them.

The politicians ran for cover. J. Neely Johnson, the Know-Nothing governor, shilly-shallied, too terrified to approve or to oppose the lawless uprising that was successfully administering the laws. In a rash moment he attempted to smuggle arms to a so-called Law and Order Committee set up in feeble opposition to the Vigilantes, but the shipment was intercepted, and Rube Meloney, the Broderick bully who was convoying them, was arrested.

In the act of making this arrest, the Vigilante's police officer was stabbed by David S. Terry, a justice of the state supreme court and member of the Law and Order Committee. Terry was a Texan with a violent temper, although as a judge he was respected. The Vigilantes arrested him, too, for assault, tried him in their own court, and found him guilty. However, when his victim recovered, he was let off with a denunciation as unfit to sit on the bench, and was advised to resign. Throughout the episode he loudly protested the illegality of his detention and had seriously embarrassed the committee; he did not resign. Ruby Meloney, Broderick's dummy, was deported.

3

The Vigilante upheaval rendered Gwin's position precarious. As a man, he sympathized with the movement, and privately showed his satisfaction that order was being restored to the distracted city; it was well known that he had participated in a similar outburst when he served as one of the judges at the equally illegal roundup and trial of the Hounds in 1849. But that episode had been a three-day commotion, at a time when there was no real government in California; now the state was established and armed interference with its authority was insurrection. As a senator and a conspicuous public figure, Gwin could not afford to approve the Vigilantes openly. For a while he was in cautious communication with the Law and Order Committee, but saw its impotence. Surrounded by pitfalls, he discreetly withdrew to a suburb, where he remained quietly until the storm blew over.

Broderick had only one possible choice of action — immediate disappearance from the city — and with him he took Baker, Casey's defender. A born improviser, Broderick turned this reverse to account by journeying through the back country and bringing his personality to bear upon people who had never seen him before. The result was a wave of sympathy for the boss who presented himself as both the personification and the champion of the "common people" against the arrogant "Chivalry." Every supporter he won was one lost by Gwin, who hitherto had been supreme in the country districts. During this period of lying low, Broderick was hard up for money, and frequently was forced to accept loans of small amounts from newfound friends. This dependency galled him, but those "touches" bound the lenders to him with additional ties of intimacy.

Meanwhile, the Vigilance Committee pushed ahead with its task. Its members were not interested primarily in politics, not being politicians; they were businessmen temporarily neglecting their affairs in order to make the city safe for ordinary citizens, and the sooner they could complete their work, the better they would like it. In August the job was believed finished; whereupon the committee staged a solemn review of their well-drilled forces, comprising infantry, cavalry, and artillery units, and then became dormant again, without formally disbanding. But they kept an eye on the elections in September, and endorsed a slate of honest candidates for the municipal offices. That ticket won right down the line, and the victory ended Broderick's hold on the city government for good.

He had returned to take part in this campaign, which also involved the Presidency. Gwin, too, campaigned for the Democratic nominees, James Buchanan, of Pennsylvania, and John Cabell Breckenridge, of Kentucky. "Buck and Breck" carried the state and the nation against the newly formed Republican party, whose standard-bearer was California's own John Charles Frémont. In the wake of this victory, California's Democrats looked forward to enjoying a generous slice of the federal patronage, and it was plain that the man who would dispense the rewards would head the party in the state. That man had been Gwin. Who would dispense the patronage in the coming administration would depend in part upon the outcome of the senatorial election in the coming January. Gwin and Broderick again were the principal candidates.

Chapter IV

THE PUBLIC, SURFEITED with excitement and its nerves frayed by the violent events of the Vigilante regime, looked forward to a renewal of the political tussle over the Senate seats with acute distaste. The *Alta California* voiced the feeling held by perhaps a majority of the voters when it stated that since 1849, "no question, of howsoever great moment to the State, has been entertained or acted upon, without first being so framed as to operate as a lever to lift some man into the Senate, or to check the aspirations of some other. Once more this nightmare is to fall upon the head of the commonwealth."

Respect for politicians was at a low ebb. When the *Alta* looked over the qualifications of the two outstanding candidates for the Senate, it was forced to turn thumbs down on both. It conceded that Broderick was "a man of quickness of perception, a fair judge of human nature in its worser aspects, a shrewd tactician, an indomitable worker, unscrupulous as a partisan, true to his friends, implacable to his enemies, but bold, frank, and manly to both." Yet in his entire record, the *Alta* could find not one action "calculated to create a claim upon the confidence or admiration of his fellow citizens. [He is] totally unfitted, by education, reading, habits of thoughts and action, and the natural constitution of his mind, for the position to which he aspires." If elected, the *Alta* concluded, he would only bring contempt and ridicule upon the state.

As for Gwin, *Alta* made little more of him. It granted that he had ability, a vigorous mind, extensive information, long experience and perfect familiarity with public affairs, but found

that he lacked "one element of a statesman, and that is, moral
and political integrity." He was deemed "avaricious," "crafty,"
"selfish," and "unprincipled." This castigation was not backed
up by any concrete instance in which these traits were supposedly displayed, and the same weakness was inherent in the
Alta's condemnation of Broderick. In both cases the men were
damned in general terms.

Harshly though Broderick was judged, Gwin seemed to draw
more scurrilous attacks than his rival, and they came from unexpected sources. The *Bulletin,* which had excoriated Broderick before, now under the direction of James King's brother,
endorsed him, calling him "honest" and "straightforward in
manner. His veracity is undoubted. His word is as good as
the bond of most men." By contrast, the *Bulletin* disparaged
Gwin, terming him "mean and contemptuous. .... His associations are among the class that scorns the poor. The clink
of gold is music in his ears."

Besides its direct editorial attack, the *Bulletin* gave space to
subscribers who dredged the dictionary for words to denounce
Gwin. One letter to the editor, signed pseudonymously,
called the ex-senator a "political pirate," and said his "primary,
if not his sole, object in the exercise of his senatorial functions
was the acquisition of money." That he was "elegant, polished
in his manners, energetic, industrious, persevering" merely
made him the more sinister, the writer went on:

> Having exhausted Tennessee, Mississippi, and Louisiana, and
> gone to Texas, you turned your eyes — keen and vulture-like
> eyes — upon this State, and like some bird of prey you swooped
> upon it, and for five years, with beak and talons, you have
> lacerated and devoured it . . . I would prefer you to the Devil,
> but I would prefer the Devil to a Whig!

Broderick was not alone in hoping to topple Gwin from party
leadership. The squabbling Democrats included many who,

formerly loyal to the doctor, had turned against him since his absence from office, and had seized the opportunity to improve their own fortunes by ruining his. Gwin and his record were under fire from many quarters, particularly from the native Californians. Intense bitterness had been aroused by the operation of the system of settling land claims which Gwin had embodied in his act of 1851. This law, welcomed at the time of its passage, had opened the way to the perpetration of widespread injustice, and Gwin was saddled retrospectively with blame for its defectiveness. It was charged that he had slyly contrived to entangle further, rather than untangle, property titles so that he might speculate in the disputed claims. Gwin's contention, given currency by his supporters, was that the law had not been administered in good faith. He never dignified his accusers by directly denying the charge of profiteering, but he did sanction denials by others, including a categorical rejection of the accusation sent by a friend to the *Alta California*, saying:

> For years after the passage of the [land claims] measure, Doctor Gwin was not interested in a foot of land in this State, and never has speculated to the amount of a dollar in any land claim.

No instance of his speculation in California lands was offered by his critics, and no instance has since been traced, although his enemies would have jumped at the chance to prove him venal. The denial must therefore stand until rebutted by concrete evidence.

2

That cruel injustice was done under the act is true; but the causes were rooted in more than the actions of any one man. The whole temper and trend of the times must be taken into account.

During the gold rush, immigrants swarmed into California by the tens of thousands. Most of these newcomers mentally associated California with Oregon, which also was opening up to immigration then. But important differences existed between the two areas and their conditions. Oregon was a wilderness, inhabited by Indians, possessing neither a government nor social institutions, and virtually every foot of it was national land, public domain, open to settlers. California, however, was populated by a civilized people, who had their long-established laws and institutions, and who held their property under legal conveyances issued by Spanish and Mexican authorities. As a result, the gold rush immigrants found most of the desirable land in California already in the possession of the native population.

By the treaty of Guadalupe Hidalgo, the property rights and laws of the Californians were recognized by the United States, which undertook to confirm them in American forms. But the American immigrants could not, or would not, suffer this. After all, they reasoned, California had been conquered "fair and square," and should not the conquerors be able to occupy the country they had won? What rights had the native Californians, once they were defeated in war? In substance, this was the feeling of perhaps most of the men arriving in California from 1849 on. It was a point of view which had been expressed against the Indians and other alien minorities time and again. The native Californians were an alien minority; and under forms of legality the Americans despoiled and evicted them from lands they had held for generations.

By the time California entered the Union, relief from the intolerable confusion of land claims was imperative, and Gwin's act of 1851 provided this in a manner which, at the time, seemed just and equitable. Under it, a general review of all land titles was to be conducted. Owners holding their property by virtue of Spanish or Mexican grants could validate their titles before a board of commissioners to be appointed by the President, and if the evidence was clear, the titles would be confirmed without further fuss. Validation could be made in several ways, none of them onerous. One way was by the mere presentation of a recorded deed, or by undisputed occupation of the land for a period of years. Claimants who could not furnish some proof of ownership would forfeit their claims, and their lands would revert to the public domain, subject to sale or other disposition by the government. In all hearings the United States was to be represented by counsel as a technical counterclaimant; and if either side dissented from the land commissioners' rulings, appeal could be taken to the federal courts, up to the Supreme Court in Washington. The method seemed fair enough. In practice, however, it became something else.

Gwin's sympathies were with the American immigrants, but he recognized the prior rights of the native population. As an expansionist, he reflected the sentiments of most of his generation, and he had no apology to make for those of his countrymen who, like himself, had pushed into new frontiers. When the land claims bill was under debate in the Senate he had made his sympathies known. Senator Benton having assailed the measure as unfair to the Californians, Gwin replied in a speech which, contrary to his custom, he read from manuscript to emphasize its importance. He quoted the sections that were designed to safeguard the legitimate rights of the prior inhabitants, some of them being extremely liberal and easy of compliance, and reminded Benton of the vast snarl over land titles in Louisiana, after that territory was acquired from France. As a result of Congress's failure to legislate promptly and wisely at the start, litigation was still going on a generation after the event, he pointed out, with no end in sight. Gwin's bill was passed, and he always ranked it as among his greatest contributions to California's welfare.

After its passage, there had been delay in putting the meas-

ure into effect. President Fillmore did not appoint the board
of land commissioners for several months, and it was a year before the hearings started. During that time, the confusion grew
worse, and California became a hunting ground for unscrupulous pettifoggers who, by legal tricks and chicanery, promoted
litigation for the sake of collecting fees from their unwary and
timorous native Californian clients, who were at a double disadvantage because they were both ignorant of American process and hardly spoke the language of their conquerors. When
suddenly called upon to justify rights which had never before
been called into question, they suspected that they were marked
for elimination. This was indeed the case, and they fell an
easy prey to glib lawyers who used up the Californians' slender
cash resources, and then induced them to mortgage their estates at ruinously high interest rates in order to carry on inter-
minable litigation.

A greater injustice, however, was the policy laid down by
Washington, whereby the government automatically appealed
every decision of the land commission that upheld the rights of
the native claimant. This meant that the owners of the land,
after, at much trouble and expense, having succeeded in getting
their titles confirmed by the commission, faced further complications, with a final settlement perhaps years off, to be rendered in Washington, thousands of miles away. Meanwhile,
the proprietors could not sell their property advantageously,
for they could not give clear title. The upshot was that many
families who had lived on their estates almost from time im-
memorial, were impoverished by the long, incomprehensible
struggle, and in the end lost everything, while the lawyers grew
rich.

❂

3

For this perversion of his act Gwin denied responsibility. There was an aspect of the situation, however, which affected him as a politician. Certain extremists among the "squatters" organized a party at Sacramento, and pressed for the outlawing of all land claims under Spanish or Mexican grants — in other words, a clean slate and a fresh start. This "squatters party" for a while exercised considerable influence, though the absurdity of their program of confiscation brought about their dispersal in the end. Gwin, and others like him, was sympathetic to the American immigrants who longed for a stake in the country they were helping to build up — for homes and farms. As a politician, he was sensitive to the wishes of his constituents, and the "squatters" were far more numerous than the Californians and their supporters. In 1852 he so far heeded the demands of the "squatters" that he submitted an amendment to the 1851 act which provided that any person who had acquired land in California in good faith could retain it, as against a prior claimant; the loser in such a situation being recompensed with an equal number of acres, which he could choose from anywhere in the public domain. The catch was that almost all the arable land in California (only a small fraction of the state's area at best) had long been preempted, and only desert and mountain terrain was left.

This amendment was righteously condemned, although Gwin defended it in the Senate, protesting against the ignominy attached to the word "squatter." Of the frontier in general he said:

> Who is there with mercenary rancor enough to pursue such settlers, and denounce and stigmatize them in opprobrium as "squatters"? A class of men whose triumphs are everywhere written upon the face of this continent — the men, bold and adventurous, who fled from the tyranny of the Old World, and

at Jamestown, Virginia, and the Plymouth Rock of Massachusetts, and at St. Mary's in Maryland, laid the foundations of the settlements which have spread over the broad bosom of this mighty Republic from the Atlantic to the Pacific, from the icy streams of the North to the tropics; before whom forests have disappeared, under whose hands cities have arisen, with whom the arts and sciences are in their highest development; by whom tyranny in every form, political, social, and religious, has been overthrown, the dignity, glory, and independence of man have been asserted and maintained, and the American Republic advanced to the front rank of the nations of the earth. That is the class of men whose interests I am proud to advocate; to whose cause every faculty I possess shall be devoted, and for the protection of a small portion of whom I invoke the sanction of the Senate to the measure I have presented.

On those who crassly speculated in disputed land claims he poured scorn, but the settlers he extolled; and though the amendment failed to pass, he would always frankly regret its rejection.

Chapter V

WHEN THE STATE legislature convened in Sacramento on Monday, January 5, 1857, legislation was not in the minds of its members. They had come together for one purpose, namely to elect two United States senators.

For days before the session the aggressive, noisy forces of the opposing candidates poured into the placid capital. The supporters of Gwin and Broderick were the most numerous and vociferous, although other candidates had their workers, all of them sanguine of success. Senator Weller was in Washington, but his managers were on hand, and he hoped and expected to win a second term. Another strong candidate was Milton S. Latham, young man in a hurry, who was climbing the ladder of political preferment with phenomenal swiftness. Born in Ohio, Latham had taught school in Alabama, where he imbibed Southern views. Coming to California, he had aligned himself with the "Chivalry" led by Gwin, and had been elected to a term in Congress. President Pierce then appointed him collector of the port of San Francisco. This was a tremendous political plum to be awarded to so young a man (Latham had not yet turned thirty), and he had been recommended for the post by Senator Gwin.

A coolness had grown up between Latham and his sponsor thereafter, because upon taking over the customshouse the new collector had struck out for himself, to build his own political machine. Turning Gwin appointees out of their jobs and replacing them with his men, he acquired a following and had become of some account in the Democratic party in the state. Naturally Gwin regarded him as an ingrate. Latham's Southern prejudices had precluded any personal compatibility with Broderick, although there was no active antagonism between them. In the coming showdown for the Senate, Latham would occupy a strong position as a possible makeweight between Broderick and Gwin, able to throw the election to one or the other, and thereby carry off the second senatorship himself. That was his intention.

The balance of forces was rendered more precarious by the fact that nominally the Know-Nothings controlled the legislature, clinging to the fag end of their terms as "lame ducks." In the previous autumn election, their party had been repudiated as decisively as it had been swept into power two years before. Most of the members were intent upon extracting as much as they could in the way of personal profit from the brief remainder of their grasp upon power. Nearly all were vulnerable to bribery, and while they would prefer cash, they were ready to accept promises if nothing more substantial offered. The Democrats in the legislature were so divided that no one of the factions could elect its man without Know-Nothing assistance. Apart from the mass of legislators were a few honest members who had open minds and were willing to listen to reasonable arguments.

The rival candidates and their managers set up headquarters in Sacramento so close to each other that activity in any one camp could be observed from the others. Broderick was installed in room 6 of the Magnolia Hotel, on J Street below Second. Gwin was in an upstairs room at the Orleans Hotel, on Second Street between J and K. Latham camped in the Fashion Hotel, on J Street just above Second. Weller's managers had separate quarters in the Magnolia Hotel.

*

2

The electioneering previous to the convening of the legislature had been intense. Gwin had been actively lining up votes all during December of 1856, rallying the undecided, exerting pressure, dangling prospects of political rewards. So had the other contestants, and in this bout there were to be no holds barred.

A paradoxical situation developed as between Broderick and Gwin. Both intended to carry out their pledge of mutual aid, but with opposite expectations. Loyal to the letter of their agreement, both would prove flagrantly disloyal to its spirit in the course of their grim pursuit of power.

The understanding between these long-time rivals was, of course, secret, known only to a handful of their most trusted associates. Neither man could risk letting the deal become known generally among their adherents, for bitter partisans on both sides would likely construe it as a sellout, and in disgust swing to some third man. Until after the election, no disclosure could be ventured; on the contrary, every precaution must be observed to conceal the facts.

Gwin's advance agent at Sacramento was James Wylie Mandeville, who himself was not fully in the doctor's confidence as regards Broderick. To Mandeville went a flow of letters from Gwin at San Francisco, instructing and advising on the conduct of the opening skirmishes. On December 19 Gwin wrote that "everything looks well," then went on:

> I think it important that you should visit Walkup [one of Senator Weller's managers]. The impression must be eradicated from his mind that there is any concert between Broderick's friends and mine, as there is none. Capt. Fry can tell you that it is more like a combination between Latham and B[roderick]. If Latham had any [political] capital to put in, they would combine, but out of the votes he claims in your county, Placer & El Dorado . . . I do not think he will get a vote.

The intention behind these subtle asseverations is plain. First, if Latham's stock, as that of a probable loser, could be sufficiently depressed, some waverers of lukewarm loyalty would sheer off from him. Second, if they could be made to suspect that a Latham-Broderick combination was in the making, the Wellerites, most of whom hated Broderick inordinately, would turn against Latham also.

There had been tentative *pourparlers* between the Gwin and Weller camps looking to combined action to elect those two men jointly. Gwin adroitly dashed cold water on this possibility, and in a letter to Mandeville on December 22 urged his lieutenant to impress upon Walkup, Weller's principal manager, the folly of such a commitment. In his opinion, said Gwin, it could not be successful, and its defeat might well sink both candidates instead of only one. He wrote:

> He [Walkup] should not sacrifice me if he finds it impossible to elect Weller and myself. His determination to that effect may not only not elect both, but most likely will defeat both. I do not think Broderick can be defeated, and if [he is] elected, who is so important to our section of the party to be his colleague as myself?

As the recognized leader of the "Chivalry," the doctor did not hesitate to assert his prerogative, or to stress the advantage he held by being on the scene. "I know the anti-Broderick party is very strong in the Legislature," he pointed out, "but with Weller away it cannot be concentrated on him." Moreover, the combination of Gwin and Broderick in the Senate would be no more incompatible than that of Gwin and Weller, he contended, since Weller was "known to be as bitterly opposed to me as Broderick, and no greater harmony could properly exist between us than if I had Broderick for a colleague. . . . I do not see any reason why if he [Weller] cannot be elected I should be defeated. A half loaf is better than no bread."

Mandeville was informed that Broderick's men were watching the movements of ex-Governor Bigler very narrowly, and bets were being laid that Bigler would be taken into the cabinet of incoming President Buchanan. That would mean Bigler's defection to the "Chivalry," bribed by a cabinet offer; if that should happen, Gwin concluded, "Broderick is overboard." Close watch also was being kept on Latham, but in that quarter Gwin was less concerned; Latham, he judged, had "to make up for his lack of strength by bragging."

The letters to Mandeville breathed confidence of success, and the doctor ticked off member after member of the legislature who was "at present all right." In regard to the all-important appointments to federal jobs that would follow his election, Gwin assured his lieutenant, "I have no concealments from you. What I have said to you shall be executed to the letter if I am successful & live."

3

It is likely that Gwin felt no uneasiness about his ability to dominate Broderick as a fellow senator, once they reached the familiar ground of Washington. There Gwin's branch of the Democracy, the Southern "Chivalry," had the whip hand, and Gwin as an old stager was fully capable of strewing the path of a novice on the national scene with booby traps.

Broderick, meanwhile, though equally confident, indulged exactly opposite expectations. He was prepared to redeem his promise of support to Gwin, but to give that support in a way that would reduce the doctor to political impotence, to political vassalage, indebted for his very reappearance at Washington to the poor stonecutter's son. Far from being averse to having Gwin for his colleague in the Senate, Broderick now fiercely desired his rival's reelection — but on Broderick's terms. His mind was vengeful; he brooded upon his plan to humble the man

who had come to symbolize everything the boss had been forced
to overcome in his struggle upward — pride of birth, influence,
wealth, privilege, arrogant self-sufficiency. Let Gwin cringe
and beg for his senatorship; under those conditions Broderick
would toss the prize to him as contemptuously as he would toss
a bone to a cur. This was the boss's scheme. He told it to no
one. Duplicity, deception, and an iron nerve would be required
to bring it to fruition. Obsessed by accumulated hate and
thwarted ambition, Broderick would commit — and cause
Gwin to commit — an irreparable mistake.

The first step in his program was to acquire control of a majority of the Democratic members of the legislature. The party
caucus would nominate their choices for the Senate, and since
the four leading candidates — Gwin, Broderick, Latham, and
Weller — were all Democrats, two of them were foredoomed
to disappointment.

After careful computation, Broderick found that he lacked
two votes of commanding a majority in the caucus. The necessity of picking up those two votes he used as a lever to jimmy
and pry Latham and Weller out of the race plausibly, and narrow the field to himself and Gwin without exposing their pre-
meditated collusion. In the process of doing this, he intended
to disguise his real intent so thoroughly that he would always
retain the initiative, and not fall into a situation where he could
not change his mind and withhold the vital cooperation from
Gwin at the last moment, should the doctor balk at submitting
to certain conditions.

Weller was first adroitly removed from serious contention.
Broderick despised the senator personally and politically, knowing him to be of mediocre ability and possessing proofs of his
venality. Besides, Weller belonged to the "Chivalry." Calling
in Weller's representatives, Broderick offered to back Weller
for the short term (Gwin's vacated seat) in return for two of
Weller's votes. The offer was specious but it sounded well, for

Broderick had said that he would settle for nothing less than a full six-year term in the Senate. The managers, however, replied that they had no authority to agree to a deal that would deprive the senator of two years in office; only Weller himself could make such a concession, they said. The senator, as Broderick knew, was inaccessible, there being no telegraphic communication with the East; but choosing to interpret the manager's hesitation as a snub, Broderick withdrew his offer and coolly eliminated Weller from further consideration. He had made a record: he had offered to cooperate and had been turned down, and that was all he wanted.

Broderick next approached Latham. Calling that eager young man to his room in the Magnolia Hotel, the boss proposed that they merge forces, and by acting in harmony elect each other to the Senate. Latham listened to this proposal delightedly and instantly agreed. Then Broderick named the price he set upon his cooperation: Latham must relinquish all claim to the federal patronage. This demand took Latham aback, for it meant surrendering his effectiveness in the party, relegating him to the status of a figurehead. But the lure of a seat in the United States Senate was too tempting, and reluctantly he gave in, begging only to retain the right to recommend a candidate for the post of collector of the port of San Francisco. He explained that he had rashly promised this place already, in writing, and to go back on his written word would be ruinous. Broderick grumbled, but finally yielded and consented to allow the single exception.

Then, having bound Latham to him, the boss came to the real point of the conference. By precedent, the caucus would first nominate a candidate to fill Gwin's vacant seat (the short term); and after that senator had been elected, the caucus then would nominate a candidate for the long term, to succeed Weller. Broderick told Latham that he was determined that the caucus should reverse this procedure, and nominate for the long term first; in other words, Broderick intended to get himself nominated and elected before the caucus took up the question of nominating a candidate for the short term. Seeing little difference whether his own nomination came first or second, so long as he was elected, Latham agreed to help put through the change of rules when the caucus met.

By falling in with this ruthless suggestion, the overanxious and overcredulous Latham showed political naïveté. He failed to perceive that Broderick, once nominated and safely elected, would have no further need of an ally, but could then dictate the choice of the candidate for the short term, and lay down his own terms. Relying on the vaunted sanctity of Broderick's pledged word, Latham tumbled into the trap. At that moment, in his secret mind, the boss was able to write off Latham as a serious contender equally with Weller. The winning cards were in his hands, and if all went as he intended it should go, he would have Gwin at his mercy.

At his headquarters in the Orleans Hotel, where he had dug in on the eve of the legislature's convening, Gwin sensed that Broderick was contemplating some slippery treachery; various slight clues seemed to point toward that eventuality, and the doctor cast about vainly for an answer to the puzzle. He was too steeped in the cynicism of politics to be shocked, but he was aroused to vigilance. With or without Broderick's assistance, he estimated that he had a very good chance of winning the election, but he prepared to encounter unexpected obstacles, and match trick for trick. Between the Gwin and Broderick camps, of course, there was no communication, the appearance of unreconciled hostility being sedulously preserved.

Gwin by this time had become as obsessively resolved to return to the Senate as Broderick was to enter it. The doctor felt that he had served the state well, and his two-year obligatory retirement had been galling. He longed for vindication, and his wife longed as ardently to resume her position of social prominence in Washington. Under the Presidency of a gentleman such as James Buchanan, recently his country's minister at the court of St. James's, Mary Gwin foresaw an era of brilliant entertainments, and she fretted with impatience to shine in that setting. Thus Gwin, impelled by his ambition and desire for reparation for the political wrong that had been done him, and egged on by his wife's social craving, was in a mood to adopt any means to achieve his goal at this crisis of his career.

4

On Thursday, January 8, Broderick dramatically disclosed, to those who believed they could read the event correctly, his evasion of the pledge of frank cooperation with Gwin. The Democratic members of the legislature met in caucus, and the Broderick and Latham forces ostentatiously joining hands, changed the order of business and without pause named David C. Broderick for the long term in the Senate.

The boldness of the maneuver, and the rapidity with which it was executed, threw Gwin's camp off balance temporarily. The doctor perceived the tactical advantage that had been seized by Broderick. The caucus was bound by the unit rule, which required all the members to vote in the legislature in accordance with the action of the caucus. Thus, when Broderick's nomination should come up for a vote in the legislature, Gwin would be compelled, under the rules of party discipline, to instruct his forces to vote for his rival. Party regularity was a cardinal principle with Gwin; he could not and would not disregard it. He realized that he had been outwitted, and he appreciated the strength of the position in which Broderick suddenly had entrenched himself.

On Friday, January 9, the two houses of the legislature met in joint convention and the entire Democratic delegation, aided by breakaways from other groups, elected Broderick on the first

ballot to a six-year term in the United States Senate. His commission had been engrossed in advance, and Governor Johnson
was waiting in an anteroom to sign it. Broderick was handed
the coveted document fifteen minutes after the vote was tallied.

With the prize in his hand, Broderick felt himself in a position to overthrow the hated "Chivalry" forever. Flushed with
success, he exulted to a friend:

"It is my turn now! Not one of them shall get his head to the
front until I have pulled out his claws and put my brand on
him!"

Tension in Sacramento mounted during that weekend. The
legislature stood adjourned until Monday, and Gwin's camp
was jittery, chagrined at having been tricked by Broderick and
alarmed by the steady drift of supporters from their camp to
that of Latham. Men whom Gwin had put in positions of afflu-
ence, men whom he had trusted, were seen in the bar of the
Fashion Hotel, where Latham had his quarters, and the tide of
rumors indicated that Latham was the man selected by Broderick to share Senate honors.

On Friday evening, after Broderick's election, the Democratic
caucus had met again and tried in four ballots to nominate a
candidate for the short term. Each time Gwin led, with Latham second, but enough votes were scattered among minor
candidates to prevent either from racking up a majority. Forty
votes were required to nominate, and Gwin never received more
than twenty-six. After the fourth inconclusive ballot, a Broderick spokesman had moved for adjournment until Saturday evening.

All day Saturday, lookouts kept watch on the hotels where
electioneering was going on. Every caller passing in or out was
spotted and identified, and the conversation in the bars was
anxiously dissected for clues to Broderick's intentions. All signs
seemed to point to Latham, and by noon on Saturday Gwin was
so disheartened that he announced he was abandoning the

contest. He made plans to return to San Francisco on the boat leaving at two o'clock.

Then suddenly Latham's cause received two setbacks. How this came about, nobody seemed able to say. But the first blow came when the man to whom Latham had promised the col- lectorship burst into the Fashion bar shouting that his room had been broken into, his papers ransacked, and the letter contain- ing Latham's promise abstracted. Cursing Latham as the in- stigator of the theft, the irate politician hurried off to see Brode- rick.

At Gwin's headquarters it was cynically suspected that Broderick had engineered the burglary in order to undercut Latham.

A second blow was dealt to Latham almost simultaneously. From some source, never identified, a paper was circulated charging that Latham had cooperated secretly with the Vigi- lance Committee in San Francisco. The statement was signed by a member of the Vigilantes' executive committee, and it added that Latham's brother had actually joined the Vigilantes, and yet had been retained on the customshouse payroll. Coop- eration in any form with the noxious Vigilance Committee was the unpardonable sin in Democratic eyes, for the machine that had been smashed was Democratic, and every victim of the committee had been a member of that party.

As the outrageous revelation passed from hand to hand, Latham's stock sank sharply. Gwin canceled his plan to leave the city.

Broderick remained secluded at the Magnolia Hotel, his in- tentions still undisclosed. To a friend he partially revealed his thoughts. In the previous autumn election, two Democratic Congressmen had been elected — Charles L. Scott and Joseph C. McKibben. Both were attached to Latham, and in this com- bination Broderick saw a danger to himself. To his friend he pointed out:

"If I go to the Senate with Latham, Scott and McKibben being his friends in the lower house, I'll be a mere cipher. But if I go with the other man [Gwin], I can have things my own way."

How he would contrive to have things his own way he did not specify.

Saturday afternoon the town was rank with rumors. That evening the Democrats caucused again. The session was opened by state Senator William I. Ferguson, a man who was believed to be in Broderick's confidence. Ferguson announced that he wished to withdraw the name of a token candidate for whom he had been voting; and it was inferred from this action that Broderick was prepared to show his hand. It was a cause of further confusion, therefore, when four ballots brought no majority to either Gwin or Latham, and the caucus was adjourned until Monday.

5

On Sunday, January 11, there was little praying in Sacramento; the politicians filling the hotels were otherwise engaged. Broderick remained aloof and silent, in mysterious isolation. At Latham's headquarters there was gloom, but at Gwin's, although there was no apparent cause for optimism, spirits seemed high. Gwin himself was genial and confident, telling callers that he was going to get a good night's rest in preparation for an active day Monday. About eleven o'clock he said good night to all, went to his room, and watchers at Latham's hotel saw his light go out. Visitors after that were told that the doctor was sleeping.

But Gwin was not asleep. Shortly after midnight, muffled in a cloak, he stole down a back stairway to the alley that ran behind the Orleans Hotel. There he met a man, also wrapped in a cloak, who was waiting in the shadows. The alley — a mere track of mud with a few planks thrown across the puddles —

led to J Street, and on the opposite side of that Street resumed and ran along the rear of the Magnolia Hotel. Since in that block there was not a single barroom, at midnight J Street was deserted.

The two cloaked men crept along the alley in silence, darted across J Street, and entered the alley beyond. At a rear door of the Magnolia, Gwin's escort rapped in a peculiar way. The door opened, and a man inside silently beckoned them to follow him up a staircase that ended, one flight above, almost at the door of room 6. A discreet tap on this door, and it was opened by a tall, brawny man with a ruff of reddish whiskers encircling his chin. It was Broderick.

"Good evening, gentlemen," he said. "Walk in. Dr. Gwin, I am glad to see you. Be seated."

The rivals shook hands. Broderick pushed forward one of the two chairs in the room, which was otherwise furnished only with a table, bureau, washstand, and bed. Gwin sat down. His companion hunched down on the bed. After a little desultory talk the companion left, closing the door softly behind him.

About one hour later, the door of room 6 reopened and Gwin emerged. He stole down the stairs, rejoined his escort, and furtively they regained the Orleans Hotel. Gwin mounted to his room undetected and went to bed.

In the Magnolia, Broderick sat alone in room 6. The curtain was drawn across the window; the lamp on the table burned with a steady flame. Beside it lay a piece of paper covered with writing.

What Broderick, regarding that paper, could not foresee was there lay the death warrant for two men — one, state Senator William I. Ferguson — the other, Broderick himself.

Chapter VI

On Monday, January 12, 1857, the drama reached its denouement when the Democrats caucused and without ado nominated Gwin for the short term in the United States Senate. On Tuesday, January 13, the legislature met in joint convention and elected him; at 1 p.m. the word was flashed to San Francisco over the "new magnetic telegraph": "Gwin elected on the first ballot. A salute is firing on the levee."

The correspondent of the *Bulletin* sent a more extended account of the election, with a commentary somewhat sardonic:

> The entire ignorance of the people at large, and even those in this city, as to what will be the action of their own representatives, is a beautiful instance of the way in which politicians carry out true republican principles, when the power is once fairly in their hands. . . . Some folks here pretend to believe that the steamship companies, knowing the impoverished condition of the State Treasury, patriotically determined to save the people a useless waste of public money, and sent up for distribution among the Democracy large sums of hard cash. . . . Gwin, they say, held on to it until the last moment, and it was not forthcoming until all other chances had failed him. Such stories always are in circulation in times like the present. Your readers, however, know politicians too well to place *too much* confidence in their reliability.

The same writer reported that after Gwin's election "the champagne flowed in torrents, to say nothing of commoner liquors, although the rejoicings were not as noisy as those upon the announcement of Broderick's success."

Dr. Gwin was aboard the boat for San Francisco one hour after his election, having issued to every member of the legislature an invitation to join him in a "victory collation" at his home in the city on Thursday, two days hence.

A hundred-gun salute fired from Telegraph Hill welcomed the senator home. He greeted his jubilant followers with an air of triumph not unalloyed with bitterness. Mary Gwin was overjoyed at the prospect of reestablishing herself in Washington society.

Hard on Gwin's heels came Don Pablo de la Guerra, a member of the state senate from Santa Barbara. A man of probity, well known in his district, he laid before Gwin evidence of Broderick's double-dealing that had aroused his indignation. The story he unfolded was this:

Until Monday morning (the morning after that midnight meeting in the Magnolia Hotel) Don Pablo had been committed to vote for a minor candidate. On Monday morning Broderick had asked him to shift his support to Gwin, and he had assented. He sent word of this changeover to Gwin's headquarters, and Gwin had been apprised of the fact; therefore he readily credited the rest of de la Guerra's report.

Just before the Democratic caucus assembled on Monday evening, Don Pablo said, Broderick had sent word to him again, requesting him to withhold his vote from Gwin. As a man of honor, who had pledged his word to vote for Gwin, this Don Pablo refused to do. But the strange reversal on Broderick's part had aroused his suspicions, and during the caucus he had noted carefully the floor maneuvering, and had become convinced that Broderick, at the last minute, was doing his utmost to throw the nomination to Latham.

This disclosure was to have far-reaching effects, for it rendered impossible, from that time on, any cooperation or harmony between Broderick and Gwin. On the doctor's part, every feeling of obligation was canceled.

The next day — Thursday — the day of the scheduled "victory collation" — another strange development transpired. The Sacramento *State Journal,* a newspaper controlled by Broderick, published an "Address to the People of California" over Gwin's signature, which raised a furor. An astonishing document to be published at any time, its appearance at that moment led to the wildest speculation as to what lay behind it, for the wording seemed to conceal more than it conveyed. The only inference that could be drawn from it was that a corrupt bargain had been struck between Broderick and Gwin at Sacramento, which reduced Gwin to a position of dependence and inferiority. In part, this pronouncement read:

> I have thought it proper, in view of the senatorial contest that has resulted in the election of Mr. David C. Broderick and myself to the Senate of the United States, to state to the people of California certain circumstances and facts which compose a part of the history of that arduous struggle. . . .
>
> A representative whose evil destiny it is to be the indirect dispenser of federal patronage will strangely miscalculate if he expects to evade the malice of disappointed men. But the hostility, malignity, and abuse which have pursued my senatorial career, when at a distance from my maligners, and which have accompanied me during the strife just closed, are such, I believe I may say, as a representative has never before endured to survive.
>
> The opposition I sustained came from an unexpected quarter, and from those whose friendship, I had believed, strengthened as it was by personal obligation, nothing could weaken or sever. Ardent, devoted, and disinterested friends I had . . . but even the force of their attachment . . . would have proved unavailing, if unaided, to meet and conquer the opposition which open hostility and secret treachery had arrayed against me. I had learned . . . in the struggle that he who confers great official power upon individuals does not always secure friends, and that the force of deep personal obligation may even be converted into an incentive to hostility and hate. In a word, to the federal patronage in the State do I attribute, in a great degree, the malice and hostile energy which, after years of faithful public service . . . have

nearly cost me the endorsement of a re-election to the United
States Senate.
From patronage, then, and the curse it entails, I shall gladly
in the future turn. . . .
I have hinted above to aid other than that received from those
whom I had regarded as friends. I refer to the timely assistance
accorded to me by Mr. Broderick and his friends. Although at one
time a rival, and recognizing in him a fierce but manly opponent,
I do not hesitate to acknowledge, in this public manner, his for-
getfulness of all grounds of dissension and hostility in what he
considered to be a step to allay the party strife . . . which has
distracted . . . the State. To him, I conceive, in a great degree,
my election is due; and I feel bound to him and them in common
efforts to unite and heal, where the result heretofore has been
to break down and destroy.

This voluntary abnegation and severance from all participation in the patronage which had formed the basis of Gwin's political power bore the date, "Sacramento, Jan. 13, 1857" — the
day Gwin had been reelected. It appeared on January 15, and
produced a shocked reaction.

All that lay behind this "Address" is not, and never will be,
known. It implied a mixture of motives, but its publication precisely on the day set aside for Gwin's victory celebration
brought charges of a breach of faith on Broderick's part. He
controlled the *State Journal,* whose editor was one of his most
loyal partisans, and the statement would never have been published without his authorization. The connotations of a disgraceful bargain, in connection with the election, were inescap-
able. The reaction in San Francisco was stormy. The "Chivalry" was outraged, and at Gwin's victory party there were
grim faces; some leading Democrats stayed away altogether.
Throughout the city ran a whisper about a mysterious paper —
something in writing — that would confirm the most malignant
construction that could be placed upon the "Address." Close
associates of Gwin and Broderick professed to know nothing
about any such paper, but the rumor would not subside.

Gwin remained outwardly unperturbed, and offered no explanation. Broderick returned to San Francisco and was welcomed like a conquering general, with civic ovations. The conventional courtesies were observed between him and Gwin, and in a few days they sailed on the same ship for Panama and Washington. Accompanying them, besides the two new Congressmen, was former Governor John Bigler, whose brother, William Bigler, was a United States senator from Pennsylvania; the Biglers together were intent upon getting something worthwhile when the patronage was handed out.

The trip was uneventful. From New York, Gwin hastened at once to Washington, while Broderick tarried in the metropolis to receive the plaudits of his former Tammany associates.

2

Gwin reached the capital and resumed his place in the Senate just in time to save the bill that provided for United States participation in laying the Atlantic cable. He was intensely interested in this project. Promoted by Cyrus W. Field with the assistance of an array of scientists, it had received the approval of the British government, and Parliament had voted a subsidy and the loan of a warship to carry out the work. In Washington the notion of stretching a wire across the ocean, in the expectation that it would transmit intelligible messages, had met with ridicule, and when Gwin arrived the bill proposing American cooperation on a par with the British seemed headed for defeat. The day after he took his seat the measure was passed, the vote being 20 to 19; Gwin's "aye" being decisive.

His reception at Washington was mixed, for rumors had preceded him regarding the peculiar circumstances of his election. Some of his friends feared that he had compromised himself; but he soon dispelled this impression, blaming the exceptional virulence of California politics; and in Democratic circles he resumed the prominence to which his experience, seniority, and party loyalty entitled him.

Broderick aroused Washington's curiosity. His dramatic return to his birthplace, at thirty-nine years of age, to sit in the Capitol his father had helped to build, occasioned admiring comment, and there was a good deal of pious talk about this example of the opportunity which America afforded to all, high or low, etc. A few senators (Robert Toombs of Georgia was one) responded favorably to Broderick's obvious force and courage; but by and large there was little warmth in his reception, and his harsh, forbidding air discouraged what slight warmth he inspired.

Sworn in as a senator on Buchanan's inauguration day, Broderick lost no time in paying his respects to the chief of his party at the White House. His reception deeply offended him; to an acquaintance he said angrily that he had found the executive mansion "cold outside, and icy within." Buchanan had been polite but reserved, and when Broderick alluded to patronage, the President had blandly told him to submit his recommendations in writing. When Broderick observed that this seemed a departure from custom, Buchanan replied that it was a new rule he was laying down, and then closed the interview. Broderick came away fuming. Was it to be the same story all over again — the stonecutter's son frustrated, thwarted, brushed aside by a supercilious aristocrat? He was hurt as well as incensed.

Broderick's expectations appear to have been both naïve and provincial. During his struggle to reach the top, he had never clearly envisioned what he would find when got there, but had dimly assumed that having entered into the Nirvana of the Senate, his long quarrel with circumstances would be ended. Therefore, when he realized that in Washington he was only the junior senator from California, and socially was considered still a stonecutter, his disillusionment was painful. The Southern society that dominated the capital ignored him without pretense; in the Senate his colleagues treated him with formal respect, but nothing more. How completely the Senate was controlled by his opponents of the "Chivalry" was shown in the distribution of committee chairmanships: Southern senators and Gwin headed every important committee except that on the territories, which was headed by Senator Stephen A. Douglas of Illinois.

Also, Broderick found himself floundering politically. Having achieved his ambition, he was at a loss to know what to do with it. His talent had consisted in playing party factions against each other, in manipulating conventions, and controlling offices. But in Washington he had no faction, and Congress was not a political convention. Furthermore, his defiance of party discipline in California weighed against him with the national leadership; he was a maverick, and they kept him at a distance.

Rebuffed and baffled, surrounded by unfamiliar and (he was convinced) hostile influences, he became morose. Soon he began to suspect that Gwin was going back on his pledge to abstain from the distribution of the patronage. Place after place went to men recommended by those friendly to the "Chivalry," while the candidates for federal jobs who were urged by Broderick were passed over. To Broderick this was plain evidence that Gwin was faithless, and he became furious with his fellow senator.

The fact was that, blinded by hatred of Gwin and all that the latter stood for, Broderick was unable to take into account the realities of the situation; yet he reached the right conclusion in an exaggerated, distorted form.

Gwin maintained (and there is no proof to the contrary) that, with one exception, he held aloof from making any recommendations for federal appointments in his own name or personally. But although he adhered to the letter of his "Address to the People," there were channels of communication with the White House that could be used by so deft and discreet a manipulator as the doctor. President Buchanan, for instance, was a long-time party associate, and Representative McKibben enjoyed ready access to the White House through his father, Chambers McKibben, a hometown neighbor of Buchanan's in Pennsylvania. The President naturally would be interested in Senator Gwin's views on matters affecting California and the Democratic party there, as mutual associates might relay these.

How the wheels were revolving to discomfit Broderick was disclosed by Gwin in confidential messages to his man Friday in California, Mandeville. The administration had hardly been installed when letters began posting westward, in which Gwin took pains to elucidate the inner workings of the machine, both for his lieutenant's enlightenment and to account for the delay being encountered in procuring for Mandeville a promised government job. This assignment, Gwin stressed, was the sole exception he was making to his announced policy of strict separation from all recommendations; he also implied that Broderick knew about this exception and had raised no objection.

On March 19, 1857 — two weeks after Buchanan's inauguration — Gwin advised Mandeville that "we are rather in a fog about the appointments. . . . Scott and McKibben have assumed to control the patronage of the State against Broderick." The Congressmen, friends of Latham, presumably were smarting over the latter's betrayal and were not above expressing their resentment. Scott, Gwin said, was proving uncooperative. "You," he told Mandeville, "they have failed to recommend for anything." He went on:

> Scott sent word intimating his willingness to recommend you for [illegible] place, when he knew Broderick and McKibben had urged [another man] for the same. I sent word to him to unite upon you. . . . He sent word he would see me on the subject and

that is the last of it. . . . They are a nice set. I have no fear I
will get you the appraiser's berth . . . [but] there will be some
delay about it.

As concerned his own relations with Broderick, Gwin added
significantly:

> I had my first interview with Broderick yesterday since we left
> [California]. He is for you for that place, as he told me. . . . I
> have determined to become no partisan. Yours is the only original
> appointment of importance in the state . . . and you could have
> been named but for the base act of Scott and McKibben in uniting
> on [a rival claimant]. Is this not a commentary on decency?

At the start of April, a number of patronage appointments
were announced, from which Broderick was shut out. The rebuff added gall to his rancor, and the sense of loneliness that
had oppressed him ever since the loss of his family became
deeper; the fruits of success seemed turning to ashes in his
mouth; and his wrath against Gwin, the personification of all
his enmity, reached an explosive pitch.

This reaction Gwin was aware of, and he interspersed progress bulletins to Mandeville with warnings of Broderick's
mounting infuriation. The appraisership prospect not having
panned out, the doctor was pressing for Mandeville's appointment as superintendent of the mint at San Francisco.

On April 3 Gwin wrote that Broderick was about to head back
to California in a fighting mood:

> Broderick leaves on the 5th in a great rage. His object is to
> carry the State convention, nominate his friends for the State
> offices, and censure the administration for the appointments
> made. . . . His denunciations of the President . . . are gross in
> the extreme.

Some observers at the capital were inclined to suspect
Broderick's great choler was "a ruse to get clear of the multitude

of promises he had made and could never fulfill if he had all the patronage." Gwin doubted this, though he failed to grasp, or at least omitted to acknowledge, the profounder causes of the estrangement. A few days before the appointments were made public, he said, he had had an interview with Broderick, at the instance of Robert J. Walker, Gwin's old friend in Mississippi. The meeting, he said, was outwardly harmonious:

> It obliterated all causes of contest for the present. Patronage was not named. . . . Since the appointments were made we have met once on business and he was very social. I have never heard of his saying a word against me or blaming me in any way, although [and then came the significant phrase] he must have known where the blow came from.

Scott, on the other hand, now was behaving "very well," Gwin reported, and in regard to an appointment for Mandeville, the doctor was prepared to make a "strong move":

> I intend to see the President in the morning and make a strong appeal to him. Of one thing you may rest assured. I will give the government no rest until you are provided for. It may be a work of time but I will never cease or tire until it is done.

Two days later — on April 5, the very day Broderick departed in a dudgeon to stir up trouble in the West — Gwin had news for Mandeville that shed more light on the intricacies of the political game as it was played in Washington:

> Since I wrote you I have ascertained that old Bigler, true to his instincts, has been urging great exertions to have a number of Broderick's men appointed to office under the guise that they where *his* friends and he and Broderick had fallen out, and had very nearly succeeded.

This harked back to the supposed split between Bigler and Broderick that had been rumored on the eve of the Senate election. It was all a pretense, Gwin scoffed, which the pair now were trying to turn to their profit. Bigler's trickery had been exposed in the nick of time, after the cabinet had already agreed on his nominee for the superintendency of the mint, and the move had been blocked partly by Gwin's prompt action. This he reported laconically: "I spent yesterday with the cabinet and the President. They will not forget us."

The sly chuckle that must have passed between the two old stagers at that White House meeting, Buchanan and Gwin, was conveyed with relish:

> It was our first meeting [since the inauguration], of which I informed him, when he replied it was true I did not come near him and was committed to no appointment, yet how the devil did it happen that all my friends were appointed? I replied because they were the best men.

Yet at the close the suppliant Mandeville was again put off with the pabulum that is fed perennially to those who wait on the pleasure of politicians:

> I think your appointment as superintendent of the mint is as certain as any future event can be in this uncertain world. If you are appointed, the only request I have to make is to bestow your patronage, which is large, on worthy members of the party, and second, dismiss all of Latham's and Birdsall's kin. The mint is full of them. Don't leave a vestige of them.

In the midst of considerations of "practical politics," the senator's constant care for the building up of California cropped up. Should Mandeville get his appointment, Gwin requested,

> I wish you would hold open one place for a lady who lives in San Francisco. She is a native of Germany now there with her father. . . . I am hoping to get a large emigration of Germans

to Southern California to cultivate the grape. Drop me a note if you are appointed saying whether you can give her the berth so that I can send it to her. She is well qualified for the place.

This project to introduce German viticulture into the state, fostered by Gwin, materialized with the founding of the town of Anaheim.

A footnote to this letter informed Mandeville:

> I go to New York this evening to see the steamer off . . . and will then go to Missi[ssippi] on a . . . visit to my old mother whom I have not seen for eight years. I will then return here to determine whether I will or not go to California but I think I shall not.

By "seeing the steamer off" at New York, Gwin was able to get his letter aboard the ship that carried Broderick to Panama on the way back to San Francisco. In the same mail was another letter from Gwin alerting party workers regarding Broderick's intentions, characterizing these as

> a bold game, in which he loses everything if he fails; and can he succeed? . . . If Mr. Broderick succeeds, he will break up the Democratic party in California; and if he fails, he breaks himself. . . . I beg of you, and every friend, to canvass [the State] thoroughly, and carry the delegates to the State convention.

The imminence of the danger Gwin did not underestimate; while he was safeguarding the interests of his faction at Washington, his seconds must head off Broderick on the home grounds.

3

The effectiveness of Gwin's watchful activity burst upon Broderick with unexpected force as soon as he arrived at San Francisco. Everywhere he found a recrudescence of sympathy with Gwin and support for the "Chivalry"; his own position had been seriously undermined during his absence. The non-performance on patronage was a source of unpopularity; some supporters had turned from him in disgust, and there was widespread questioning of his motives. In response to Gwin's urging, a group of party leaders called Broderick on the carpet to answer charges of disloyalty to the administration.

Forced to defend his actions — a situation new to him, for his tactics had always been to attack — Broderick fumbled, blundered, and finally took the worst possible course — he lied. He protested that he harbored no subversive plans, and assured the Democratic leaders that no undercover bargain had been struck between Gwin and himself in connection with their election. He had been elected, he maintained, "without bargain, contract, alliance, combination, or understanding with anyone." The rumors hinting at a "corrupt deal" regarding the patronage, he avowed, were false.

These private denials Broderick reinforced by publishing a "Letter to the People of California" that closely paralleled Gwin's now notorious "Address."

"Between Mr. Gwin and myself there was no condition whatever in regard to the distribution of the patronage," this statement affirmed. What had happened, he said, was that after the election he had learned that Gwin "had agreed with others to take no part in the recommendation of a single federal officer"; but this decision had been taken entirely independently of Broderick, and he challenged anyone who doubted his statement to "produce a man within the length and breadth of the State whom I ever deceived, or to whom I ever falsified my word."

His customary tactical address failed him, for the July convention which he had determined to dominate turned down his slate of candidates for state office, and nominated a "Chivalry" ticket, headed by ex-Senator Weller for governor. Weller blamed Broderick for his failure to get a second term in the Senate and was hot for revenge. The Democratic ticket won in the election, and with Weller as governor Broderick was deprived of any voice in handing out the state jobs. His isolation seemed complete.

4

Broderick returned to Washington brooding upon his grievances and casting about for ways to retrieve his position of strength.

Gwin, whose outlook was neither naïve nor provincial, meanwhile had been constructively active. His interest in Alaska and the Atlantic cable had led him to note the steady advance of Russia down the Amur River in Siberia, and he proposed the construction of a round-the-world telegraphic connection. This would stretch from California to Alaska, be carried across the Bering Strait to Siberia, up the Amur River to Russia in Europe and St. Petersburg, and thence to Great Britain, where it would hook up with the transatlantic cable. The scheme was opposed as merely visionary, although Gwin was convinced that it was feasible, and when the Atlantic cable actually began relaying messages, he tried to get action on his plan. But the temporary failure of the cable after three weeks of operation dampened people's enthusiasm. Not until after the Civil War, under better conditions, would Field succeed in laying another cable which would prove a success. Gwin followed Field's struggle with sympathy throughout.

The acquisition of Alaska occupied the doctor again at this time. With the approval of the President, he opened a roundabout negotiation looking to purchase of the territory by the United States. The correspondence, kept unofficial with great care, was routed through Gwin as a middleman: Secretary of State Lewis Cass gave the senator a message orally, which

Gwin embodied in a private letter to the Russian minister at Washington, Baron Edouard de Stoeckl; the minister passed the information along as a "confidential aside" in his dispatches to his Foreign Ministry, and the replies were returned from St. Petersburg by the same route. Progress was made, but despite Gwin's urging, the negotiations were not brought to a head. Nevertheless, it was upon these preliminary discussions that Gwin's friend, Seward, would base his successful effort to acquire Alaska years later.

Upon returning to the Senate, Gwin had been named to the Committee for the Post Office and Post Roads, and he was chairman of the Senate Conference Committee that perfected the bill creating the Butterfield stage line to California by way of Santa Fe. Speedier, more convenient communication between the East and West coasts never ceased to preoccupy him. In presenting his first railroad bill in 1852, he had urged Congress to "bind these Pacific possessions to the rest of the Union with hooks of steel, regardless of cost," and from that position he never deviated. The sectional conflict was the insuperable obstacle as bill after bill failed to pass. Some disgruntled Californians blamed their senior senator for these failures; but it would require a Republican Congress and the exigencies of the Civil War to resolve the dispute and bring the railroad into being.

The social position in the capital of Senator and Mrs. Gwin was unrivaled. The first two years of Buchanan's administration were gay; times were flush, money was plentiful, and a galaxy of hostesses, almost all of them Southern, entertained lavishly. The charms of that brief period have been recounted in memoirs; it was as if society realized that it was dancing on a volcano and was determined to make the most of the lull before disaster. Senator Gwin was reputed to spend at the rate of $75,000 a year, mainly for entertainment, and the parties and dinners in his mansion at Nineteenth and I streets, just off

Pennsylvania Avenue, were among the liveliest of that time.

Mary Gwin's tact enabled her to carry off some situations that would have "sunk" less capable hostesses. One of her feats — and a triumph for the senator also — was her successful introduction of Senator Seward to the exclusive circle of Southerners. As a "black abolitionist," Seward at first was shunned by the capital's best society. His Southern colleagues might fraternize with him in the Senate, but they did not invite him to their homes. Their wives, in some instances, had announced that they would not speak to the man, should anyone have the ill-breeding to introduce him.

Seward, who was gregarious and liked good conversation and sprightly company, found his ostracism hard to bear, and he appealed to Gwin to break down the barrier. While the latter was doubtful of success, for he knew the temper of his Southern intimates, he consulted his wife and they agreed to try. Seward was invited to a dinner at which the other guests belonged to the ultra Southern set.

The company had assembled in Mrs. Gwin's drawing room before the New Yorker arrived. Mary Gwin confessed that she quaked inwardly when she heard Seward announced, and an icy chill descended upon the room. Seward entered, bouncy and affable, ignored the air of constraint, and was appropriated by Mrs. Gwin herself, who immediately led the way to the dining room. The dinner began dismally enough, but Seward could be a captivating talker, and gradually his geniality and flow of anecdote thawed the ice, and the evening wound up pleasantly.

A story was told that the next day, Senator Hunter of Virginia encountered Toombs of Georgia at the Capitol and said, "I just met Seward, and he said, 'How are you, brother?' "

"Did you knock the fellow down?" demanded Toombs.

"No," replied Hunter. "You can hardly knock down a man who has just called you brother."

Seward became a frequent guest in several Southern homes, including that of Jefferson Davis and his wife, Varina, and Mrs. Gwin's triumph of social diplomacy was a prized feather in her cap.

5

The high point of Mary Gwin's social achievements, however, was the fancy dress ball she gave that lasted from dusk to dawn on April 19, 1858. President Buchanan received at the side of the hostess, and everyone of consequence attended. Seward was there, and other senators (but not Senator Broderick), making the most of their exemption from donning a costume. In his invitation to them, Gwin had stressed that in his opinion no garb so well became a senator of the United States as that in which he daily transacted the business of the nation.

The doctor and his wife had resolved that this entertainment should eclipse anything ever seen in the capital, and with the cooperation of every segment of society — the army, the navy, the diplomatic corps, the cabinet, the Senate, the House, and the executive mansion — they succeeded. The ball, coming just when political rancor was rising to its culmination, was later compared to the Waterloo ball given by the Duchess of Richmond in Brussels on the night before the battle, and it inspired much quotation of Byron's impetuous lines:

> There was a sound of revelry by night,
> And Belgium's capital had gathered then
> Her beauty and her chivalry, and bright
> The lamps shone o'er fair women and brave men;
> Hundreds of hearts beat happily; and, when
> Music arose with its voluptuous swell,
> Soft eyes look'd love to eyes that spake again,
> And all went merry as a marriage bell.

For weeks the excitement had been working up. There were consultations about costumes, mantua-makers were swamped with orders, special effects were procured from Paris and New York, books of history were pored over for details of stuffs and ruffs.

The press reported the affair elaborately, and a former army major, John von Sonntag Haviland, composed a "Metrical Glance at the Fancy Ball" that was printed in the Washington *Star* and copied widely for years afterward. Taking for his model Pope's "Rape of the Lock," Haviland invoked the "Muse of Fashion" in lines that might apply to Washingtons of other eras, too:

> To that gay capital where congregate
> The worst and wisest of this mighty State;
> Where patriot politicians yearly wend
> The Nation's fortunes, and their own, to mend;
> Where snobbish scribblers eke the scanty dole
> By telegraphing lies from pole to pole;
> Where bad hotels impose their onerous tax,
> And countless Jehus sport untiring hacks;
> Where murder boldly stalks, nor cares a straw
> For useless Police or unused Law;
> Where Gamblers bland with Statesmen freely mix,
> And seem sometimes to make exchange of tricks;
> Where Party decks the brawling partisan
> With wreaths and spoils — no matter what the man.
>
> Thither, O Muse of Fashion, wing thy flight,
> And shed the radiance of thy varied light.
> For lo! amid the night of Fashion's din
> A bright idea lights the mind of GWIN,
> And see, responsive to her welcome call,
> All parties vie to grace her Fancy Ball.

The rhyming author, who danced out the night clad in ar-

mor, as Richard Coeur de Lion, depicted the jocund evening
in couplets "topical and timely":

> No carking cares of State can enter here
> To damp the spirits or repress the cheer.
> Frowns and annoyance are denied the door,
> And pleasure rules upon the waxen floor.
> No Slavery, but to Beauty, here is seen;
> Nor Abolition, save of Discord's mien.
> Chivalric sway all hearts and minds maintain,
> From sunny Texas up to snowy Maine,
> And Concord circles, with her flowery hand,
> All parts and sections of a happy land.
>
> Fear not to yield to Pleasure's syren spells,
> But gladly borrow Folly's cap and bells.
> Appareled thus, in form and spirit, now
> To the bland Hostess make your grateful bow.

According to the prosaic press, Mrs. Gwin received her guests
"with a courteous affability that set them at ease at once." She
was costumed as the Queen of Louis Quatorze. ("Skirt of white
moiré antique, trimmed with flounces of *pointe aguille;* train of
cherry satin, trimmed with a ruche of white satin; coiffure of
the time of Louis XIV.") Wrote Major Haviland:

> Not California's produce could content
> The large abundance of her kind intent;
> Nor California's boundless mines command
> The generous hospitality her hand
> Would scatter lavishly, with liberal power,
> To heap the gladness of the festive hour.
> In regal guise, no less with royal port,
> She smiles sweet welcome to her gathering Court —
> The frolic subjects of a sportive Queen
> Whose kindness rules the gay, fantastic scene.

Mention next was due of the host; in Haviland's words:

> Close by her side, in form and stature great,
> As well became a pillar of the State,
> With ready tact and all-attractive art,
> The good Amphytrion plays his graceful part.

With perhaps more literal exactitude, the newspaper reports said that "Senator Gwin, in citizen's dress, was ubiquitous, and unceasing in his endeavors to promote the enjoyment and amusement of his guests, exhibiting a genuine California hospitality."

Both the Gwin daughters were on hand, in fetching costumes, although William Gwin, Junior, the son, was away at school. Lucy, the elder daughter, made a charming picture as a Greek girl, a character irresistible to that romantic generation brought up on Byron's "Maid of Athens" and the Greek war of independence. Lucy's costume was: "white satin skirt, and full white satin pantalettes; boots of silver and blue satin. Over the white satin skirt, which was trimmed with strips of cherry satin, was a skirt of tulle trimmed with silver. Tunic and bodice of blue satin, trimmed with silver. Necklace of pearls, hair pleated with braids, and a Greek cap of blue and white satin, trimmed with silver and two silver tassels — a bewitching costume, charmingly worn." Beside this description Haviland's complimentary couplets seemed perfunctory:

> . . . The daughter of the house, arrayed
> In the rich costume of a *Grecian Maid*,
> With charming frankness, and with winning grace,
> Reflects the kindness of the mother's face.

The couplet he bestowed upon Carrie Gwin, dressed in boy's clothing as a Page, was even briefer:

> While yonder *Page*, in splendid court array,
> Bespeaks the triumphs of a future day.

The newspapers were more enlightening as to Carrie's costume: "white satin trousers, full to the knee; long stockings of silk, boots black, coat of maroon velvet, trimmed with gold; cap of velvet and gold, with white plumes."

Down the long list of notabilities went rhymster and reporter, describing the costumes, beautiful, saucy, and ingenious: a Vivandière, a Quakeress, Robin Hood and Friar Tuck, a Matador, a Gypsy Girl, a Milkmaid, a Queen of the Night, a Ranchero, with lasso; a quartet of Pierrots from the French Legation; dukes, duchesses, peasant girls and brigands; Highlanders and The Star-Spangled Banner impersonated by the daughter of Francis Scott Key. The British minister, Lord Napier, appeared in the dress worn by Britain's first envoy to the United States. North and South mingled in amity. Mrs. Senator Butler of South Carolina (aunt of the Preston Brooks who assaulted Charles Sumner in the Senate) came as The White Lady of Avenel, while Mrs. Senator Hale of New Hampshire was admirable as a Spanish Duenna. "Prince John" Magruder, the dandy of the army, was magnificent as the King of Prussia; Mrs. Stephen A. Douglas, a beauty among beauties, was Aurora; and Representative Clingman of North Carolina wore a costume of his own designing, intended to represent A Gentleman of the Twentieth Century.*

Mrs. Daniel Sickles, wife of the Tammany Congressman and a pet of the President's, made a demure Red Riding Hood, while Philip Barton Key, "the handsomest man in Washington," dashed about as a Huntsman in cherry velvet jacket, white satin

---

* As a curiosity, this was the garb a gentleman of the nineteenth century imagined a gentleman of the twentieth would wear upon such an occasion: "A blue coat with metal buttons, faced and lined with white satin, except the velvet collar. Two vests, the outer one white, the under one red. White satin breeches with red bands at the knees, white silk stockings and black pumps." Remarked the Washington *Star:* "If all those beaux who live in the Twentieth Century look as well as did the honorable and gallant member from North Carolina, the appearance of ballrooms will be improved."

breeches, lemon-colored high-top boots, jaunty cap, and slung across his chest a silver bugle on which he blew a blast from time to time. Mrs. Rose O'Neil Greenhow, in apron and mob cap, represented A Housekeeper of the Old School, and her daughter, Kate, was one of several White Ladies. Mrs. Jefferson Davis, as Madame de Staël, spoke in French and broken English and was voted to have the most authentic costume, while Representative Lawrence Keitt of South Carolina lent a dashing air to his characterization of Charles XII of Sweden.

For many who danced across "Mrs. Gwin's beautifully waxed floors" that April night was indeed a Waterloo Ball. In less than a year, Philip Barton Key would be murdered by Daniel Sickles in Lafayette Square, as the lover of that demure Red Riding Hood. Three years from that night Rose Greenhow would be an inmate of the Old Capitol prison, to be brought to trial before a military board in that same ballroom, by then transformed into a dingy government office. After suffering the bitterness of war and catastrophe, Varina Davis would be reduced to begging her husband's life from a President whom she despised. Daredevil Keitt's epitaph would be soldier-like: "Killed at Cold Harbor."

6

These developments lay unguessed in the future while the Gwins rounded out their climactic social year. That summer and autumn Mary Gwin spent in Europe with Lucy and young William, Junior. The senator was in the thick of the political turmoil and busy furthering measures to benefit California, especially the transcontinental railroad. His correspondence grew slack, and it was Christmas day before he got around to writing an old friend, Benjamin Davis Wilson, at Los Angeles, the news long overdue of himself, his household, and his legislative expectations:

A merry Christmas to you and Mrs. Wilson. . . . I begged Mandeville to write you and explain how much I was pressed by the Pacific Railroad question, which occupied every moment of my time and caused me apparently to neglect my friends. I occupy my Christmas in the agreeable duty of doing what the adjournment of Congress for ten days gives me leisure to do — write to those friends whom I value so highly.

First, for news of the family:

Mrs. Gwin and Lucy are at home in fine health, after an extensive and delightful tour through Europe. They left Willie at school in Paris. Carrie did not accompany them. She has grown so much you would scarcely know her.

Then concerning business:

I will press your patent through the General Land Office and you may rely on getting it an an early day, and also [the] resurvey of the harbor plan. . . . As yet I have not seen Professor Bache, for he has been absent, but I will keep him up to that work. I am his friend whenever [he is] attacked in the Senate, which is very often, and he must stand up to my friends.

Regarding the railroad bill, Gwin had a promoter's prescience of success during the current session of Congress, though he appended a note of caution:

It has great difficulties to contend with and I shall feel anxious until the last vote is called. It has been under discussion two weeks and will come up again when we meet, which will be on the 4th of January. It is stronger than I have ever seen it in Congress. I sent you my speeches by the last mail. You will see they are elaborate and intended to cover the whole subject, but I fear I did not do it justice. But what mortal can? My last speech created quite a sensation and no attempt has been made to answer it. The facts cannot be controverted, and if truth, justice, and patriotism prevail, our success is certain.

The letter closed affectionately:

> God bless and prosper you and yours. All my family join me in our warmest love to you and Mrs. Wilson. As ever very truly, your friend, Wm. M. Gwin.

The Professor Bache whose battles Gwin fought in the Senate was the physicist, Alexander Dallas Bache, who held the position of superintendent of the Coast Survey and was a member of the Lighthouse Board. A few months later Gwin would be appealing strongly to Bache on behalf of the construction of a much needed lighthouse on Point Lobos, outside the narrow entrance to San Francisco Bay. Bache had turned down the proposal once, but Gwin felt that he had acted on the basis of incomplete and faulty data. He urged a reconsideration, and reminded Bache:

> You know how I have labored for the Coast Survey in California, and don't let any of my constituents say that it has stopped the building of lighthouses that they think, and so does Congress, are indispensably necessary. We must have the lighthouse and you must help us get it.

Preoccupations of this kind took up much of Gwin's time and energy; but the political pot was seething again, and as a Senate leader he was required to give that careful attention. A storm of cyclonic fury had roared out of the West, darkening the Washington sky. Slavery was the issue, and the watchword, "bleeding Kansas."

Chapter VII

LECOMPTON IS A name seldom encountered today outside a gazetteer. In 1858 it was a flaming beacon of war.

The details of the dispute are complex, but the events leading up to the Congressional turmoil may be summarized quickly. At stake was the admission of Kansas to the Union as a free or slave state.

People from both the North and South had poured into the Territory, with the Northerners predominating. A convention of free-state men, meeting in Topeka, had, in 1856, drafted a state constitution that banned slavery. President Franklin Pierce denounced this action as illegal, and the constitution was turned down by Congress. The following year another convention, composed of pro-slavery men, met in Lecompton and drafted a constitution that sanctioned slavery.

This so-called Lecompton constitution was submitted to Congress, and President Buchanan urged its adoption. Three weeks after his recommendation, the constitution was certified as having been ratified by the people of Kansas in a plebiscite, although the total number of votes cast was absurdly small. This was because the free-staters boycotted the polls in protest against the form of the ballot, which allowed only a vote for or against permitting slavery, but not for or against the constitution as a whole. The constitution also contained a clause forbidding interference with slaves already in Kansas.

The outcry against the tenuously certified result of the plebiscite was so great, a second election was ordered; and this time the pro-slavery forces boycotted the polls. Even so, the

Lecompton constitution was rejected by some ten thousand votes to one hundred.

In an angry message to Congress, Buchanan declared the people of Kansas to be in virtual insurrection, and demanded that Congress accept the "legal" — that is, the Lecompton — constitution in spite of the outcome of the second plebiscite.

Stephen A. Douglas, Democratic senator from Illinois, told the President that he would never consent to such a fraud, whereupon Buchanan threatened to read him out of the party. Since Douglas had Presidential hopes, this was a grave matter to him; nevertheless he joined battle with the administration, attacking the Lecompton swindle. Among members of his party he met with almost no support. The entire Southern delegation stood with Buchanan, and Gwin, as administration leader in the Senate, voted with the South. The Republicans were anti-Lecompton, but they were a small minority. Senator Broderick was one of the few Democrats who rallied to the side of Douglas.

Until this time, it would have been difficult to determine what were David C. Broderick's political beliefs on any question except that of slavery versus free labor. There he spoke out not from sympathy with the slaves, but in defense of white workingmen. He had been a "practical politician," concerned with winning elections and not with abstract doctrines. His feeling on the subject of slavery, as indicated in his speeches, had reflected the aims of the Free Soil party of the fifties — "free soil, free speech, free labor, free men." It did not take in the rights of Negroes at all. But diverse as were his views on slavery from those of the strong Southern element in the party, Broderick had never swerved from the Democratic ranks, nor, probably, had he ever contemplated such a defection. His early training in party loyalty at Tammany Hall would have militated against it.

✿

2

The Lecompton struggle brought to light a different Broderick. Here was an issue that touched his origin and his personal experience, and on the question of free labor he was inflexible. In 1851 he had tongue-lashed Douglas for the latter's support of the Fugitive Slave Act; not because it was inhumane, despotic, and unjust, but because it was a concession designed to shore up the South's system of slave labor. Now he spoke out in Douglas's behalf. Broderick's power in attack had always been remarkable, and in a series of outbursts he drove home his points with a logic and energy that bordered on ferocity.

He announced his break with the administration on the issue of Lecompton soon after Congress reassembled in December, 1858. In reply to the Presidential message, he recalled that he had worked for Buchanan's election, and then added defiantly:

"But I do not intend, because I am a member of the Democratic party, to permit the President of the United States, who was elected by that party, to create civil war in the United States."

What puzzled him in this whole Kansas conflict, he went on, was the amazing forbearance of the free-state people there. "If they had taken the delegates to the Lecompton convention and flogged them, or cut their ears off and driven them out of the country, I would have applauded the act," he cried.

This taunt to the administration infuriated its leaders, but Broderick had only begun. On December 23 he made a speech of such boldness it focused national attention upon him, and in the West he loomed up suddenly as a new champion of the aspirations of the North against those of the South — of freedom against slavery. The metamorphosis was a unpremeditated as it was dramatic, and to a certain extent it belied his real sentiments; but there was no mistaking his courage.

"How foolish of the South to hope for success!" he chided his party mates, and especially Gwin:

> Slavery is old, decrepit, and consumptive; freedom is young, strong, and vigorous. There are six millions of people interested in the extension of slavery. There are twenty millions of free men to contend for these territories out of which to carve themselves homes where labor is honorable. Has it ever occurred to Southern gentlemen that millions of laboring free men are born every year, who demand subsistence and will have it? That as the marts of labor become crowded, they will crowd into the territories and take possession of them?
>
> I represent a State, sir, where labor is honorable, where the judge has left his bench, the lawyer and doctor their offices, and the clergyman his pulpit for the purpose of delving into the earth; where no station is so high and no position so great that its occupant is not proud to boast that he has labored with his own hands.

Here he turned toward Senator H. H. Hammond of South Carolina, one of the richest and suavest spokesmen for the Southern slavocracy. A few days before, Hammond had referred slightingly to the poorly paid wage earners in the North as the "mudsills of society," faceless drudges, whose condition was more degraded than that of the slaves on his plantation. Hammond's epithet was being quoted in the capital's drawing rooms as a stroke of wit, and Broderick spoke with a warmth of feeling he seldom displayed:

> I suppose the senator from South Carolina did not intend to be personal in his remarks to any of his peers on the floor. If I had thought so I would have noticed them at the time. I am, sir, with one exception, the youngest in years of the senators upon this floor. It is not long since I served an apprenticeship of five years at one of the most laborious trades pursued by man, a trade that from its nature devotes its follower to thought, but debars him from conversation.
>
> I would not have alluded to this if it were not for the remarks of the senator from South Carolina, and that thousands who know

that I am the son of an artisan and have been a mechanic would feel disappointed in me if I did not reply to him. I am not proud of this. I am sorry it is true. I would that I could have enjoyed the pleasures of life in my boyhood days, but they were denied to me. I say this with pain. I have not the admiration for the men of that class from whence I sprang that might be expected; they submit too tamely to oppression, and are too prone to neglect their rights and duties as citizens. But, sir, the class of society to whose toil I was born, under our form of government, will control the destinies of this nation. If I were inclined to forget my connection with them, or to deny that I sprang from them, this chamber would not be the place in which I could do either. While I hold a seat here, I have but to look at the beautiful capitals adorning the pilasters that support the roof to be reminded of my father's talent and handiwork.

The chamber sat silent during this tribute, though Seward murmured praise of "the courageous young senator." But Broderick was not finished. He wished to deal with the gay bachelor in the White House and with party leaders, like Gwin, who presumed to pronounce political doom upon Democrats who rejected their authority. The power to establish tests by which a man must stand or fall, he said, rests not with party leaders, but with the people; and never would he join in coercing the people of Kansas to accept a constitution which they abhorred. The President, he said, must accept the guilt for the bloodbath that was drenching "bleeding Kansas," for the President knew that the Lecompton constitution and every vote endorsing it were founded in fraud. Contemptuously he concluded:

> I hope, sir, that the historian when writing the history of these times will ascribe the attempt of the executive to force this constitution upon an unwilling people to the fading intellect, the petulant passion, and the trembling dotage of an old man on the verge of the grave!

❊

3

The debate launched upon this note was pursued with mounting bitterness throughout that session. Douglas was reviled
and ostracized by his party, but Broderick stood by him. Gwin
listened indignantly to the speeches. As a Jacksonian he held
party loyalty to be the first duty of a politician, and as a leader
he had always enforced party discipline rigorously. Now Douglas and Broderick and a scattering of others were rending the
Democratic party to the joy of the Republicans. Even Gwin's
customary self-control failed him, and he grew uncharacteris-
tically irritable in debate. When Senator Henry Wilson of
Massachusetts scoffed at Gwin's pretensions to speak for California, Gwin taunted him with "practicing demagoguism."
Wilson flung back that he would "sooner be charged with demagoguism than with stealing," and Gwin leaped to his feet,
assailed the Massachusetts senator as "a liar, a cowardly, slan-
derous traducer of character," and threatened to horsewhip
him. Strenuous intercession by Seward and Jefferson Davis, the
minority and majority leaders, was required to restore a measure
of calm.

Gwin's temper was tried again when Broderick threw down
the gauge to the California legislature. Feeling about Lecompton was running high at Sacramento, and the legislature, over-
whelmingly Democratic, adopted resolutions instructing the
state's senators to remain true to their party and vote for the
disputed constitution. This action was in line with accepted
practice, for United States senators were deemed to represent
the legislatures that elected them, rather than the people of
their states at large, and as such were subject to instruction and
reprimand by their "constituents" — the legislators.

Gwin read the resolutions before the Senate and said that he
would respect his constituents' wishes; but Broderick defiantly
retorted that he would not heed the resolutions "here, now, or

in the future." He was satisfied, he said, that "four-fifths of
the people of California repudiate the Lecompton fraud. I shall
respect the wishes of the people."

This was heresy in the eyes of Gwin and all straight-party
men.

The uproar so frightened Buchanan that he was ready to
abandon the fight. Gwin, hurrying to the White House, pleaded
with the President, pointing to the political consequences that
would follow such a surrender. But it was impossible to inject
steel into the backbone of that timorous gentleman farmer.

Under the pressure Douglas wilted. He was facing a rugged
fight for reelection in Illinois and would require the full support
of his party; therefore, he agreed to accept a compromise on
the Lecompton issue.

When word of this weakening reached Broderick, he at first
refused to believe it. Let Douglas come and say for himself
that he was giving up — or giving in — he demanded. And so
great was Broderick's magnetism, Douglas came, "sweating
blood," according to a witness of the meeting. Meekly Douglas explained why he felt that policy required a compromise of
the question. At that, Broderick gave a bellow of rage:

"You had better, sir, go into the street and blow your damned
brains out! I shall denounce you! You came to me of your
own accord and asked me to take this stand, and I have followed you. I have committed myself against this infernal Lecompton constitution. Now, if you desert me, God damn you,
I will make you crawl under your chair in the Senate!"

Before that blast Douglas cowered, and he promised to
vote against the compromise. Keeping one eye upon his terrible supporter from California, this he did, although the compromise was passed just the same.

*

4

The session adjourned on June 14, and, having no social or other duties to detain him at Washington, Broderick set out at once for California. His political stock there was at a low ebb, for he had incurred the hostility of the legislature; Governor Weller and Gwin's "Chivalry" ruled the state; federal office-holders were beholden to his enemies; and the national Democratic leadership had, in effect, dropped him from consideration. The legislature had officially censured him for defying its instructions. Never, since the start of his rise, had he fallen so low in point of power. But he had an issue — Lecompton — and his courageous stand on that question had set up an undercurrent of popular sympathy in the state.

His mind, however, was filled with foreboding. Friends noticed that he was possessed of a new thoughtfulness; he brooded often, and seemed in the grip of a fatalistic gloom.

Broderick had denied, publicly and categorically, that any corrupt bargain had attended his election and that of Senator Gwin; yet he knew that proof of such a bargain existed — the fatal letter which Gwin had written under Broderick's dictation during that hush-hush midnight conference in room 6 of the Magnolia Hotel.

This letter Broderick had not dared either to destroy or to make known. As long as he held it, he had a weapon against Gwin that could be used in the last extremity. The document he had entrusted to a reliable friend — the man who had arranged the meeting in room 6 — State Senator William I. Ferguson.

With startling suddenness, Ferguson became involved in a duel just before Broderick headed west. During a political argument in a barroom, Ferguson was provoked to a point where retreat was impossible, and his opponent sent a challenge. The quarrel had flared up so quickly that Ferguson's sus-

picions were aroused, and before going to the dueling ground
he passed the Gwin letter to another friend of Broderick's. Then
he and his antagonist met with rifles on Angel Island, and Ferguson was killed.

As if in confirmation of Ferguson's guess, while the encounter
was taking place, his desk was broken open and his papers were
stolen.

News of all this had reached Broderick in the East, and while
in New York, waiting to board the ship for Panama, he had confided to a friend that his enemies were plotting his death, also,
by means of a trumped-up duel. As he spoke, sitting in a Bow-
ery saloon, he was set upon by two bruisers, whom, however, he
drove off with his cane. There, he remarked, was proof of his
premonition: he was certain the two men had been hired to involve him in a brawl during which he would be killed, probably by confederates lurking nearby. Ferguson's death, he
was convinced, had resulted from an attempt to get possession
of the "scarlet letter," and he expected his enemies now to recoil from nothing in their determination to obtain that document and destroy him.

Broderick was in this fatalistic mood when he returned to
Washington in the autumn. He had spent his time in California
attending to his tangled business affairs, mingling little in politics. This time he came east by the overland stage, desiring to
judge for himself the practicability of the central route and its
possible use for a railroad. Along the way, to his surprise, he was
received enthusiastically. At Salt Lake City a large crowd welcomed him, and at other stopping places he was the subject of
civic receptions. His fame outside California was on the rise,
and he enjoyed the agreeable sensation of learning that his following was not negligible. The journey imposed a succession
of physical hardships, and he arrived in Washington exhausted.

During his absence the party lash had been laid on both him
and the insurgent Douglas. Gwin, as chairman of the Senate

Democratic caucus — acting in concert with Senator John Slidell of Louisiana, and with the full approval of President Buchanan — had stripped Douglas of his chairmanship of the Committee on Territories, the position that had brought Douglas into national prominence. And Broderick had been disciplined by removing his name from the list of Democratic senators who were invited to attend the caucus meetings. For all practical purposes, Broderick now was a renegade from his party and isolated in the Senate.

Chapter VIII

THE 1859 SESSION of Congress was more turbulent than its predecessor. Members went armed, knives were flourished on the floor of the House, and in the Senate the debates crackled with acrimony. The administration's prestige was gone. Buchanan found himself tossed upon the horns of a dilemma and pursued a policy of vacillation that satisfied no one. The fire-eaters of the South cursed him for being too grudging in granting their demands, while Northern firebrands inveighed against him for kowtowing to slaveholders. The White House weather vane did not veer more erratically than did the executive policy. Gwin tried in vain to hold the President to a firm course midway between the sections, and increasingly deplored the baleful influence of Slidell upon the pliant, well-meaning, but bewildered Buchanan. Gwin knew Slidell thoroughly and placed no trust in either his sincerity or his political wisdom.

To Gwin, party loyalty took precedence over sectional prejudice, but the issues had divided the Democrats nationally. In California, where the party was deeply split, the disruptive factor, as Gwin saw it, was Broderick. Compromise had become unthinkable: Broderick's break with the administration stigmatized him as a traitor in Gwin's eyes. Party unity depended upon the elimination of Broderick — or Gwin — and a united Democracy was going to be needed in the coming Presidential contest.

Broderick saw the situation in the same light, but reversed, and with even greater intensity of feeling. Having declared war upon the administration, he realized that he was marked for liquidation. Gwin was the administration's viceroy in California, and the "Chivalry" were allies of the Southern, administration wing of the party; hence they must be unseated, finally, completely, and mercilessly. With his usual audacity Broderick resolved to get rid of Gwin; not merely to check him in his personal ambition, but to obliterate him as far as meaningful connection with the Democratic control in California was concerned. It was a move of desperation, and Broderick was indeed desperate: believing that his enemies were plotting to remove him by death if need be, he felt he must liquidate his arch foe before the latter could liquidate him. The Democratic party was Broderick's home, he had fought its battles, and he did not propose to be driven out. Reckless in his courage, he was ready to risk all rather than try to temporize; as for the outcome, he was fatalistically prepared to accept it.

Thus it came about that when Broderick and Gwin returned to California at the close of the Thirty-fifth Congress, in March, 1859, they had the same purpose in mind. With Broderick traveled Congressman McKibben, who had been among the few supporting Douglas in the Lecompton fight; accompanying Gwin was Representative Scott, a staunch administration man.

2

They found the state much agitated over the Lecompton question. Gwin set about allaying the turmoil, but Broderick furthered and capitalized upon it by setting up his own anti-Lecompton organization in every county. This forced Gwin to assume a more vigorous pro-Lecompton attitude, and on that basis he called the regular party faction into convention to nominate candidates for state offices, to be elected in the au-

tumn. Broderick called a separate convention of his delegates
to put a rival ticket in the field.

This pitting of Democrat against Democrat gave hope to the
Republicans, and their national leadership contributed toward widening the rift among their opponents. Senator Seward
secretly fed funds to Broderick, and the latter's insurgents in
return nominated a Republican for governor. This shattered
any semblance of party unity, and the point was reinforced
when Representative McKibben, after receiving the Broderick
convention's nomination for another term in Congress, was also
endorsed by the Republicans.

The so-called Lecompton Democrats under Gwin's direction
nominated Milton S. Latham for governor; Latham was willing
to make common cause with Gwin against Broderick, in retaliation for his betrayal (as he thought) in the 1857 Senate election. Thus the battle lines were drawn, with Broderick — although clinging to his identity as a Democrat — working in
alliance with the antislavery Republicans.

Against the advice of friends, Broderick took the stump in behalf of his ticket. He had never campaigned before; he had
been a behind-the-scenes manipulator; he was not sure that he
could address a popular audience effectively, but he plunged
ahead. Gwin likewise took the stump, although he professed
to be no spellbinder. But eloquence would have been wasted
in the contest of vituperation that developed. Both men knew
they were fighting for survival.

Broderick made clear at the outset that the struggle was between himself and Gwin. The candidates for election were all
but ignored, the ostensible issues thrown overboard, while the
leaders slugged it out. Speaking before a crowd at Sacramento,
Broderick sounded his keynote when he said:

"I come tonight to arraign before you two great criminals —
Milton S. Latham and William M. Gwin."

This was the preamble. In tones of loathing he pictured Gwin as "dripping with corruption" and faithless to California's interests.

This descent to personal abuse angered Gwin, and he departed from his custom and dealt out scurrility in reply. In words calculated to whip and sting he poured scorn upon Broderick as a party deserter, a turncoat, a vulgarian, a cheat, not a gentleman, a failure in the Senate and a liar to boot, and he challenged him to make good his indiscriminate charges of corruption.

Then Broderick played his trump card, and produced the "scarlet letter" written by Gwin, the existence of which he had so strenuously denied. From the platform he read what Gwin had written in abject submission, that midnight in room 6 of the Magnolia Hotel. It ran as follows:

Sacramento City, January 11, 1857

Hon. D. C. Broderick,

Dear Sir, — I am likely to be the victim of the unparalleled treachery of those who have been placed in power by my aid and exertion. The most potential portion of the federal patronage is in the hands of those who, by every principle that should govern men of honor, should be my supporters instead of my enemies; and it is being used for my destruction. My participation in the distribution of this patronage has been a source of numberless slanders upon me that have fostered a prejudice in the public mind against me and have created enemies that have been destructive of my happiness for years. It has entailed untold evils upon me, and while in the Senate I will not recommend a single individual to appointment in the State.

Providing I am elected, you shall have the exclusive control of the patronage, so far as I am concerned, and in the distribution I only ask that it may be used with magnanimity, and not for the advantage of those who have been our mutual enemies, and unwearied in their exertions to destroy us. This determination is unalterable; and in making this declaration I do not expect you to support me for that reason, or in any way to be governed by it. But as I have been betrayed by those who should have been my friends, I am in a measure powerless and dependent upon your magnanimity.

Very respectfully,
Your obedient servant,
Wm. M. Gwin

Here, cried Broderick, flaunting the letter, was proof that Gwin, the proud aristocrat, was "dripping with corruption." He had sold himself to get back into the Senate, and then had violated his word, trampled on his vaunted "honor," and treacherously and deceitfully had manipulated the patronage in favor of his friends.

Latham did not get off any easier. Latham, said Broderick, had come crawling to him in disguise to beg help in getting elected; and when another visitor chanced to enter the room, he had crouched in the privy to escape being seen and recognized.

That these disclosures sullied himself as much as his targets Broderick did not seem to appreciate, or indeed to care. His purpose was to humiliate, humble, and ruin Gwin. He challenged Gwin to meet him face to face and refute the charges. Gwin did not meet him, but in town after town he replied in kind. At Yreka he told a cheering crowd:

> My colleague in the Senate, David C. Broderick, has chosen to take the stump for the avowed purpose of assaulting private character. He has selected me as one of those whom he wishes to "bully down" to his own degraded level. He has in addition picked out the governor of your State [Weller] and the Democratic candidate for that office [Latham] to assail with senseless vituperation. It therefore becomes necessary for me — for the first time in my life — to use language that should never be indulged in upon the stand, and never would be by me if I had a gentleman to deal with.
>
> I acknowledge with shame that for a time I was deceived by him, and am willing to atone for it in sackcloth and ashes. To suppose he was my friend was of itself a degradation that noth-

ing but the passion engendered by a bitter contest could justify.
. . . Latham was a victim of Broderick's villainy in that senatorial
contest. I have abundant proof of these facts, and had prepared
them for publicity in Washington two years ago last spring. But
Broderick heard of it, and like a cowering hound, begged for
mercy.

Gwin described the misery that responsibility for the federal
patronage had brought to him, how he had been hounded
and badgered by office-seekers until he had resolved — months
before the so-called "corrupt bargain" — to forgo all future participation in that accursed privilege. As for the "bargain" Broderick was mooning about:

> He does not attempt to disguise the fact that he was prostituting
> the high office that had just been conferred upon him [the senator-
> ship]; whilst it is false that I intended, by any act of mine, to say
> or do more than to abstain from the contest for the federal offices
> in this State, as I had said a thousand times before I had any in-
> tercourse with him. He acknowledges that he was in the market.
> His own election will, in my opinion, prove to have been brought
> about by promises he never intended to perform, and other base
> acts that no one else would have resorted to.
> He challenged me to this discussion. We shall see if he will
> challenge me again to meet him, after what I have said tonight —
> for me to expose to his face his robberies on the State and San
> Francisco treasuries, whence he got the plunder funds that he
> collected to spend, as he says, in favor of the Democratic party —
> but in fact to procure his election to the Senate by bribery and
> corruption.
> Under the guise of friendship he concocted a conspiracy against
> me that is without parallel in this or any other State. He deceived
> me and then tried to ruin me. . . . He is infamous. . . . He
> hates the Democratic party. . . . We have served two years to-
> gether in the Senate. He has returned home, disgraced. . . . He
> will slander and lie about me; it is his vocation. . . . This is
> strong language and I intended it to be so.

Attacking Broderick on another score, Gwin asked his
audiences:

Are you aware that your senator, before taking his seat in a
regular session, announced that he would not speak to members
of the cabinet, not even officially, if he could help it? He thinks
he is in a position to neglect the important business of his constituents, and is lazy enough to throw the labor on his colleagues.
He boasts that he did not speak to the cabinet officers because
he differed with them!

This claim, Gwin said, was utterly false and misleading. In
refutation he gave the dates of visits he and Broderick had paid
to cabinet members, going together on official matters.

Broderick replied by harping on Gwin's self-abasement as
shown in the Magnolia Hotel surrender. He gloated when he
recounted the scene:

I had then my commission as United States senator in my
pocket, when old Gwin came begging at my feet for favor and
help. I remembered all that he had said and done against me;
and before I would have refrained from my opportunity to humiliate him, I would have torn my credentials into pieces and thrown
them into the fire!

3

Up and down the state the two men traveled, lunging at each
other, seemingly bent upon mutual destruction. The press
generally was hostile to Gwin. The Sacramento *Union* assailed
him as "an artful plotter, whose first step to power was one of
meanness, cunning, and hypocrisy." The San Francisco *Bulletin* spoke of "the obsequious, unmanly, contemptible Gwin."
And the *Alta California* (which Broderick had purchased, to
utilize as his mouthpiece) heaped invective upon him: "this
political parasite and montebank . . . this political huckster,
who barters the power which his position gives him for filthy
lucre, and bedraggles the toga of a senator of the United States
in the slime and filth of political corruption!"

It was everywhere assumed that a duel would result from
the exchange of such insults. Broderick remained convinced

that a conspiracy existed to egg him on to a fatal contest, since only by that method could the "Chivalry" silence him. One newspaper spoke for many when it commented:

> We speak the convictions which have been forced upon all men who have read the speeches of Broderick and Gwin, that a bloody termination of this controversy is expected by the friends of both senators.

Gwin made no effort to avoid a challenge, nor did Broderick, but neither issued one. Sneered Broderick:

"If I have insulted Doctor Gwin sufficiently to induce him to go about the State and make a blackguard of himself, he should seek the remedy of every gentleman who feels offended."

The debate raged on, yet cool observers of the political winds were never in doubt as to the result at the polls. Broderick was drawing crowds, but Gwin controlled the party machinery and party workers, and on election day the Gwin candidates — the Lecompton slate — won everywhere. Broderick's hopes were tumbled in the dust.

Seward's confidential agent in California — Cornelius Cole, Republican district attorney of Sacramento County — put his finger on the cause of Broderick's downfall in his report to the Republican managers in the East:

> The attempt was made to reprove Democracy with Democracy. It failed as expected. The Broderick-Douglas men carried on the war under the Democrat flag, but fought with Republican weapons and used Republican ammunition.

In almost everything but name, Broderick's wing of the California Democracy had swung into line with the emergent party, the Republicans. Because they had hesitated to cross over boldly into the new camp, they had fallen between the two forces and had been crushed.

The day after his repudiation at the polls, Broderick received the long-expected challenge to a bloody climax.

Chapter IX

THE CHALLENGE did not come from Gwin; he needed no better revenge than that which had been administered by the voters. Two years after Broderick had "put his brand" on him, he had humbled his humiliator, and Latham, the rejected, had been elected governor.

Dueling was not uncommon in California, although unlawful. The practice, brought along by men from the South, was viewed with toleration, and not to accept a challenge was to risk incurring odium among a large portion of the community.

Broderick's challenger was David S. Terry, the justice of the state supreme court who had run afoul of the Vigilance Committee in 1856. A man of violent temper, a former Texas Ranger, brawling and aggressive, Terry habitually carried a Bowie knife under his shirt front ready for instant use. He was that sort of quarrelsome man.

Terry had been elected to the supreme bench by the Know-Nothing party, and upon its disintegration he had reverted to his former connection with the "Chivalry." As a Southerner he hotly supported the pro-Lecompton stand taken by Gwin, but he was never particularly close to the senator. The previous June he had made a bid for nomination for a second term on the bench at the convention of the regular Democrats, but had been disappointed.

Just before the convention adjourned, he had addressed the delegates, thanking those who supported him, and at the close going out of his way to insult the anti-Lecompton wing as "a miserable remnant of a faction sailing under false colors, trying to obtain votes under false pretenses. They are the followers of one man, the personal chattels of a single individual, whom they are ashamed of. They belong, heart and soul, body and breeches, to David C. Broderick. Yet they are ashamed to acknowledge their master and are calling themselves 'Douglas Democrats,' when it is known that the gallant senator from Illinois has no affiliation with them."

Then, his voice dripping with the hatred of a Southern firebrand for Northern abolitionism, he sneered:

"Perhaps, Mr. President, I am mistaken in denying their right to claim Douglas as their leader; for it is the banner of the black Douglass, whose name is Frederick, not Stephen!"

Frederick Douglass was the former slave who had become an ardent propagandist for abolition. To suggest intimacy with him was an insult that no Democrat could overlook.

Terry's attack caught Broderick's eye as he read a newspaper in the dining room of the International Hotel in San Francisco. Flinging down the paper, he exclaimed to the friends who were with him:

"The damned miserable wretch, Terry, after being kicked out of their convention, went down there and made a speech abusing me. I have defended him at times when all others had deserted him. I paid and supported three newspapers to defend him during the Vigilance Committee days, and this is all the gratitude I get from the damned miserable wretch for all the favors I have conferred on him!"

Sitting nearby was a friend of Terry's, a man named D. W. Perley. He overheard Broderick's outburst, and coming to the senator's table asked whether he had heard correctly. Broderick repeated his opinion of Terry, and added:

"I have spoken of him as an honest man — as the only honest man on the bench of a miserable, corrupt supreme court. But now I find I am mistaken. I take it all back. He is just as bad as the others."

On behalf of Terry, Perley immediately challenged Broderick; but the latter brushed the challenge aside, pointing out
that no quarrel existed between himself and Perley, and also
that the latter, who was a British subject, could have no legitimate interest in an American election campaign.

His action was generally approved, although expectations
of a duel sooner or later were intensified. The San Francisco
Times, a Broderick supporter, warned that "there are certain
political opponents of David C. Broderick who long for a chance
to shoot him, either in a fair or unfair fight. . . . His seat in the
Senate would be quite acceptable to a number of gentlemen in
this State."

Broderick's aspersions upon Terry were published widely,
and Terry bided his time until election day, September 7. On
September 8 he resigned from the supreme court (his term had
only a few more weeks to run) and sent Broderick a demand for
a retraction of his statement made in June. This Broderick refused, although well-wishers urged him to use this loophole
to avoid an encounter. But Broderick was irritable and apa-
thetic, worn out by the exertions of the campaign, and the
premonition of doom was upon him when Terry insisted upon
a meeting.

Pistols were chosen. Under the rules each principal had the
right to bring a set to the grounds, where choice would be made
by the toss of a coin. Terry borrowed a set that had done duty
in several encounters. They were owned by a Dr. Daniel Aylette, a resident of Oakland, across the bay from San Francisco;
Terry also was living in Oakland. Aylette's pistols were of Belgian workmanship, single-ball, with hair triggers. Terry tested
them by firing a shot from each and was satisfied; they were left
in Aylette's custody until the day of the duel.

Of Terry's two seconds, one was Calhoun Benham, United
States attorney at San Francisco and prominent in the
Buchanan-Gwin faction. Benham was well versed in affairs

of honor, having been both principal and second in several. Broderick's chief second was Joseph McKibben, the Congressman who had been defeated for a second term in the election just held. Neither McKibben nor his colleague had ever served as second in a duel before; they required coaching. Through ignorance or clumsiness, they committed several blunders. For instance: Broderick was exhausted, and he was suffering from a feverish cold that threatened to develop into pneumonia. In order to rest, he had withdrawn to the home of a friend, Leonidas Haskell, near Black Point, south of San Francisco. But on a foggy night, his seconds took him from his bed and drove with him several miles into the city in order to receive Terry's cartel formally. It was a long, cold drive, and Broderick's illness was aggravated.

Outwardly he remained confident, assuring friends that he was a skilled marksman and had emerged unscathed from a duel before.

"Don't you fear," he said to those who tried to dissuade him. "I can shoot twice to Terry's once, and beat him shooting every time."

But his pugnacity had disappeared; he seemed weighed down by lassitude. His advisers differed in their counsel, one feeling that "it has got to come, and this is the best time for it. He never had a better chance, and he is not going to get hurt. He can hit the size of a ten-cent piece at his distance every time. These Chivs have got to learn that there is one man they can't back down."

The press discussed the matter with *sang-froid*. Calculators of odds believed they favored Broderick. On the morning of the day set for the encounter, the San Francisco *Morning Call* commented, under the headline "A Dead Shot":

> It is generally understood that Judge Terry is a first-rate shot; but it is doubtful whether he is as unerring with the pistol as Senator Broderick. This gentleman, recently, in practising in a

gallery, fired two hundred shots at the usual distance, and plumped the target every time. As he is also a man of firmer nerve than his opponent, we may look this morning for unpleasant news from the field.

Although this paragraph was shown to Judge Terry, whose impetuosity was well known, it failed to ruffle him.

2

The date announced for the duel was September 12; the place, a farm near Lake Merced, south of the city. When the principals appeared, a peace officer was on hand to arrest them, this being the subterfuge commonly resorted to. The seconds drove off to confer with the judge in whose jurisdiction the location lay, and the contest was officially called off. Informally it was simply moved forward one day. In this way the authorities could later claim that the law had been enforced and that they had not known about the matter until it was all over.

At dawn on September 13, the opposing parties arrived in carriages. Each principal brought two seconds, a gun-loader, and a surgeon, and each brought a brace of pistols.

The opponents took off the overcoats they wore against the morning chill, and handed their watches and other valuables and all metallic objects in their pockets to spectators among the crowd of about eighty.

Broderick's seconds, having won the toss for choice of position, placed him with his back to the sun that was just peeping above the hills. Terry's seconds won the toss for choice of weapons, and took the Aylette pistols. These were examined by the seconds and the two gunsmiths, and the latter loaded them. The principals then took position and were handed their weapons.

The conditions provided that the duelists should stand ten paces apart, holding their pistols with the muzzles down, and as the words "Fire-one-two" were spoken they were to raise their arms and fire — neither before the first word nor after the last. Broderick seemed to find the grip of his pistol awkward in his broad palm, and later it would be said he murmured, "My seconds are children; as like as not they have bartered away my life." But this was never clearly established.

Broderick wore his coat buttoned up to his chin, and his broad-brimmed black hat pulled down over his eyes. Terry wore his hat pushed back on his head, with the brim turned up. He stood sideways, presenting as narrow a silhouette as possible, while Broderick planted himself firmly in a half-turn that exposed most of his upper body. Both men were tall, Terry slightly the taller. Both were calm and grave while the seconds searched them for chain-armor or other protective devices.

The seconds then explained how the word would be given, and asked if both men were ready. Terry answered, "Ready." Broderick, who seemed still to be having difficulty adjusting his hand to the pistol grip, hesitated, then said quietly, "Ready."

The seconds stepped back and the word was given. Between "fire" and "one" Broderick jerked up his arm and fired. The bullet dug into the earth about nine feet in front of him. Terry, taking deliberate aim, fired, and a puff of dust spurted from Broderick's coat over the upper right chest. His right arm, half-raised, slowly stretched out to full length. Then he sank on his left knee and crumpled.

Terry stood still, watching. He remarked to Benham that his bullet had struck "too far out," and he was ready for a second shot. But it quickly became clear that the duel was ended. Broderick's wound did not bleed much, but he was unable to rise. Placed in a carriage, he was taken back to the house of his friend Haskell.

There, three days later, at nine-twenty on the morning of Friday, September 16, 1859, David C. Broderick died.

✽

3

His funeral was such as had not been seen in San Francisco since that of James King of William, the victim of one of Broderick's bullies. The entire city turned out to hear the funeral oration delivered in Portsmouth Square by Edward D. Baker. With emotion the speaker quoted his friend's purported dying words:

"They have killed me because I was opposed to slavery and a corrupt administration."

More poignant and more credible, because they expressed the invincible spirit of the man, were the words Baker said Broderick had gasped in telling how he had fallen:

"I tried to stand, Baker, but the blood blinded me."

The blood blinded California, too, and overnight Broderick — the politician so recently repudiated at the polls — became a martyr in the cause of freedom, the symbol and emblem of the rights of the common man against privilege. In death he triumphed as he had never triumphed in life.

The reaction against his enemies was terrible. Charges of treachery were raised. At the inquest (another formality devoid of significance) the gunsmith who loaded Broderick's pistol testified that he had found the hair triggers of the two weapons unequal, that of Broderick's being so delicate a mere jar would trip it. He said he had called the attention of Broderick's seconds to this defect; but the latter — when testifying under oath, and in print, in one of Broderick's newspapers, the San Francisco *News* — denied this, and alluded to the gunsmith's reputation for finding fault with any pistol not of his own make. The controversy would never be cleared up.

But ugly talk swirled through the state, and cast in the villains' role were the "Chivalry" and Gwin. No evidence ever was produced to indicate that Gwin had any connection with

Terry's challenge, but he was covered with opprobrium nevertheless.

Four days after Broderick died, Gwin and Congressman Scott left San Francisco on their way back to Washington. The *Alta California* reported the departure of their steamer as the most subdued ever experienced. Despite the multitude of people at the dock, there was none of the usual "shouting or loud, boisterous mirth; there was no pelting of oranges and apples between those on the wharf and those on the steamer; the very newsboys and peanut vendors were quieted. The only thing which caught the eye as unusual was an immense placard, six feet long and three feet wide, wreathed in mourning, with a photograph of the late lamented David C. Broderick in the center, and the following words in unmistakable characters inscribed above the picture: 'The will of the People — may the murderers of David C. Broderick never return to California.' "

Such, in *Alta's* words, was the "bitter parting salute to the *Honorable*, who was returning to Washington to represent the people of California and gaze upon a vacant chair."

Gwin and Broderick. Their drama had ended and yet not ended. Broderick lay in a grave at Lone Mountain with James King. And Gwin would move on to a larger stage, where momentous changes were pending, in which he would play a part brilliant, equivocal, and subtle.

Two hitherto unpublished photographs of Senator Gwin now in the possession of Mr. R. Pierson Eaton, grandson of Colonel Samuel G. Hamblen, Gwin's official jailer at Fort Jackson after the war. According to family tradition, the bearded photograph was taken during Senator Gwin's confinement at the Fort and was presented to Colonel Hamblen in token of the friendship between them formed then and continued in later years. After Gwin's release and return to California, the tradition goes, Gwin sent Hamblen the clean-shaven photograph, taken in Sacramento at about the time of Broderick's death, as proof that "I do not always look like an old bear." Belonging to a clean-shaven generation, Gwin never succumbed permanently to the postwar fashion of beards. *Courtesy of R. Pierson Eaton*

Left:
David Colbreth Broderick, son of an Irish immigrant stonecutter, who became San Francisco's political boss during its most turbulent era and struggled successfully against overwhelming odds to achieve his ambition, a seat in the United States Senate. Gwin's indomitable antagonist, Broderick was killed in a politically inspired duel in 1859. *Courtesy of Library of Congress*

Right:
Edward Dickinson Baker, United States senator from Oregon, friend of Abraham Lincoln and colonel in the Union army. An orator gifted with a rare power of impromptu eloquence, he was a close associate of Broderick, and ardently defended the Union cause. He fell in battle in the opening stages of the war. *Courtesy of Library of Congress*

Marshal Achille Bazaine, commander of French forces in Mexico under Maximilian, and his seventeen-year-old Mexican heiress bride, Doña Josefa Peña. Their marriage in Mexico City in 1865 was celebrated with imperial panoply and festivities that lasted for weeks. This preoccupation further distracted the amorous, vainglorious marshal from providing Gwin with the vital military support promised, and thus sounded the knell of the Sonora colonization project. *Courtesy of Anne S. K. Brown Military Collection, Providence, R. I.*

Left:
Napoleon III, Emperor of the French, who was fascinated by Senator Gwin's account of the immense mineral wealth of the Mexican border province of Sonora, and heartily assured Gwin of French military backing to open up the province to immigrants from the United States—mostly Confederate refugees. When placed under pressure by the Washington government, Napoleon procrastinated, and finally disavowed any connection with the senator whatever. *Courtesy of The Bettman Archive*
Right:
Archduke Maximilian of Austria, handpicked by Napoleon III to become Emperor of Mexico. Affectionate and scholarly, Maximilian was sympathetic to Senator Gwin's plans for developing Sonora but on reaching Mexico became involved in a web of intrigue and took to roving the countryside and practicing taxidermy rather than attending to state business. Eventually abandoned by Napoleon, Maximilian took the field against Mexico's legally elected President Benito Juárez, and was captured and shot. *Courtesy of The Bettman Archive*

PART THREE

The Politics of Ambiguity

Chapter I

BRODERICK'S DEATH had shaken California, and the nation was absorbing a different shock when Senator Gwin reached Washington. This was John Brown's seizure of the United States arsenal at Harpers Ferry in a harebrained attempt to incite an insurrection of slaves.

The South saw red; for in the background of their society was always the spector of a servile uprising, and the atrocities that had drenched Haiti in blood were a living memory. The only possible explanation for Brown's rash act seemed to be lunacy; to most fair-minded men North and South it appeared incredible that a sane man would trifle with so appalling a danger. Buchanan's Secretary of War, John B. Floyd, a Virginian, had received a cryptic warning of the proposed raid, but paid no attention to it; later explaining that, "I was satisfied in my own mind that a scheme of such wickedness and outrage could not be entertained by any citizen of the United States." The question was immediately raised: who was behind John Brown's action? Who instigated and planned it? Where had he procured arms and money? Who were the men who plotted the devilish affair?

When the Thirty-sixth Congress met on December 5, a searching inquiry into every circumstance of the raid was demanded. "Brown, a ruffian, a thief, and a robber, nothing more, had no resources of his own. We want to know where the money was supplied," was the Southern cry. "We want to know the incentives that led him to that expedition." In the Senate the

motion for appointment of a select committee to conduct the
investigation was presented by Senator James M. Mason of
Virginia, and after a vigorous debate it was adopted.

Besides sending a thrill of horror through most of the nation, Brown's raid convinced Southern moderates that the
abolitionists, in their determination to stamp out slavery,
would recoil from no extremity, even if it involved the destruction of the government. This realization ushered in a new,
climactic phase in the long struggle. For as long as most men
could remember, there had been threats on the part of the
South to secede, and Northern states had made similar threats,
in one form or another, during the previous half-century. The
Union had been renounced as intemperately by abolitionists
as by Southern fire-eaters; William Lloyd Garrison had publicly burned the Constitution as a thing accursed, "a covenant
with hell." No more flagrant act of defiance had ever been perpetrated by a Southern disunionist. But as time had passed
without producing a definite rupture, Northern politicians
had come to scoff at the Southern fulminations, deeming them
merely rhetoric intended to bully the North into granting concessions. On the other side, the more reckless Southerners
had come to feel that "cowardly Yankees" would not
fight, should it come to a showdown. The falsity of both these
assumptions was clear to Gwin, and he had tried to alert his
Northern colleagues, especially, to the reality of Southern
intransigence.

The Congress that met just after Harpers Ferry differed from
its predecessors in that the Republican party, grown to full
stature, now marshaled a strong minority in the House and
Senate. In the 1859 elections every free state except California
had returned majorities against the Democratic administration, and there seemed to be a very good chance that if the
Democrats remained divided, the Republicans might carry the
Presidential campaign in 1860. This the Southern Democrats

saw and feared, and warnings of what would happen should the Republicans elect a "sectional President" were frequent and fervid.

Gwin's friend and sometime expansionist ally, Senator Seward, had become a principal target of Southern invective since his enunciation of the "irrepressible conflict" theory. The slave staters attacked Seward not only for what he was, but also for what he seemed almost certain to become — the Republicans' Presidential candidate in the approaching election. Louisiana's silken-voiced Senator Judah P. Benjamin purred that Seward was "the distinguished author of almost every heresy" upon the subject of slavery; while a Richmond newspaper did not hesitate to publish an offer made by a band of Virginia hotheads to pay $2,500 each "for the heads of the following traitors" — naming numerous prominent Republicans — and $50,000 *"for the head of William H. Seward."*

"You may elect Seward to be President of the North, but of the South, never!" the Virginians warned; and on December 12, Alabama's Senator Clement C. Clay, Junior, flung down the gage formally in an impassioned speech in the Senate. Pale and trembling with indignation (the motion to track down the instigators of Harpers Ferry being then under debate), he cried:

> Gentlemen of the Republican party, I warn you, present your sectional candidate in 1860; elect him as the representative of your system of labor; take possession of the government as your instrument in this "irrepressible conflict"; and we of the South will tear the Constitution to pieces and look to our guns for justice!

This sort of talk had been heard before, although seldom under such tense circumstances, and on the Republican side of the chamber it was received with the usual scorn and skepticism. Senator Gwin was distressed, for he knew that Clay was in deadly earnest, and that the determination he expressed

was common to almost the entire South. A Southerner himself,
he understood the temper of the Southern people as no North-
erner could, and he knew that secession was not only being
talked about, it was being planned. He himself would never
approve that step, but he moved among Southern disunionists, whose views were concealed from no one. Therefore the
airy scoffing of the opposition frightened him, and rising, without preparation, he made the most impressive speech of his
career. His aim, his hope, was to bring the Northern extremists to see the situation realistically, and to convince them that
unless they acted temperately in this crisis, the country —
the whole country — stood in grave and imminent peril. He
had not meant to engage in the debate at all, he began,

> But the speech of the senator from Alabama strikes me as a
> warning such as never has been given in the Senate of the United
> States before. I believe that the senator has expressed the feeling
> of a vast majority of the people of the slaveholding States. I
> believe he has stated here today what will inevitably be the action
> of those States in the event of an election of a Republican candi-
> date to the office of President of the United States. Entertaining
> this opinion, I should be faithless to the trust that has been re-
> posed in me . . . if I did not add my voice of warning at this
> particular juncture, which is fraught, in my judgment, with ex-
> treme peril.
>   Mr. President, there is a great mistake existing in the non-
> slaveholding States in regard to the public sentiment in the South.
> They seem to entertain the delusion that there is no serious idea
> in the Southern States to separate . . . in the event of the election
> of a Republican candidate for the Presidency. I believe not only
> that such is the sentiment and determination of a vast majority
> of the inhabitants of the slaveholding States now, but that it
> will be nearly a unanimous sentiment in the event of such an
> election, and that it will be carried into practice. . . . The in-
> habitants of the non-slaveholding States should no longer labor
> under the delusion that the South will not act. . . .
>   The senator from Illinois [Republican Senator Lyman Trum-

bull], the other day, asked why the South looked upon the people of the non-slaveholding States as their enemies, who wished to put the knife to the throats of their wives and children? It is because they believe the doctrines that are taught by his party lead inevitably to that result. Whether they are right or wrong, they believe it. That is the sentiment of the people of the Southern States, and I believe they intend to resist the acquisition of power . . . by his party, because they think that the election and installation of a Republican President would be their conquest.

Heretofore threats of disunion have been fulminated, but I have never believed until the last few years that the danger was so great. I have always believed that something could avert it. Why? Because the parties that existed in the country existed in all the States. But the Republican party is a sectional party. . . . It has no existence in the Southern States, and never can have any existence there. . . . I do not intend to say anything against the Republican party, but I desire to call the attention of that party to the remarks of the senator from Alabama, and I observed that the senator had spoken his true sentiments and the sentiments of those whom he represents. They believe that the principles of the Republican party are destructive to the constitutional rights of the slaveholding States, and that they can only preserve those rights by resisting the principles of that party; and if a President of that party were to be elected and installed, it would be destructive to their constitutional rights. I stated that he spoke the sentiments of his people, and that the South would act on his convictions, and break up this government, in such an event. That was all I said; it was no threat . . . I appealed to the fears of nobody, of no section, of no party; that was not my object; but I did appeal to the judgment of those who entertain certain principles, whether it was best for them to persevere in those principles when they saw that the effect of their triumph must be the destruction of the government.

Mr. President, I want this Union to be preserved and made perpetual, and in order that it may be perpetual it is necessary that the senators on the other side, when appealed to, as they have been this morning, should at least give some gleams of hope to the Southern States that the policy of their incoming administration, if they should succeed in electing a President, will be divergent from what the local policy of their States has heretofore been with reference to slavery. If not, I believe a separation will be inevitable.

Now, I do not profess to be any braver than anybody else; but I certainly am not brave enough to adopt and carry out any lines of policy that would jeopardize this glorious confederacy, and I have in a small way attested it.

Gwin then reached into the history of California's admission in 1850 to furnish an example to the Republicans to put patriotism above partisan advantage, as he, on behalf of his state, had done then. Recalling the threats of disunion that had rung through Congress upon California's presenting itself as a free state, he told how a national rupture had been staved off by Henry Clay's compromise. He had acquiesced in that compromise, he said, although it meant delay in recognizing the rights of his state — a matter of utmost seriousness to the Californians, then in a lawless chaos. He recalled:

I acquiesced in the view of the senator from Kentucky. I did not want the admission of California to cause the destruction of the Union itself, and hence I was willing to have her just rights delayed, and the privileges to which she was entitled . . . overlooked, for a time, rather than that her admission should result in the destruction of the very confederacy of which she sought to be a member. . . . I was willing to abide my time rather than to bring this injury and danger upon the country. . . .

There have been sentiments uttered [on the other side of the chamber] which are well calculated to arouse indignation, and to stir the flame that is now raging in the country. You hear it said that in the event of the election of a Republican candidate for the Presidency, if there is any resistance, they will hang those who resist. Now, whom are they going to hang? One of the senators [Senator Wade of Ohio] indicated very plainly that he intended to hang the governors of the States. How is he going to get at them? By invasion? Is it not an indication to the Southern States . . . that they will be invaded, and that their governors are to be taken and executed? Is it not a notice to the representatives of those fifteen states here, that if they dare to avow these opinions, they are to be executed, too? Is that the spirit that ought to be indulged, or are those the words that ought to be used here, if you wish to preserve this confederacy? Is it not a species of degradation to hold out to senators representing fifteen slave-holding States, that in the event of their resisting, or any portion of their population and government resisting, a Republican President, they are to be put to death as traitors? . . . It is inviting a dissolution of the Union; and it will result in that if this tone of remark is to be indulged in here and elsewhere. . . .

I say that a dissolution of the Union is not impossible, that it is not impractical, and that the Northern States are laboring under a delusion if they think the Southern States cannot separate from them, either violently or peaceably; violently if necessary. . . . It is because I believe they can separate, and that they will separate in the event to which I have alluded, that I have referred to the speech of the senator from Alabama as a warning to every man who loves this Union, that now is the time to present the question in its true form, and that the election of a Republican President is the inevitable destruction of the confederacy. I have believed it for a long time. I have stated it long since as a matter of opinion. It is not a question in which those whom I represent are particularly interested, for we are two thousand miles away from any slaves.

I have submitted to the judgment of those who represent the Republican party, even if they think it is right, whether it is proper to press the success of a political party in this country to the point of destroying the government. That was my suggestion. I said that I made the suggestion because I represent a constituency in favor of the preservation of the Union, although they are very remote from your seat of government. We revere this Union, we honor it, and we desire to preserve it. My only object in the remarks I made was to present to the country the idea that there is danger, and to submit whether it is not best to pause before parties get so much excited that it will be impossible to prevent a collision.

2

In California, this appeal to reason provoked a storm of denunciation. "Gwin's Disunion Speech," the newspapers headlined his remarks, and he was attacked in scathing terms.

It was said that in the heat of debate he had lost his usual self-control and had revealed himself as at heart a disunionist and traitor. Always the advocate of compromise that would prevent senseless strife, Gwin had stated his opinion that the South really would secede if a Republican were to be elected President. This opinion was grounded in his sympathies with the Southerners, his innate understanding of a people he had known from birth, and his grasp of the sentiment prevailing there; and he had begged the hotheads of the North to stop and consider before it became too late. Yet the partisan press of California detected in this appeal an attempt to create discord and disrupt the nation, in the expectation of some personal or political gain. Gwin was a schemer, Gwin was a traitor to his country and to his state, the press shouted.

The Sacramento *Union*, perhaps the most influential paper in the state, said that at first it had been inclined to discount the fragmentary reports of Gwin's speech that seeped through from Washington, but the full text justified the blackest construction that could be placed upon it. Had not the senator declared that the South not only would, but could, withdraw and go it alone successfully, that secession would be the easiest thing in the world? His words showed that his heart was with the South. The *Union* quoted him as saying: "They [the slave states] have the elements of power within their boundaries. . . . The shore line of the Northern States is only 9,335 miles, while that of the Southern States is 23,803 miles. . . . Their seacoast is fitted for commerce. . . . They have fine harbors, fortified. . . . If they take possession of them in advance, they can defend themselves against any enemy. . . . By waiting, they put themselves in the power of the federal government; but by preparing for the event in advance, they put it out of the power of any government on the face of the earth to inflict on them what they conceive to be a serious or fatal injury."

Did not this stink of treason, demanded the *Union*. Did it not show that the senator from California was part and parcel of the whole secession plot — daring to predict victory for traitors? What about the figures he had trotted out to contend that the Republican cause was the cause of a section only, that the Republican party had no national validity? In all the states of the South, he had pointed out, in the last Presidential election, there had been hardly one Republican vote cast; few of those states bothered to offer a Republican electoral ticket at all; yet the Democrats, who took all those states except one, had gathered an additional 1,200,000 votes in the free states — more than twice as many as they had garnered in the Southern states combined. His citing this statistical fact, the *Union* implied, was enough to show which side the senator's heart was on. Conceding that Gwin had taken "considerable pains to deny that he was in favor of disunion," the *Union* argued that he had "exhibited abundant evidence to prove that were he a senator from Mississippi, instead of California, he would proclaim himself a rank disunionist if the majority of the people of the United States constitutionally elected a Republican President. When he presents himself for reelection," the paper prophesied, "then [the voters of California] will sit in judgment upon his disunion speech — his violent, disgusting, Southern fire-eating speech in justification of disunion."

Other journals called the speech shameful — "manifest treason and sedition." Broderick's shadow lay across any action or utterance of Gwin's, and Seward's confidential informant in California — Cornelius Cole — reported, "Doctor Gwin will not be returned."

3

Seward had not been present in the Senate when Gwin made his appeal to reason; he was touring Europe, and was being received with impressive honors in all the principal capitals. When, in January, 1860, he returned to Washington, he found the social and political climate greatly changed. No Southern senator greeted him when he reappeared for the first time in the Senate; those with whom he had been on friendly and even cordial terms avoided him. From the Democratic side, only Senator Douglas crossed over to shake hands with the man whom he expected to oppose in the coming Presidential campaign. Even Senator Gwin, as he came in, merely touched Seward's hand and passed along quickly without entering into conversation. Seward smiled his enigmatic smile.

There was only a semblance of social life in the city. President Buchanan still occasionally favored a hostess with his avuncular benignity, but there was little spirit in the entertaining, and no intermingling of Northern and Southern circles. The President insisted that the storms amid which his administration was foundering were costing him not an hour's sleep, but his haggard face belied him. Here and there a hostess still attempted to blend political oil and water, and Rose Greenhow, the vivacious aunt of Mrs. Stephen Douglas, did keep up a sort of intimacy with a few prominent Republicans, but her tea table made a modest exception to the prevailing air of hostility.

The Gwins kept open house, but their hospitality was no longer inclusive. In private, Mary Gwin grew despondent over the dark outlook, yet she assured her reduced circle that all would still turn out well. Gwin hoped, but with less and less conviction. His own position was beset with difficulties.

Douglas seemed likely to become the choice of the Democrats for President, and after the Lecompton bitterness Gwin could expect no favors from him. Senator Seward, who seemed certain to be the Republican candidate, was politically useless to Gwin. In California, Broderick's ghost stalked the political halls and Gwin was anathema. The nation which he had served long, and had helped to enlarge and make great, seemed careening toward disaster, carrying him with it. He loved the South, and he reverenced the Union; he could forsake neither. He had sworn an oath to preserve, protect, and defend the United States of America, and that oath he shrank from violating. Yet every claim of parentage, education, kinship, friends, and interest drew him toward the South, and to renounce his own would be foul ingratitude. The senator was torn between conflicting loyalties; ambiguity clouded his judgment and confused his actions. As the 1860 election approached, his perplexity increased. There were many men like him, uncertain of which way to turn.

Chapter II

DURING THE REST of the first session of the 1860 Congress, Senator Gwin marked time, though his anxieties did not. At the end of February he received a sharp reminder of the cause of his current unpopularity in California when a successor arrived to fill out Senator Broderick's term. This successor was the man whom Broderick had shouldered aside in 1857 — Milton A. Latham. In the previous autumn Latham had been elected governor with Gwin's help, although without any enthusiasm on the doctor's part. He had taken office on January 9, and his first official act had been to forward to Congress a memorial voted by the legislature, petitioning that California be partitioned into two states, Northern and Southern. The memorial went unheeded, although Latham favored it.

The new legislature had faced the necessity of replacing Broderick in the Senate, and now Latham showed political finesse. The story told in Sacramento was that a group of capitalists, who were lobbying for the passage of a bill granting them rights to construct bulkheads at San Francisco, came to suspect that Governor Latham would veto the bill when it came to him. The lieutenant governor, John G. Downey, however, was understood to be friendly to the measure; so a deal was worked out, by which Latham would be promoted to the Senate and Downey would succeed him as governor. In accordance with this arrangement, five days after he was installed as governor, Latham was elected senator in Broderick's place; but unfortunately for the reputation of Sacramento politicians, Downey, upon becoming governor, vetoed the bulkhead bill.

Milton Latham had qualities that made for early success, being quick-witted, pliable, ingratiating, and sufficiently discreet. Between him and Gwin the personal relationship was so distant that the new senator hesitated to call at the Gwin home upon arriving in Washington. President Buchanan steered him into the correct channel when Latham called at the White House.

"But you haven't called on Mrs. Gwin yet," the President chided gently.

Latham murmured a vague excuse, but Buchanan, with a knowing glance, insisted, "Oh, I have heard her speak very highly of you. She hopes to see you one of her circle."

The hint was plain. Latham called on the Gwins and was received hospitably. Gwin introduced the young senator to the cream of Southern society, and in no time Latham was included in gatherings composed of men who really ruled the land. Among these were General Winfield Scott, commander of the army; Senator Hammond of South Carolina; Senator Crittenden of Kentucky; Vice-President Breckinridge, also of Kentucky; Mississippi's Senators Jefferson Davis and Albert G. Brown; Senators Mason and Hunter of Virginia; and the Georgia millionaire, Howell Cobb, Secretary of the Treasury.

Latham also explored more debatable ground. He called on Senator Douglas, whom he found drinking tea and "full of hope" regarding his Presidential chances. He also cultivated New York capitalists who were ready to finance a Pacific railroad over the central route, if government cooperation could be secured. Latham drafted a bill meeting their wishes, but when it came before the Senate Gwin voted against it, contending that in minor ways it discriminated against California. His apparent abandonment of the project he had been pushing since 1852 raised a cry of anger in the West, and the legislature reprimanded him and ordered him to reverse his vote. The measure was amended to overcome Gwin's objections, and then he did vote for it; but it failed of passage.

His enemies cited this action as an indication of Gwin's corruptibility: he was, they said, in the pay of the steamship companies, who were loath to lose their monopoly of transportation to and from the West. A rumor circulated that the bills for the sumptuous entertaining at the Gwin home were being footed by the Pacific Mail Steamship Company, and that the Gwins' social splendor was a cloak for lobbying on behalf of the shipping interests. Where formerly the senator had been extolled as a manipulative wizard, furthering California's interests at the national level, now he was depicted as a schemer acting from disgraceful motives. Just what nefarious designs he had in mind were not spelled out; the popular impression that he was working toward secession was a peg strong enough to hang a multiplicity of insinuations upon. Gwin had become a whipping boy for every sin committed by the "Chivalry," and he realized his plight.

2

Toward the close of April, Latham was startled to be given a glimpse of Gwin's anxiety. It was revealed to him during a call at the senator's home. The Democratic national convention was due to meet in Charleston, South Carolina, that month, and Washington was tense. The party was divided angrily, and the Democratic chances for success in November would depend upon the choice of the Presidential candidate. Senator Douglas was the favorite of the Northern wing of the party. The Southern Democrats had spurned him as faithless to their principles, and were insisting on an out-and-out proslavery candidate. To such a choice the Northerners were bitterly opposed.

During an after-dinner stroll, in the garden, Dr. Gwin opened his mind to Latham in reference to his own troubled outlook. The burst of confidence puzzled the younger man; it was not characteristic, and Latham listened intently, saying little. Pointing out that his Senate term would expire in less than a year, Gwin admitted that reelection seemed impossible. In any case, he could not afford the outlay that a campaign would entail; in view of the hostility that had been worked up against him, the expense was bound to be high. His best course, he suggested, probably would be to try for a cabinet post in the new Democratic administration; or in default of that, a diplomatic appointment. Everything hinged on the choice of the Presidential candidate. From Douglas he could reasonably expect nothing. But Breckinridge was friendly, and the Vice-President was out to get the nomination; coming from a border state, where free and slave elements managed to live in tolerable harmony, Breckinridge should be acceptable to all factions and sections. Yes, probably Breckinridge, the doctor concluded, would be his best hope.

Such candor on the part of the usually close-mouthed doctor seemed suspect to Latham, although he could not guess for what purpose he was being posted on Gwin's worries. When he said good-bye, he noticed that Gwin pressed his hand warmly, without saying a word. What this action signified Latham could not decide. He recorded his bewilderment in his journal; and two days later he was further perplexed by a word dropped by Mrs. Gwin on a pleasure cruise down the Potomac. From her comment, Latham deduced that Gwin had informed his wife about the garden talk, and that for some reason she was annoyed. Nodding her head emphatically, she assured the junior senator that "we intend to come back to the Senate, sir." Her reputation as a political strategist was known to Latham, and he wondered whether the doctor had some unannounced reason to hope.

The guest of honor on the Potomac excursion had been Miss Harriet Lane, Buchanan's niece and official hostess. The outing had been gotten up by Samuel Ward, man-about-Washington who knew everybody and whom everybody knew. As a Forty-niner in the gold rush, Ward had arrived at San Francisco on the *Panama* with Gwin, and between him and the doctor there subsisted a firm friendship.

3

The Democrats convened in Charleston on April 23 and at once it was clear that they were hopelessly at odds. Douglas's men overrode the delegates from the cotton states and forced adoption of a platform containing a moderate clause on slavery. This pleased Northern Democrats, but so incensed those in the Gulf states that, in accordance with a prearranged plan, their delegates marched out of the hall and reassembled in their own convention a few doors away.

Washington was feverish with suspense. Every scrap of news coming from Charleston was seized upon to raise or depress the hopes of the opposing factions. The telegraph service was unreliable, the mails were slow; hence contradictory rumors agitated the capital from hour to hour.

When balloting for the Presidential candidate started on May 1, Douglas assumed a commanding lead, but was unable to muster enough votes to nominate. All that day and the next, balloting went on.

On May 2 Senator and Mrs. Gwin were dinner guests of Senator Hammond. The South Carolinian was somewhat aloof from the turmoil, for he had no political ambition; he was rich, socially secure, and was in the Senate only from a sense of duty. His guests, however, were deeply involved in the drama unfolding at Charleston. Around the well-furnished table sat the Vice-President and Mrs. Breckinridge, Senator

Brown of Mississippi, Representative W. W. Boyce of that state, Senator Latham, and two charming ladies from Georgia, in addition to the Gwins. It was a strictly Southern gathering, and all thoughts were upon Charleston.

Midway through the dinner, Sam Ward dropped by with a message for Gwin to the effect that Douglas had withdrawn, and James Guthrie of Kentucky had surged up as a compromise candidate, capturing a hundred and ninety-six votes, only six short of the required number.

This was bad news for Gwin; Guthrie was no more acceptable to him than Douglas, for the Kentuckian had never forgotten his near duel with Gwin in Franklin Pierce's time. The other guests were silent when Gwin relayed Ward's report to them, but Latham believed he heard Mrs. Breckinridge's heart thumping, while the Vice-President turned pale; Breckinridge had been hopeful that in case of a deadlock the convention would turn to him, and to have the prize snatched by a competitor from his own state was a bitter pill.

After a pause, the conversation resumed, but there was no heart in it, and as soon as the amenities permitted, Gwin and Latham slipped away to find Ward and get a fuller report.

Ward, however, had heard nothing further. The telegraph line had broken, and the word he had relayed had come to him, he said, on the authority of the White House. Despite the late hour, Gwin and Latham posted to the executive mansion, while Ward went in search of Jefferson Davis, to see if he had received word from the Mississippi delegation in Charleston. Buchanan told his callers that he had received no information, and he knew nothing about the report Sam Ward had conveyed. Ward and Davis coming in, the latter assured the President that he, too, was in the dark regarding Douglas's withdrawal; but if the Illinois senator had indeed quit the race, the South's prospects would seem to have brightened.

All three senators and Ward next tried Howell Cobb, the Secretary of the Treasury, to learn whether he had any message. Cobb was not at home, but his wife said no word had come there. Perhaps the Virginia senators, Mason and Hunter, might have fresh information, it was suggested, and the party knocked at their doors. Hunter, also, was out, but Mason said he had received a message paralleling Sam Ward's information, and he did not relish the thought of having James Guthrie in the White House.

At this moment Hunter and Cobb came up with a wire just received: "Douglas 150½, Guthrie 68, adjourned until tomorrow." So Douglas had not been eliminated, and Guthrie was still the runner-up. Gwin was disgusted.

"Damn the luck!" he muttered as he strode away. "A pretty fist of it I've made today, sure!"

The next morning reliable dispatches revealed that the convention, boycotted by the Gulf states delegates and unable to agree on the candidate, had adjourned for six weeks, and would meet again in Baltimore.

In June delegates representing the Northern and border states reconvened at Baltimore and nominated Senator Douglas. The Southern Democrats met at Richmond and nominated Breckinridge for President and Senator Joseph L. Lane of Oregon for Vice-President, on a pro-slavery platform.

Senator Seward, watching the commotion, commented upon the historic spectacle of the breakup of the once mighty Democratic party, which had ruled the nation, except for brief interruptions, since the Presidency of Thomas Jefferson. Senator Gwin had been born during Jefferson's administration, and he, too, sensed that an era — his era — was ending. The dissolution had been coming for years; the Whig party had disappeared, the stopgap Know-Nothings had gone the way of all fads, and political discord had divided even the churches into Northern and Southern branches. Old loyalties were dissolving. Senator Seward, for one, being flexible, could bend with the change. Gwin was not so supple: he had been able to adjust within the party, but as a Democrat, a party leader, a Southern-leaning supporter of Buchanan, and an exponent of party responsibility, he could not shake off the discipline of a lifetime. Practical in tactics, he was not revolutionary; when faced with the necessity of a choice he remained loyal to what he considered the true, legitimate branch of the Democratic organization, and spent the summer of 1860 in California campaigning for Breckinridge and Lane. There he encountered still new changes, and, in one man, a portent of greater changes to come.

Chapter III

EDWARD DICKINSON BAKER was one of those predestined individuals who are born to fill a unique role in a time of crisis. In the course of an active career he had passed through many stages; but by 1860 he had arrived at full maturity, and was ready to assume his place in history as a meteor — spectacular in its transit, but even while it is being observed, extinguished. For Gwin, Edward Baker was to take the place of Broderick as a malign influence.

Before coming to California in the mid-fifties, Baker already had lived fully and adventurously. Born in England and brought to the United States as a child, he became so imbued with the ideals of America that while still a boy he was said to have burst into tears upon learning that his foreign birth debarred him from ever becoming President. As a young man he moved to Illinois, where he practiced law in Sangamon County and became a close friend of Abraham Lincoln.

Baker's greatest gift was his power of spontaneous eloquence. He had all the endowments favorable to oratory — voice, presence, magnetism, intellectual sweep, felicity of phrase, clarity of utterance, mastery of imagery. In person he was handsome, with a fresh, ruddy face and mobile features that could express every shade of emotion. His clear tenor voice possessed extraordinary range and carrying power, and filled the largest halls without strain. His gestures were vivid, and on the platform he displayed what old-time actors called *port* — a graceful dignity that riveted attention and imposed respect. When aroused, his eyes would flash and from his lips words would gush in a torrent; at such times the sheer impetuosity of his utterance was overwhelming.

As a lawyer, Baker's forte was converting juries. He could so bemuse a jury that a disgruntled opponent once expressed his belief that Baker could charm any twelve normally intelligent men "out of their five senses and six wits." This ability was displayed to best advantage in criminal cases, especially capital ones; in that field he was preeminent.

The law offering a stepping-stone to political life, in Illinois Baker had been elected to Congress as a Whig, after capturing the nomination from Lincoln. While he was a Representative, the war with Mexico broke out, and Baker volunteered, was brevetted colonel, and fought with gallantry in General Scott's campaign. During an early stage of that conflict, he became so indignant over the abominable food furnished to the soldiers that he reappeared in Congress in uniform, and by a single speech succeeded in having the situation corrected. Such dramatic strokes came naturally to him; he carried them off with superb dash and *élan*.

His having enthusiastically engaged in the war which the Whigs condemned (although steadily voting supplies to carry it on) made Baker's political future in Illinois dubious; and after the conclusion of peace he found an outlet for his superabundant energies in supervising the construction of a railroad across the Isthmus of Panama, a formidable feat of engineering. Then, returning to Illinois, he ran again for Congress as a Whig, in a district where election tellers had never been able to count more than six Whig votes. The power of his tongue elected him. Still restless, he next moved to California and quickly established himself as one of that state's foremost attorneys. His fees were large even for that day of prodigal spending. The services he performed for David Broderick were only a sideline to his general practice; his specialty was "hanging cases," and rarely did one of his clients feel the noose. Conforming to the loose legal ethics of the time and place, he had defended the murderer Cora with his best skill, and had been rewarded with a hung jury. The Vigilantes, however, in hanging Cora, annulled his eloquence.

The 1856 uprising distressed Baker as it distressed most lawyers, to whom, from either conviction or interest, the sanctity of the law was an inviolable principle. Setting aside legal authority, even for praiseworthy ends, was hard for legalists to condone, and Baker had vaguely aided the so-called Law and Order Committee. So had Gwin, who was a lawyer by education, and so had Broderick, although for more personal reasons affecting his own safety. Baker had incurred suspicion for his defense of Cora; and with the public inflamed against everyone in any way connected with the corruption of the city, he deemed it prudent to withdraw from San Francisco until the tempest blew itself out.

In 1857 he returned and announced himself a candidate for Congress on the Whig ticket. The Democrats trounced him. Perceiving that the Whig party was moribund, he joined the rising Republicans, whose antipathy to slavery he shared and whose buoyant spirit he found congenial. In 1859 he again ran for Congress, under the Republican label, and again was flattened by the Gwin-"Chivalry" steamroller.

Baker had admired Broderick immeasurably. Right or wrong, he believed that beneath the harsh exterior of that tormented man had been a passion for human freedom, which had been the mainspring of his actions. To Baker, Broderick typified the submerged, repressed, exploited portion of humankind struggling for a share in life's fulfillments. Freedom — the ideal of freedom — was Baker's passion, and the eulogy he had delivered over his slain friend, quite as much as the shock of Broderick's killing, had ignited the wildfire of revulsion against Senator Gwin.

During his years as a flashy attorney and a wanderer, thirsty for excitement and acclaim, Edward Baker had accumulated some dross; but by 1860 this had been mainly purged away, and he was able to answer a call that projected him into the very center of national affairs. Early in 1860 a delegation of Republicans from Oregon waited upon him. That state had become the political fief of Senator Lane, outspoken apologist for slavery, who was soon to become Breckinridge's Vice-Presidential running mate. The Republicans of Oregon, few and feeble, needed a candidate to run against Lane's Democratic nominee for United States senator. They offered Baker the nomination, although the cause, they warned, was probably hopeless. Baker's friends in San Francisco also rated his chances in Oregon as nil, but Baker accepted. He went to Oregon, and canvassing the sparsely settled state on horseback, roved from hamlet to hamlet and brought his formidable powers of persuasion to bear upon every voter he met. At the same time he ardently championed his friend Lincoln for the Presidency. In October not only was Baker elected, but Lincoln carried Oregon by a plurality of fewer than three hundred votes. Baker was the first Republican to be elected to either branch of Congress from the Pacific West.

2

In California, meanwhile, the Presidential campaign had become a free-for-all, four-way contest. The Democrats dominated the state numerically, as they had since 1850, but they were divided three ways. Against Breckinridge, the "regular" party nominee, were pitted Douglas, the idol of the Northern element, and John Bell of Tennessee, a middle-of-the-roader nominated by a faction calling themselves the Constitutional Union party and made up of moderate Democrats and former Whigs and Know-Nothings. Lincoln was the weakest candidate in the canvass: twenty-two newspapers in the state were trumpeting the merits of Breckinridge, twenty-four supported Douglas, and only seven came out for Lincoln. By October the Republicans despaired of success; apparently nothing could break the Democratic hold on California, and the only question was which Democrat would come out ahead.

Baker's Oregon victory resuscitated the Republicans' hopes. When his ship entered the Golden Gate on his journey toward Washington, a hundred-gun salute was fired from Fort Point. The Republicans organized a rally for October 26 which he would address, and on that evening a throng of twelve thousand gathered outside the American Theater, eager to hear him, although the building would hold only four thousand. Upon the doors being opened, the crush to get inside became so dense that several men who fainted had to be handed out over the heads of others packed in the passageways.

On the platform Baker radiated confidence, and his words were fired with assurance. Disdaining to dwell upon past defeats, he bade his listeners "look forward to the new day dawning." He went on:

> We live in an advancing generation. The prayers and tears and hopes and sighs of all good men are with us, of us, for us. As for me, I am not ashamed of Freedom. I know her power, I glory in her strength, I rejoice in her majesty. I have seen her again and again struck down, I have seen her friends fly from her. I have seen her foes gather around her. But when they turned to exult, I have seen her again meet them face to face, clad in complete steel, and brandishing in her strong right hand a flaming sword, red with insufferable light!

With a sweep of his arm he seemed to brandish that very sword, and excited hearers later would assert that they had actually beheld the blade flashing above his head. In concluding, the orator sounded a note that would be of omnious significance for Gwin. Reminding his audience that two years previously he had spoken at the funeral of William I. Ferguson, the victim of an equivocal duel, and that barely a year had elapsed since he had stood "by the bedside of my slaughtered friend Broderick, who fell in your cause and on your behalf" (at this point the shorthand reporter interpolated the word "sensation" to describe the reaction of the audience), Baker swept into an impassioned crescendo:

And I cried, "How long, oh, how long, shall the hopes of Freedom and her champion be thus crushed?" The tide has turned. I regret my little faith. I see better omens. The warrior rests. Nor word, nor wish, nor prayer, nor triumph can call him from that lone abode [*sensation*], but his example lives among us. In San Francisco, I know, I speak to hundreds of men tonight — perhaps to thousands — who loved him in his life and who will be true to his memory always. In a higher arena it may be my privilege to speak of him and for him, as I will [*tremendous applause and cheering*], and I hope, I believe, that I shall be able to say that his ashes repose among a people who loved him well; who are not and never will be forgetful of the manner of his life, nor of the method of his death [*profound sensation*]!

This speech disconcerted Democrats and reanimated the Republicans, and in November, California went for Lincoln by a plurality of six hundred and fourteen votes — all credited to Baker, the avenger of Broderick.

On November 10 Senator Gwin sailed aboard the steamer *Sonora* for Panama and Washington. Also on board were two other prominent Democrats, Reverdy Johnson of Maryland and Senator Benjamin of Louisiana, who both had been appearing as government counsel in land claims litigation. Roaming the ship in restless ebullience — fresh, confident, forward-beckoning — was Senator-elect Baker.

Dr. Gwin was not companionable on that voyage; most of the time he remained in his cabin.

Chapter IV

BOTH GWIN AND BAKER had cause to hasten to Washington, for events were rushing toward a climax, and the two men were far removed in the West from the critical center.

The California election had been held on November 6, but when the two senators sailed for the East, four days later, they were not aware of the national result. They knew that California and Oregon had gone for Lincoln, and since October 31 they had known that the Republicans had also carried the three October-voting states — Indiana, Ohio, and Pennsylvania. No further information would be available to them until they should reach Panama where they could intercept dispatches being sent westward; from these they learned that Lincoln definitely had been elected — a sectional, minority President.

At Panama, Gwin also may have learned that South Carolina was making good her threat to secede in the event of a Republican victory, and had already called a convention for that purpose. On November 10 — the day Gwin left San Francisco — South Carolina's two senators, James Chesnut, Junior, and the urbane Hammond, had resigned from the Senate. Both were Gwin's friends. The crack-up had started.

On December 5, Gwin and Baker — between whom there had been only formal courtesies exchanged — arrived separately at Washington. Baker was sworn in at once. Senator Lane, the defeated Vice-Presidential candidate, refused to make the customary introduction of the new senator from his state, and Baker was escorted forward by California's Democratic Senator Latham.

Gwin found Washington heavy with foreboding. The Gulf states, whose representatives had breathed defiance before the election, now were in doubt as to their course: to secede or to submit. Withdrawal from the Union would almost certainly mean war; radical Republican governors in the North already were preparing and calling for it. Amid the backstage scurrying Gwin remained aloof, on his guard, for his position was doubly ambiguous: though a senator from a free state, he could not endorse the extreme Northern stand, nor could he conscientiously align himself with the Southern hotheads, for he did not approve of secession. He participated in the Senate debates as little as possible, and attempted to maintain a precarious balance between the irreconcilables. The moment for decision was at hand, but he shrank from it. The dilemma in which he was caught had been foreseen by his friend Seward. In a speech on the evening before election day, Seward had reminded his audience that the appeal being made by the three candidates opposing Lincoln was an appeal to fear — "fear that if you are so perverse as to vote for [Lincoln] . . . this Union shall come down upon your heads":

> Fellow citizens, it is time, high time, that we know whether this is a constitutional government under which we live. It is high time that we know, since the Union is threatened, who are its friends and who are its enemies. I tell you that . . . when tomorrow's sun shall have set, and the next morning's sun shall have arisen upon the American people, rejoicing in the election of Abraham Lincoln to the Presidency, those men who today sympathize with, and excuse, the disunionists, will have to make a sudden choice, and choose whether, in the language of the senator from Georgia [Toombs], they will "go for treason and make it respectable," or whether they will go for freedom, for the Constitution, and for eternal Union.

Seward had not underestimated the nation's peril. "This republic of ours is in a crisis," he had said, "and I believe that if it fails to pass safely through this crisis it will languish and die." It was a time for clear-cut decisions, on the one central issue, secession or union; doubts, hesitations, equivocations would not be tolerated on either side. Gwin, who sympathized with the disunionists, although he was not one of them, faced the necessity of choosing, and the irreconcilable loyalties pulled him in opposite directions. California itself was divided on the question of secession. Its remoteness had kept alive an inclination to detach itself from the nation and establish its own government. Ever since the state's inception the agitation to split it into northern and southern sections had persisted, as it would persist a century later. Had the separation taken place in 1861, the southern portion, linked to the South by geography and temperament, almost certainly would have joined the Confederacy.

In Northern California, where unionist sentiment was predominant, the agitation over secession had not yet caused acute alarm. It seemed incredible to most people around San Francisco that the slave states would withdraw simply because a Republican had been constitutionally elected. Therefore the news that South Carolina, on December 20, had indeed withdrawn, and that the cotton states were likely to follow, startled Westerners, and adherents of both sides swung into action looking toward the election of state officers favorable to their views in the fall of 1861. In the convention of "Chivalry" Democrats secession speeches were made and calls were issued for a declaration of California's independence. Even the assassination of Lincoln was urged. Edmund Randolph, eccentric but influential Virginian, cried on the convention floor:

> For God's sake, speed the bullet, may the lead go quick to the heart, and may our country be free from the despot usurper who now claims the name of President of the United States!

This was in 1861, and Randolph's outburst was greeted with cheers.

*

2

At Washington, meanwhile, sedition seemed to find a haven in the White House itself, according to watchful Republicans. Seward was convinced that treason was brewing there. As early as December 29, 1860, he wrote to Thurlow Weed, his political partner in New York, that "the plot is forming to seize the capital and usurp the government, and it has abettors near the President." Buchanan's cabinet was disintegrating. Lewis Cass, popular elder statesman, had resigned as Secretary of State in protest against the President's submission to Southern demands, and other cabinet resignations were to follow. Seward assured his correspondents that he was not relaying alarmist rumors, but had certain knowledge of a conspiracy to "seize the capital on or before the 4th of March." He sent a warning to Lincoln in Illinois that "this, too, has its accomplices in the public councils. . . . You must not imagine that I am giving you suspicions and rumors. Believe me I know what I write."

One of Seward's sources of information was Senator Gwin. They met daily in the Senate, and Gwin was in an advantageous position to know what was going on behind the scenes; he had friends in both camps, and like Seward he recoiled from the dreadful prospect of war. Both senators were men of peace, willing to risk much to bring about a reconciliation. Seward soon felt that he was sufficiently in the secrets of the White House to tell his wife, "treason is all around and amongst us"; and in a letter to her written just after Secretary of War Floyd, a Virginian, had resigned:

This Democratic administration has run as far as its Northern members dare to go, in the way of treason, until it has to choose between absolute surrender, from now until the 4th of March,

to the seceders, or else a break. . . . The White House is abandoned to the seceders. They eat, drink, and sleep with [the
President].

Throughout December, Gwin did what he could to stem the
vacillation of the administration. His relations with Buchanan
continued to be sympathetic, and the irresolution of the timorous old man distressed him. The President veered between
domineering Senator Slidell, on one side, and pro-Union Jeremiah Black, the Pennsylvanian who had succeeded Cass as
Secretary of State, on the other.

It is arguable whether the Civil War could have been
avoided. Gwin believed that it could have been, had another
Andrew Jackson occupied the White House; and in retro-
spect he would attach principal blame for the debacle to Buchanan and Winfield Scott. Not that they were solely responsible, but between them, he believed, they had commanded the
means whereby secession could have been halted in its tracks.
Such was Gwin's feeling in those tense weeks before the outbreak of hostilities at Fort Sumter; and later he became absolutely convinced that impartial history would demonstrate, "as
clearly as a problem in Euclid," that Scott and Buchanan, by
their action and lack of action, had precipitated a needless
war. There had been no intentional error committed, he said,
for both leaders were "pure patriots and devoted to the Union";
but he felt that they had been "derelict in their duty to the
Constitution and the laws, which they had sworn to support
and maintain."

There was no personal animosity behind his conclusion, for
he was a friend of both men. Indeed, it had been Gwin who
had obtained for Scott the coveted rank of lieutenant general.
In 1855 the bill for that purpose had been defeated in the
Senate, and Scott had appealed to Gwin to move for a reconsideration. After amending the measure in line with the general's

suggestion, to make the rank expire at Scott's death, Gwin steered it to final passage. With Buchanan, Gwin had long been on the most friendly terms. But in the crisis of 1860-61, in Gwin's judgment, the President and the general failed disastrously.

"They were one thing today and another tomorrow," he recalled, "veering like a weathercock to the right and to the left, at the very time they should have been most firm and determined." On December 15 Scott had said of the seceding states, "Let the erring sisters go in peace," and on the twenty-ninth and thirtieth of the same month he had recommended vigorous military measures to crush South Carolina's aggressive defiance. "Instead of this," Gwin pointed out, "Scott immediately afterwards drew back from the enforcement of the very policy he had just outlined." And Buchanan he found equally unstable:

> When Congress assembled, just after the Presidential election, [Buchanan] was completely under the control of Senator Slidell and his Southern associates. . . . Black and Slidell had been Mr. Buchanan's most trusted friends, and their bitter opposition to each other at this time caused him much annoyance and great distress of mind. He would say "yes" to Mr. Slidell today, and the same to Black tomorrow, until Mr. Slidell left him, a bitter enemy, and Judge Black tendered his resignation as chief cabinet adviser.

If Buchanan had added to his December message to Congress, in which (as Gwin put it) "he demonstrated to his own satisfaction that he had no power to coerce a seceding State, these words: 'But notwithstanding what I have just written, in the language of the immortal Jackson I say, "The Union! It must and shall be preserved!"' and then had acted up to that declaration, there would have been no Civil War."

The parallel between the Nullification crisis of the 1830s, which he had lived through as a young man, and the crisis of

1861 was constantly present in Gwin's mind. Jackson's "most cherished friends and warmest adherents were nullifiers," he pointed out:

> During the Senatorial tournament between Webster and Hayne, he sent a note of congratulation and commendation to Hayne upon his great and successful oratorical effort. Three years later, after reading the "Nullification Proclamation" of Hayne (then governor of South Carolina), he exclaimed, "The traitor! I'll hang him as high as Haman!" . . . That was the end of nullification, and such would have been the end of secession if Mr. Buchanan had followed in the footsteps of his . . . predecessor. Jackson's nearest friends were nullifiers, and Buchanan's, by a singular coincidence, were secessionists. John Slidell had more influence with Mr. Buchanan than any dozen men in the country. Slidell was an arrogant dictator and despot. Mr. Buchanan succumbed to his influence up to the last, when Slidell quit him in anger. No closer ties would have been broken between Buchanan and his secession friends than were broken between Jackson and his nullification friends when the general announced the celebrated sentiment: "The Union! It must and shall be preserved!"

Though sympathizing with Buchanan's plight, Gwin deplored the President's variability and lack of firmness. Yet in a way Gwin experienced the same difficulty in striking out boldly for one side or the other. His loyalties confused him. His attachment to the Union was genuine and sincere, but so was his affection for the region of his birth. He liked to describe himself as "a stern party leader and a successful one," and up to now he had not hesitated to choose a side and stick with it. But now, while waiting for some sign of Jacksonian vigor from the White House, he was caught in the drift himself, and the confusion and ineptitude shown at the opposite end of Pennsylvania Avenue increased his own confusion on Capitol Hill.

❋

3

At the end of December, 1860, Secretary of War Floyd resigned amid a flurry of financial scandals and rumors of schemes to subvert the North's military might. In one of these purported schemes, affecting California, Gwin's name was freely used. It was said that just after the election, the senator had hastened back to Washington to urge the assignment of a commander of United States military forces on the West Coast who could be counted upon to side with the South.

The Western area was organized in two military departments, one under Winfield Scott Hancock, stationed at Los Angeles, and the other under Philip Sheridan, stationed in Washington Territory. On January 15, 1861, an order reached San Francisco which merged the two departments into one, and placed that under the command of Albert Sidney Johnston. The order had been signed by Secretary Floyd a month before, and Johnston was known to have pronounced Southern sympathies.

This shift in command alarmed Northern sympathizers. The alarm was increased when a plot was reported to have Johnston "neutralize" California and hold it aloof from either North or South, in the event of hostilities. Whether this plot existed or not is beside the point; although reported on the most tenuous grounds, such was the excitability of men at the time, that it was given credence in the Northern camp. Word of the supposed conspiracy was brought to certain Northern leaders by a Negro who had been acting as nurse for Edmund Randolph, then gravely ill. The servant said he had overheard whispered conversations between his patient and some visitors who behaved in a conspiratorial manner. The purport of these whisperings was that Johnston could be persuaded to proclaim the state's neutrality, and to serve notice that the soldiers under his orders would not be used against the troops of either North or South, should war break out. This arrangement would avoid formal secession and leave California technically in the Union until such time as it would be feasible to attach it to the Confederacy. The force Johnston commanded was insignificant, but he could augment it by calling out units of the state militia who were favorable to the Southern cause, and there were many of these.

The frightened Northerners sped warning of this proposed mutiny to Washington by pony express, urgently requesting that Johnston be replaced by an officer of unquestionable loyalty. At the eastern end of the line, Senator Baker had been using his influence with Lincoln to make the same change. Should California split off, he told the President-elect, Oregon, Arizona, and Nevada would follow; and with a Southern insurrection on its hands, the federal government could never muster sufficient strength to reclaim the Pacific West. Baker was giving valuable aid to the Union cause in the Senate, where his powers as a speaker were demonstrated almost from the first.

Neither Gwin nor Latham made any secret of their expectation of seeing California independent, should the Union definitely break up. Gwin was being quoted as having said that "in case of a dissolution of the Union, California would unite herself to the South," and he took pains to deny this and make his views clear in these categorical terms:

> I have never made that statement upon any occasion. I hope, Mr. President, that this Union will be imperishable; but if it is ever broken up, the eastern boundary of the Pacific Republic will be, in my opinion, the Sierra Madre and Rocky Mountains.

Senator Latham was no less frank in predicting an independent Republic of the Pacific unless the North and South composed their quarrel:

We have resources not possessed by any other State of the Union, while our population comprises the most enterprising and energetic men of the country. Why should we trust to the management of others what we are abundantly able to do ourselves? Why depend on the North and the South to regulate our affairs? This, too, after the North and the South have proved themselves incapable of living in harmony with one another?

As state after state seceded — Florida, Alabama, Mississippi, and Georgia, soon to be followed by Louisiana and Texas, while the border states, Virginia, Arkansas, North Carolina, Kentucky, Tennessee, and Maryland, teetered — the crisis deepened hourly. The "war party" among the Republicans called for troops to quell the "rebellion," but the Southerners went their way, organized the Confederate States of America at Montgomery, Alabama, and elected Jefferson Davis provisional President and Alexander Stephens Vice-President.

4

On February 11 President-elect Lincoln left Illinois for Washington. Barely had he started eastward when the insurgent government at Montgomery voted to seize, by force or otherwise, all federal installations within its borders, including Forts Sumter and Pickens. These United States military bases, located at Charleston, South Carolina, and Pensacola, Florida, were lightly garrisoned, and already South Carolina had been peremptorily demanding that Sumter be surrendered — a demand which President Buchanan had temporarily sidetracked by begging for time to pray before making a decision. Meanwhile the Confederates served notice that any move toward strengthening the forts would be considered an act of war.

To preserve the peace at all costs was the overriding desire of Senator Seward, soon to head Lincoln's cabinet as Secretary of State. He appreciated that the vital issue was perpetuation of the Union; besides that, the issue of slavery was subordinate;

and he was bending every effort to calm the hysteria. In his belief secession was like a disease, which would run its course and eventually bring about its own cure; that the Southern states, if treated with leniency and understanding, would sooner or later realize their folly and come back into the Union peaceably. For this temporizing attitude he was accused of "appeasement" by the radical "war Republicans."

Seward's feeling was shared in large part by Senator Gwin. His supreme concern, also, was to head off hostilities; so long as no blood was shed, some accommodation might be reached.

Although Seward had accepted Lincoln's invitation to be Secretary of State, he would not exercise authority until March 4. Meanwhile, the belligerency exhibited at Montgomery caused him the sharpest anxiety. "Mad men North, and mad men South," he told his wife, "are working together to produce a dissolution of the Union by civil war. . . . Once for all, I must gain time for the new administration to organize and for the frenzy of passion to subside."

In the emergency he appealed to Gwin for help. Seward had a talent for intrigue, and the plan he had in mind was subtle. The men of the Confederate government at Montgomery were former Senate colleagues and in some cases personal friends of both Seward and Gwin. These men, on their side, knew the cordiality that existed between the New York and the California senators; therefore, Seward reasoned, he might be able to transmit to the highest quarters at Montgomery assurances which they would deem convincing, that the policy of the incoming administration would be one of patience and forbearance, not one of force and coercion. As a prospective cabinet member, Seward could not extend such assurances himself; decidedly, he must not appear in the transaction at all. But through Gwin he might be able to get word to Jefferson Davis and his advisers.

Seward never doubted that he could speak authoritatively

on the subject of administration policy, because he expected to set that policy himself. Seward conceived of Lincoln as a country lawyer unversed in national affairs, who would be grateful for tactful guidance in dealing with the vast and unprecedented problems raised by the secession. With this in mind, the prospective Secretary of State asked Senator Gwin to write to his fellow Mississippian, Jefferson Davis, and convey, as coming from an unimpeachable source, the pacific intentions of the new government. If the letter were phrased adroitly, Davis and his colleagues should be able to detect Seward's voice disguised as Gwin's. That was Seward's hope.

Gwin hesitated, for he realized the responsibility this would place upon him, and already his situation was ambiguous. As his intimacy with Seward was known to Jefferson Davis, probably the latter would give full credit to anything he relayed and infer that it came from Seward. Davis then presumably would shape his own policy accordingly. For Gwin to guarantee that the new administration would not use force against the Confederacy would be hazardous in the extreme, for how could he be sure what would be the policy of Lincoln? No policy had been announced yet, and none could be set definitely until the new administration was organized.

One wing of the Republicans — the more vociferous branch — was clamoring for war. At dinner tables, Michigan's Senator Zachariah Chandler was saying that "a little blood-letting would do this Republic good." Ben Wade of Ohio was so spoiling for a fight that he could bring a brace of pistols into the Senate, plank them down on his desk, and glare around in hope of a challenge. Governor John Andrews of Massachusetts was equipping his militia for instant service in the field. These warmongers were as ready to fight as were their counterparts at the South; and their spokesman, Salmon P. Chase of Ohio, was being pushed for the cabinet as a counterpoise to Seward. How could Gwin foretell which faction would prevail?

Gwin weighed the risks to himself and to his friends at the South; for they were his friends, although he could not endorse their conduct. Should Jefferson Davis suspect that Washington contemplated war, it would be his duty to arm for resistance, to raise troops, procure weapons, erect fortifications, lay in military stores. On the other hand, should he be convinced that the Lincoln administration intended to pursue a policy of peace, it would be to his interest to restrain his own fire-eaters and refrain from warlike preparations, lest they provoke some rash act among the corresponding hotheads of the North. Gwin was ready to seize any chance, however faint, of heading off catastrophe; but he shrank from inadvertently relaying misleading or false information, and in spite of Seward's and his own sincerity, this was a possibility. Still, after the most careful thought, he acceded to Seward's request, and wrote a letter to Davis setting forth Seward's assurances of a policy of peace. The letter was mailed in the ordinary way, for the postal service had not been interrupted, and Gwin waited uneasily for word of its safe arrival.

Personally he was not hopeful. His political judgment told him that the break, which had been building up for a generation, probably was past mending, barring some miraculous shift in sentiment on one side or the other. But a practical politician does not count upon miracles. With luck, Gwin believed, the South might be able to go it alone; and there was the vision cherished by many Southern statesmen of expanding into Mexico, Cuba, and Central America, to create a Caribbean empire that eventually would overawe the diminished United States.

On February 18 Gwin wrote pessimistically to the San Francisco attorney, Calhoun Benham (the man who had seconded Judge Terry in the fatal duel with Broderick):

> The cotton States are gone forever. The border States will follow; it is only a question of time. If no collision takes place,

reconstruction [of the Union] is barely possible. The chances are
there will be two republics, North and South, with amicable relations. Time will probably turn it into three.

5

During that February, Washington's aspect changed so
greatly that Gwin could hardly recognize the city where he had
dwelt so long. Gone were Democratic colleagues with whom
he had been intimate; in the Senate their chairs stood empty;
their houses were shuttered; their families had departed to
plantations or hotels and boardinghouses in overcrowded Montgomery. There was no social life to speak of. Mrs. Gwin was
desolate. The last gala event had occurred in December, on
the day South Carolina "went out"; it was a fashionable wedding, which President Buchanan had honored with his presence, and was, of course, a Southern affair. Midway in the evening, the President remarked upon a sudden commotion in
the outer hall; was the house on fire? he asked. The blaze was
greater than that: a telegram announcing South Carolina's
secession was being handed around among the guests, and men
and women were capering for joy. "Thank God!" cried Keitt
of South Carolina. "At last we are free! I feel like a boy let
out of school!"

Buchanan turned ghastly pale, and shaking as with a sudden
palsy he had called his carriage and returned to the White
House, where for hours afterward he had been forced to listen
to delirious congratulations from his Southern supporters —
congratulations inspired by his refusal to take up arms to prevent the step.

By February social gatherings had been almost suspended.
Strange men were filling the capital, men from the West, uncouth in appearance, rough in dress, earnest in manner. Among
them were place hunters and antislavery politicians, conserva-

tive ex-Whigs and rabid abolitionists, old hands and newcomers to the intricacies of wire-pulling, high-minded gentlemen and time-serving scoundrels. The city was periodically swept by panic at rumors of an imminent attack. It was said that the Confederates planned to seize the city before Lincoln could be inaugurated. There was also reported a plot to kidnap President Buchanan, spirit him to some place of safekeeping, and install Breckinridge as his successor, and that Breckinridge would at once recognize the Confederate States of America as sovereign and independent. After Texas left the Union, a rumor spread that the cutthroat frontiersman, Ben McCulloch, was encamped in nearby Virginia with five hundred of his Texas raiders, prepared to dash into Washington on March 4, murder Lincoln in the inaugural parade, and take over the capital. McCulloch was said to be flitting in and out of the city, hiding by day in the Gwin mansion; and it was even reported that rough Ben was romantically smitten with Lucy Gwin.

The linking of Gwin's name with that of McCulloch — an Indian fighter who was believed to be capable of any atrocity — intensified the unpleasantness of the senator's position. Seward felt it was no longer safe for them to meet outside the Senate chamber, and an unobtrusive channel of communication was opened with the help of their mutual friend, Samuel Ward. On February 15, Ward renewed the lease on his house at 258 F Street, next door to Seward's home. Hospitable Sam Ward's visitors included men of all shades of political opinion, and no special notice would be taken of anybody's dropping in there. Notes began to flow from 258 F Street to the house next door. On Sunday, February 17, Seward received the following, written in Sam's hasty script:

Hon. W. M. Seward

Dr. Gwin dines alone with me today at five and thought that, if not elsewhere engaged, you might find it a relief from the cares and questions to join us, which I would esteem a great pleasure as well as a high honor.

There will be no other guest.

Yours with great respect
SAM[1] WARD

There was nothing to compromise a statesman in accepting such an invitation, and the indication that there would be "no other guest" meant that the conversation could be uninhibited. Under this innocuous cover, other meetings took place between Gwin and Seward. To further the appearance of mere sociability, Ward forwarded chatty messages of his own, sometimes accompanied by a gift. Sending along a case of wine, he pointedly described it as guaranteed to induce "pacific inspirations. . . . Its soothing influence upon our friend Dr. Gwin in some of his most irascible moods sustains this theory. . . . I wish I had a shipload of it to send to Montgomery."

As February waned and Lincoln neared the capital, rumors of assassination plots multiplied. In New York the President-elect received a serious warning, and at about the same time General Scott in Washington got wind of a plot to kill Lincoln as he passed through Baltimore, a changeover point between two railroads, where the cars were drawn slowly through the streets by horses from one terminus to the other. Seward sent his son, Frederick, to intercept Lincoln at Philadelphia; and since this warning tallied with the one received at New York, Lincoln agreed to push on to Washington in secrecy. Frederick Seward carried back word of this change of plans to his father.

The capital swarmed with Confederate spies, and Seward was apprehensive. Getting Lincoln safely from the railroad station to his hotel presented a problem, and the nervous Seward hit upon an expedient which seemed to answer. This was to borrow Senator Gwin's carriage and bring the President-elect to the hotel in that. Dr. Gwin's equipage was well known in Washington; no Southern malcontent would cast a suspicious glance at that smart turnout. Seward appealed to Gwin, who himself dreaded some desperate act, and the carriage was turned over at once.

At 6:30 A.M. on February 23, the night train from Baltimore pulled into Washington station, and a lanky passenger, supposedly an invalid, who had made the trip in a curtained berth, shuffled down the steps of the car between two guards — one of them Ward Hill Lamon, six-footer from Springfield and future marshal of the District of Columbia, and the other Allan Pinkerton, the detective, who was traveling incognito as Mr. Allan. On hand to greet the shawl-wrapped "invalid" was Elihu B. Washburne, Congressman from Illinois. The four bustled into the Gwin carriage, and without drawing the least attention from anyone were driven to Willard's Hotel, where Seward was waiting.*

---

* Authority for this episode is Gwin, and the probabilities favor its acceptance as true, because of the circumstances under which he revealed it — at a time when his motive was to prove his loyalty to the government, and when Seward, both as a man and as Secretary of State, would have had an interest in exposing its falsity, had it been untrue. Seward never did contradict the story. The men participating in Lincoln's reception at the station set down their own accounts years later, when their memories inevitably were more or less blurred. In some respect these accounts are contradictory; although one point in which all concur is the intense excitement under which they were laboring. Lamon, for instance, failed to recognize Washburne at the station when the latter popped out from behind a pillar, although the two knew each other in Illinois. Naturally Seward had sent no advance word of his ruse, but had merely provided a waiting carriage. The loan of the carriage under such dramatic circumstances was precisely the sort of thing that would stick in Gwin's memory; while the significance of the action, showing the complete trust Seward placed in Gwin's discretion and loyalty, is obvious.

Chapter V

THE INAUGURATION WAS nine days off. Gwin's term as senator had nine more days to run. Already his successor was in town: a Douglas Democrat named James A. McDougall (not the "I, John McDougal," we have met before, but a politician whose capacity for whiskey was almost as spacious), and Mrs. Gwin was in the melancholy midst of packing. She had disposed of their wine cellar and was letting go at a fraction of their cost the sumptuous furnishings of their great house. It was dismally clear that the Gwins contemplated a long absence from the city. About his plans, however, the senator was reticent; he was still a public official, he would say when quizzed, and change the subject. Daily in the Senate he encountered the man who had eulogized Broderick — Edward D. Baker — a close confidant of Lincoln. The auguries for Senator Gwin were not propitious.

Some time before March 4 (the exact date is uncertain), Gwin was involved in another devious errand on behalf of Seward. The latter, prompted by motives which perhaps only his devious nature could divine and may not have been entirely clear even to himself, developed a professed reluctance to enter the cabinet. He had experienced previous hesitations. While Lincoln's offer of the Secretaryship of State was still pending, Seward had been thinking of retiring from public life altogether. His disappointment at not having been elected in Lincoln's stead was keen, although to his credit he never allowed this to make him resentful. But he liked to be wooed, and although he had convinced himself that he would be the policy-maker of the new administration, still, the President-elect was an unknown quantity, untested and hence uncertain; he might be capable of springing surprises, and Seward did not like to be disagreeably surprised. There was also the question of rivalry inside the cabinet; the "war party" was strong, and many of its aims Seward opposed, while the changes which the nation was undergoing made the nature and gravity of the opposition he would face difficult to assess.

Whatever his reasons, shortly before the inauguration Seward made his doubts known to Lincoln, who received the information noncommittally.

Coincidentally, however, Seward made an appeal to Gwin, which was so extraordinary the doctor was startled. Seward asked him — a "lame duck" Democrat about to leave office, well known for his Southern connections — to go to Lincoln and impress upon the President-elect the soundness of Seward's view of the secession crisis, and the urgency, if war were to be averted, of Seward's becoming Secretary of State.

Gwin objected that he doubted that Lincoln would even see him, let alone listen to his advice; but Seward was sure he could arrange an interview through Lamon. Gwin alluded to his own ticklish position; he could scarcely afford to be seen hob-nobbing with the Republican President. Seward guaranteed secrecy. Gwin sincerely believed that the presence in the cabinet of a moderate like Seward was necessary to check the radicals, and he was willing to do anything that would head off a bloody conflict. Therefore he agreed to meet Lincoln.

The meeting took place in the newly finished President's room at the Capitol. Vice President-elect Hannibal Hamlin was present throughout, but did not participate in the conversation, which was almost wholly one-sided. Gwin spoke for nearly an hour, stating why he believed Seward should be retained, and Lincoln listened attentively. At the close the President-elect expressed himself as gratified that the talk had taken place; and in the Senate the next day, Seward told Gwin that he definitely would become Secretary of State.*

2

The question of peace or war was still unresolved, although the Montgomery government had appointed three commissioners to go to Washington and negotiate the surrender of the forts and other federal property in the seceded states. On March 3 the first of these commissioners, Martin J. Crawford of Georgia, reached Washington, and attempted to obtain an interview at once with the prospective Secretary of State. This ran counter to Seward's policy of dodging definite commitments. "Cheerfulness and hope are now the needful watchwords," he had written to Thurlow Weed; and repeatedly he told friends, "I must gain time." Continuing to play for delay, he made use of Gwin again in fending off the importunities of the Confederacy's commissioners.

March 3 was a Sunday, and the Senate remained in session all day winding up its affairs. Spokesmen for the contending factions exchanged final taunts; Andrew Johnson of Tennessee denounced secession as unadulterated treason, and retiring Senator Lane of Oregon defended it as the South's only recourse in the face of Northern tyranny. Seward was able to ignore the inconvenient presence of Crawford in the city that day.

Monday, March 4, dawned with rain, gusty and raw. Under tight security precautions Abraham Lincoln took the oath as

---

* Authority for this episode is Gwin's *Memoirs*. There is no corroborating evidence, but since the story was told by Gwin more than once, Hannibal Hamlin, an abolitionist and no friend of any Southern sympathizer, could have denied it had it been false. The *démarche* fits in with Seward's character and known last-minute hesitations. Lincoln's caution in consulting with a man of Gwin's connections is indicated by his having Hamlin present as a witness.

President, and was introduced by Senator Baker to the crowd spread out before the steps of the Capitol. As the President read his speech, above him towered the columns chiseled by Broderick's father. That day Dr. Gwin became an ex-senator. He did not participate in the ceremonies at the Capitol. That afternoon Samuel Ward found him in his study, discussing the situation with Senator Hunter of Virginia. Ward had brought a copy of the inaugural speech, which neither Gwin nor Hunter had read, and they agreed that it was about what had been expected, although ambiguously phrased.

During the discussion an acquaintance walked in, fresh from Montgomery, and Gwin was relieved to learn that his letter to Jefferson Davis had been received and read. Gwin expressed his opinion that the secession movement had about reached its limit. Virginia, at any rate, he was sure would not "go out."

Ward mentioned Seward's quandary in respect to the Confederate emissary, Crawford, with whom Ward himself had spoken, and whose colleagues, John Forsyth of Alabama and A. B. Roman of Louisiana, were due in the city at any moment. Hunter and Gwin suggested that the best course for Seward would be to refer the matter of their reception to the Senate; they estimated that he could count on Democratic votes to sustain him in that case. Ward said that Crawford had made clear that the commissioners must be received promptly, or it would be impossible to control the war fever in the South, and that Sumter and Pickens surely would be attacked.

Already Gwin had developed suspicions about the policy the government would adopt. When Lincoln, just before the inauguration, announced his cabinet officially, and included Chase, the leader of the "war radicals," as Secretary of the Treasury, Gwin had feared that this indicated a yielding to Chase's belligerent supporters; and he had tried to protect himself and to alert his friends at Montgomery by sending a telegram expressing this fear. The draft of this telegram he had

submitted to Seward, by means of Sam Ward, to be checked for
accuracy. Seward had changed the wording to alter the meaning into an assurance that *in spite of* Chase's inclusion, the government's policy would be one of peace. Believing that Seward
was better informed than himself, Gwin had authorized Ward
to file the message as amended; and ever since then he had
been uneasy.

Now, with Seward installed, Gwin was still apprehensive,
and he requested Ward to arrange another unobtrusive meeting with the secretary. On the evening of March 4, therefore,
Ward wrote out a summary of the views expressed by Hunter
and Gwin that afternoon, and sent it to his next-door neighbor
with the following scribble:

> Dr. G. desires to see you and begs you will be kind enough to
> send me word as early as you please tomorrow at what hour it
> will be convenient for you to meet him at 258.

Before that meeting, Gwin himself interviewed the Southern
commissioners, and when he joined Seward (presumably on
March 5) he was able to inform the secretary of their demands
in detail. They insisted that Seward receive them at once, he
reported, and they warned that refusal to receive them would
precipitate war.

Seward sparred for time, citing the confusion inseparable
from moving into office and the horde of job hunters who must
be placated. He did not repulse the commissioners outright;
but he was not wholly frank with Gwin. Now that he was
Secretary of State, he was bound to be more circumspect.

It happened that the commissioners also were playing a waiting game, hoping to give the Confederacy time to fortify itself
against an expected attack. They did insist upon being received by Seward immediately; but once they had been recognized, they would be willing to let the negotiations drag along.
Recognition was the all-important step, and they believed they

could trick Seward into it; privately they sneered at him for
his gullibility. Seward, however, who was quite as wily,
adroitly eluded their trap.

In all this Gwin was an intermediary, accepting a role distasteful to him and fraught with grave risks. Both sides were
confiding in him, but neither trusted him wholly; at any moment it might suit the purposes of either party to repudiate him
— and "communication with the enemy" could be a serious
matter, with Washington full of rumors. True, Lincoln had
not been assassinated, and Ben McCulloch had never been
closer to the Capitol than Arkansas, but public toleration was
wearing thin and the door to some compromise of the quarrel
was rapidly closing. Yet as long as it remained even ajar, Gwin
was reluctant to give up all attempt to stave off catastrophe.
He hoped that Seward's peaceful intentions would be imple-
mented; but he watched anxiously for the first sign that the administration was swinging toward a tougher attitude.

The commissioners from Montgomery kept up the pressure
upon Seward. On March 8, Crawford wrote to the Confederate
Secretary of State, Toombs, in language scarcely veiled, that
"a late distinguished senator of the United States" had consented to carry the commissioners' ultimatum to Seward. This
was in the form of a memorandum setting forth the terms on
which the commissioners would remain in Washington. These
included the calling of a twenty-day truce, during which neither side would make any military move, while negotiations for
a permanent settlement were under way. Seward was requested
to initial this memorandum and return it in token of acceptance.

The paper was entrusted to Gwin, with the oral addition
that in the event of rejection, the South stood "prepared to
accept war." Gwin made an appointment to see Seward at the
secretary's home on the morning of March 8. He called, and
was told by the servant that the secretary had suffered an overnight attack of lumbago, and had been ordered to bed by his
doctor, and forbidden visitors.

Gwin was a medical man, and he detected something fishy about this sudden diplomatic illness. Intuitively he sensed that Seward had reneged upon the appointment, without wishing to say so, and was in this way giving him a hint of an impending change in the administration's attitude. If this were so, Washington had become untenable for him; he must break off the dangerous game and look to his own safety. Returning home, he hastily packed and that same day left the city. The next month he would spend in the South, setting his affairs in order and studying the chances of the Confederacy's success in a war with the United States.

Chapter VI

SHORTLY AFTER LINCOLN'S inauguration, Gwin had paid a call on ex-President Buchanan, who was leaving Washington that day. He found his old friend disconsolate, and noted the sadness with which Buchanan remarked that Gwin was the only senator who had come to see him since he had left the Presidency. Buchanan wondered whether he would be able to reach Wheatland, his home in Pennsylvania, without being lynched, and Gwin had come away mentally contrasting the fate of the wavering, infirm, irresolute Buchanan with that of Andrew Jackson. Years later he would put down his thoughts on that day:

> Mr. Buchanan, abandoned by his most cherished friends, left Washington in gloomy despair. Both factions heaped curses upon his head, as the man who, from want of firmness of character and stability of purpose, was responsible for the impending conflict. He went to Wheatland . . . a hopeless, broken-hearted man, and passed forever from the public gaze.
>
> How different was Jackson's retirement from the Presidency! He remained for years afterwards a colossus in the political world, and his party bowed before him in reverence. Many a pilgrimage was made to the Hermitage by the most distinguished men of the country; and up to the last he enjoyed the obedience and admiration of his party and personal friends. Buchanan's name might well be blotted out from history; while Jackson's would adorn the annals of any nation. The one will pass away and be forgotten; the other will live on and be imperishable.

His own fate doubtless also preoccupied the doctor's thoughts as he came away from that sorrowful good-bye to the last Democratic President Washington would see for two decades. Gwin was only fifty-five, energetic and hearty. He had been in public service for thirty years, and had years of life in him still. He believed that he had served his state and his nation well. He was proud of the United States; but he loved the South, where his roots lay, although its leaders had taken a course which he deplored. Thus his loyalties still tugged at him as he headed into the Southern states in search of a guide to his own future actions.

Going south presented no difficulties at that date. One took the steamboat down the Potomac to Acquia Landing and boarded the "steam cars" there for Norfolk, Richmond, and points beyond. The trains ran regularly (the railroads were owned mainly by Northern stockholders, though the trainmen were Southern), and the mails and other public services still functioned normally.

Gwin could have noted the bellicose crowds collected at each station, where young men strutted and old men spouted. There were hurrahs for Jeff Davis and jeers for the pusillanimous Yankees. Everywhere — in the Carolinas, Georgia, Alabama, Mississippi — the people seemed eager for a fight. These were Gwin's own people, whom he comprehended; and in spite of much silly bragging, he felt that they seriously intended to make good their claim to independence. Everywhere he was received with consideration, but he avoided making commitments, and one month after leaving Washington he returned, his mind now made up. He had decided to remain — at least for the time being — neutral.

On April 10 he discussed the impressions gained on his trip with another prominent Democrat, Edwin M. Stanton, who had been Attorney General during the closing weeks of the Buchanan administration. Gwin and Stanton had met in Cali-

fornia, where the latter had been sent by Attorney General
Black to unsnarl land claims. This task Stanton had carried
out with a ruthlessness that had earned him a multitude of enemies. Later, as White House intimates, the two men had
come to know each other better, although there was not much
compatibility between them.

After the talk with Gwin, Stanton wrote to Buchanan:

> Doctor Gwin has just returned from Mississippi. He speaks
> with great confidence of the stability and power of the Con-
> federacy, and evidently sympathizes strongly with them. . . .
> Every day impresses stronger convictions upon the public mind
> that armed collision will soon take place.

On April 12 Confederate guns began to blast Fort Sumter,
and Stanton dashed off another note to the ex-President:

> The impression is held by many . . . that in less than thirty
> days [Jefferson] Davis will be in possession of Washington.

The war which Seward and Gwin had striven to circumvent
had begun, and there could be no neutrality now.

2

In both the North and the South, the attack on Sumter
lighted fires of patriotism. Lincoln called for seventy-five thousand troops to suppress rebellion and convoked Congress in
special session. Virginia seceded, followed by Arkansas and
North Carolina, with Gwin's native Tennessee, although divided in allegiance, allying itself to the Confederacy.

On April 19 the first troops responding to Lincoln's call, the
Sixth Massachusetts Regiment, were attacked by a mob in
Baltimore and fought their way clear with the loss of several
men. Thereafter for ten days the capital was isolated from the

rest of the country, and its seizure by surrounding Confederates was hourly expected.

During this tumult Dr. Gwin remained inaccessible in his home. As more soldiers from the North arrived over the hastily restored rail lines, the panic subsided; and about the first of May, Gwin decided that it would be safe for him to make a quiet exit. Going to New York, he embarked for Panama on his way back to California.

The reasons for his going west can only be surmised. He left his family — his wife, two daughters, and seventeen-year-old son — in Washington, preparing to depart. They would not say where they intended to go, but already they felt like aliens in a strange land.

About one month after Sumter, Mrs. Philip Phillips, wife of a former Congressman from Alabama, writing to Mrs. Clement Clay, Junior, described the altered capital: "Despair . . . broken hearts . . . ruined fortunes . . . the sobs of women, and sighs of men. . . ." On rambled this tearful lament:

> I am still in this *horrible city* . . . but distracted as I am at the idea of being forced to remain, we feel the hard necessity of keeping quiet. . . . For days I saw nothing but despairing women leaving suddenly, their husbands having resigned and sacrificed their all for their beloved States. You would not know our beautiful capital, desecrated, disgraced with Lincoln's low soldiery. . . . The Gwins are the only ones left of our intimates, and Mrs. G. is packed up ready to leave. Poor thing! Her eyes are never without tears.

Mary Gwin had reason to weep. Her former kingdom was now an armed camp; her friends were scattered, and their homes were put to ignoble uses. "There are 30,000 troops here," wrote Mrs. Clay's informant. "Think of it! They go about the Avenue insulting women and taking property without paying for it. . . . Such are the men waged to subjugate us of the South."

Mary Gwin would have to join the dismal exodus; but for a while she tarried, and the capital speculated why. The Gwin plantation near Vicksburg, in Mississippi, had usually been considered the family seat, where the senator expected to retire and where he had accumulated his papers and documentary library. With the way still open to the South, why, it was wondered, did Mary Gwin linger in Washington, and why had the doctor himself gone west?

A clue to his motive may perhaps be contained in a letter Gwin had written to two friends in Los Angeles on February 2, 1861, just one month before he was cast adrift by Lincoln's inauguration. In the midst of legislative news, the senator had interpolated: "Everything seems going to ruins on this side of the mountains. You ought to thank God your destiny is cast in the favored country where you live." In California the situation was still fluid, and it may be that he wished to look over conditions there before deciding where to dispose his family. His career as a politician was finished, at least for a long while to come; that much seemed sure. No matter what might be the outcome of the fighting, the nation would never be restored to what it had been. He had served California well and was proud of his record; right up to the last feverish weeks, he had been watchful of the state's interests.

An irony was that one of Gwin's notable contributions to California's progress would be used against him in the near future. That was the pony express. During the encounter with Broderick in 1859, the latter had taken credit for this dramatic speeding up of communication between East and West; and Gwin had pointed out in reply that the credit lay quite elsewhere. The pony express operated between St. Joseph, Missouri, and San Francisco, and it had been in collaboration with Missouri's senators that Gwin had prepared the bill underwriting the service. He had piloted it through the Post Office Committee, of which he was a member, in the last days of the session. In the rush toward adjournment, the bill seemed to stand little chance of passage, if it were to rely on Democratic votes alone; the Southern bloc disliked the choice of the central route, and were opposed to the expenditure on principle. Gwin therefore had turned the bill over to Broderick, rather than see it die, counting upon his rival's friends among the Republicans to push it to passage in the brief time remaining. Broderick had presented the report and the bill was passed, but Gwin always considered the pony express one of his most valuable achievements. As it turned out, the pony express would play a vital part in holding California in the Union by keeping Washington informed more speedily of critical developments in the West.

Gwin had never withdrawn from business entirely. In this respect he had violated the code of the true Southern gentleman, who would not deign to sully his hands with commercial enterprise. The doctor had irons in the fire in both the South and the West, and quite probably it was partly for the purpose of settling his business affairs in California that he returned to San Francisco in June, 1961. Although he went into seclusion in his home on Jackson Street, and made no public statement, his reappearance set off furious speculation as to his objective, especially among Northern radicals, who were suspicious of his every move.

3

In California, a struggle was in progress to hold the state in the Union, and to many observers the outcome seemed doubtful. The state government was composed of Democrats, some of whom were frankly disloyal. There were schemes afoot to proclaim the state independent, or to attach it boldly to the Confederacy. While Gwin was touring the seceded states, a crisis over alienation of the military establishment in the Pacific area had gravely alarmed Union supporters.

On April 9, Albert Sidney Johnston had resigned from the United States Army. But until his resignation could be acted upon at Washington he remained in command. The War Department, meanwhile, had taken fright, and even before the Sumter attack, General Edwin V. Sumner, a tough cavalry officer, had been ordered to proceed to San Francisco with all haste and relieve General Johnston. Sumner, told to observe utmost caution so as to elude the Confederate spies who swarmed in both the capital and New York City, was rowed down New York harbor at night to board the steamship for Panama in the lower bay. The secret orders he carried he was instructed not to open until he was well at sea on the Pacific side.

It was afternoon on April 24 when Sumner stepped ashore at San Francisco, and special editions of the newspapers were just then appearing on the streets with the first word of the bombardment of Sumter. The dispatch had been transmitted across the continent with what was regarded as phenomenal speed — in twelve days. ("Per telegraph to St. Louis; thence by telegraph to Fort Kearney; thence by pony express to Fort Churchill; thence by telegraph to San Francisco.")

General Sumner went directly to the Presidio and relieved Johnston that afternoon. The latter yielded without remonstrance, and left for Los Angeles; Southern sentiment was strong in that region of the state. Sumner set to work energetically, called in his widely dispersed forces, and, to the best of his ability, placed the state in a posture of defense. It appeared that he had arrived none too soon, for even while he was taking his measures the Bear Flag of the short-lived California Republic of 1846 was hoisted in several inland towns and Southern sympathizers drilled openly. Public opinion was divided; friends of the North were more numerous but sympathizers with the South were more aggressive. The Knights of the Golden Circle, a secret organization of Confederate agents, was understood to be spreading throughout the state; and about the time Gwin reached San Francisco, Johnston rode away from Los Angeles with nearly two hundred fighting men, bound for Dixie. This expedition was intercepted at Fort Yuma by United States dragoons, and all except about thirty were turned back; the remainder, including Johnston, succeeded in eluding the regulars, and upon reaching Richmond, Johnston was commissioned a major general in the Confederate army.

Gwin saw the unfolding of this episode and felt the tension around him. There is no indication that he joined in any of the abortive plots. His visitors were few, mainly political associates, but since these were Democrats they aroused the suspicions of observant unionists. Calhoun Benham called, and he had never concealed his Southern leanings. Some of those watching the doctor's movements were convinced that Gwin was biding his time, waiting for California to swing one way or another — into the Confederacy or into independence — but he gave no sign. His discretion appears to have been complete.

In July the rout of the Northern army at Bull Run sent a shiver of dread through California's unionists, as it did through the North generally, and pro-Southern belligerency flared up afresh. The moment seemed ripe for a decisive, disrupting blow; and it was at this precise moment — perhaps the moment for which he had been distined — that Senator Baker loomed up as an unexpected, powerful rallier of Northern confidence. A summons that aroused the nation from the despair into which Bull Run had plunged the most sanguine came from the first Republican elected to Congress on the Pacific coast.

❖

4

At the outbreak of hostilities, Baker had been commissioned
a colonel to raise a regiment of California volunteers. (With
modesty rare in those hectic days, he had declined Lincoln's
offer of the rank of brigadier general on the grounds of inexperience.) Since then he had shuttled between the drill camp
and the Senate chamber, where he spoke vigorously in favor of
giving the President all the men, the money, and the power
needed to crush the rebellion. Lincoln, Baker insisted to his
colleagues and indirectly to the nation, had asked for four
hundred million dollars, but the loyal men in Congress proposed to give him five hundred million:

> He has asked for four hundred thousand men; we propose to
> give him half a million. And for my part, if, as I do not appre-
> hend, the emergency should be still greater, I will cheerfully add
> a cipher to either of these figures. . . . Whether the peace shall
> be conquered at Richmond, or Montgomery, or New Orleans, or
> in the wilds of Texas, I do not presume to say; but I do know
> that the determined, aggregated power of the whole people of
> this country — of its treasure, of its arms, of its blood, of its en-
> thusiasm — kindled, concentrated, poured out in one mass of
> living valor upon any foe — will conquer!

At the same time the senator warned the North to expect
temporary setbacks. "I am not quite confident," he said with
effective understatement, "that we shall overrun the South without severe trials."

That prediction was fulfilled at Bull Run on July 21, and the
demoralizing reverse spread trepidation throughout the North
— nowhere more than among the friends of the Union in California. Sedition was being uttered in the streets when Baker's
forthright words rallied the Northern element in that state. It
was on August 3, at the very nadir of the depression caused by
the military disaster, that the senator made his great appeal.

Senator Breckinridge of Kentucky, the former Vice-President and recent candidate for the White House, provoked Baker's outburst. Breckinridge was stubbornly opposing all military measures, dwelling upon the futility of bloodshed, picturing the entire nation as wearied by the struggle and longing for peace. He assailed the use of military courts in areas occupied by federal troops, a practice despotic and unconstitutional, he said. The whole tenor of his speech was defeatist, and Breckinridge exerted great influence upon Democrats in the North. Many of these were lukewarm for the war anyway, and as the Kentuckian droned on in accents of gloom, the leaders of Lincoln's party in the Senate became increasingly alarmed. A hurried call was sent for Baker. He was with his regiment nearby, and when told that not a minute was to be lost, he sprang on his horse and galloped back to the Capitol. Running up the steps, he strode, booted and spurred, into the Senate chamber, in his dusty uniform. Unbuckling his sword, he laid it across his desk, then sat down and listened to Breckinridge inveighing against "unconstitutional acts of war." From time to time his face flushed, and he shifted restlessly in his seat. When Breckinridge concluded, he arose to reply.

Beginning courteously ("for nobody is more courteous and more gentlemanly than the senator from Kentucky"), he asked Breckinridge to specify which "unconstitutional acts of war" he proposed to set aside, but drew only evasive, petulant replies. At that Baker opened up:

> The honorable senator says there is a state of war. What then? There *is* a state of war. None the less war because it is urged from the other side; not the less war because it is unjust; not the less war because it is a war of insurrection and rebellion. It is still war. What then? Shall we carry that war on? Is it his duty as a senator to carry it on? If so, how? By armies, under command; by military organization and authority, advancing to suppress insurrection and rebellion. Is that wrong? Is that unconstitu-

tional? Are we not bound to do with whomever levies war
against us as we would do if he was a foreigner? There is no
distinction as to carrying on war: we carry on war against an
advancing army just the same whether it be from Russia or from
South Carolina.

Will the honorable senator tell us that it is our duty to stand
here, within fifteen miles of an enemy seeking to advance upon us
every hour, and talk about nice questions of constitutional construction as to whether it is war or merely insurrection? No, sir.
It is our duty to advance, if we can; to suppress insurrection; to
put down rebellion; to scatter the enemy; and when we have
done so, to preserve the liberty, lives, and property of the people
of the country, by just and fair regulations.

Warming to his theme, he pointed out:

The Constitution does not provide that spies should be hung.
Is it unconstitutional to hang a spy? The Constitution does not
provide for the exchange of prisoners; indeed, the Constitution
does not provide that a prisoner may be taken at all; yet his
captivity is perfectly just and constitutional. . . . Bayonets at
best are illogical arguments; but, sir, it is part of the law of war.
You cannot carry in the rear of your army your courts; you cannot organize juries; you cannot have trials according to the forms
and ceremonial of the common law amid the clangor of arms.
I ask the senator from Kentucky again, respectfully — is that unconstitutional?

By now Breckinridge sat glowering in silence. Baker swept
on:

Now, a few words as to the senator's predictions. The senator
of Kentucky stands up here in a manly way, in opposition to what
he sees is the overwhelming sentiment of the Senate, and utters
reproof, malediction, and prediction combined. Well, sir, it is
not every prediction that is prophecy. I confess, Mr. President,
that I would not have predicted three weeks ago the disasters
which have overtaken our arms; and I do not think (if I were
to predict now) that six months hence the senator will indulge
in the same tone of prediction which is his favorite key now.

I would ask him, what would you have us do now — a Confederate army within twenty miles of us, advancing, or threatening to advance, to overwhelm your government, to shake the pillars of the Union, to bring it about your head, if you stay here, in ruins? Are we to stop and talk about an uprising sentiment in the North against war? Are we to predict evil and retire from what we predict? Is it not the manly part to go on as we have begun, to raise money, and levy armies, to organize them, to prepare to advance? . . . Can we do anything more? To talk to us about stopping is idle; we will never stop. Will the senator yield to rebellion? Will he shrink from armed insurrection? Shall we send a flag of truce? *What would he have?* These speeches of his, sown broadcast over the land, what clear, distinct meaning have they? Are they not intended for disorganization in our very midst? Are they not intended to dull our weapons? Are they not intended to destroy our zeal? Are they not intended to animate our enemies? Sir, are they not words of brilliant, polished treason — even in the very Capitol of the nation?

The crowded galleries burst into applause, and Baker stood immobile in his uniform, his face alight, until order had been restored. Then his words tumbled out with impassioned earnestness:

What would have been thought if, in another capitol, in another republic, in a yet more martial age, a senator as grave, yet not more eloquent or dignified than the senator from Kentucky, had risen in his place, surrounded by all the illustrations of Roman glory, and declared that advancing Hannibal was just, and that Carthage ought to be dealt with in terms of peace? What would have been thought if, after the battle of Cannae, a senator there had risen in his place and denounced every levy of the Roman people, every expenditure of its treasure, and every appeal to the old recollections and the old glories?

Impetuously Senator Fessenden of Maine cried out, "He would have been hurled from the Tarpeian Rock!" — Rome's punishment for traitors. Baker took up the words:

Sir, a senator tells me that he would have been hurled from the Tarpeian Rock! It is a grand commentary upon the American Constitution that we permit these words to be uttered by the senator from Kentucky. I ask the senator to recollect what, save to send aid and comfort to the enemy, do these predictions of his amount to? Every word thus uttered falls as a note of inspiration upon every Confederate ear. Every sound thus uttered is a word (and, falling from his lips, a mighty word) of kindling and triumph to a foe that determines to advance. For me, I have no such words to utter. For me, amid temporary defeat, disaster, disgrace, it seems that my duty calls me to utter another word — and that word is, bold, sudden, forward, determined war!

In vain the chairman appealed for order. Over the applause Baker went on:

I do not consider whether it is subjugation or not. It is compulsory obedience, not to my will, not to yours, sir, not to the will of any one man; but compulsory obedience to the Constitution of the whole country. . . . There is not a man among us who dreams of causing any man in the South to submit to any rule, either as to life, liberty, or property, that we ourselves do not willingly agree to. Did he ever think of that? Subjugation for what? When we subjugate South Carolina what shall we do? We shall compel its obedience to the Constitution of the United States, that is all. Why play upon words? If it be slavery that men should obey the Constitution their fathers fought for, let it be so. If it be freedom, it is freedom equally for them and for us. We propose to subjugate rebellion into loyalty. We propose to subjugate insurrection into peace. We propose to subjugate Confederate anarchy into Constitutional Union liberty. The senator knows that is all we propose. When the Confederate armies are scattered; when their leaders are banished from power; when the people return to a late, repentant sense of the wrong they have done to a government they never felt but in benignancy and blessing, then the Constitution made for all will be felt by all. Is that subjugation? To restore what was, as it was, for the benefit of the whole country and of the whole human race? That is all we desire and all we can have. . . .

Sir, while I am predicting, I will tell you another thing. This threat about money and men amounts to nothing. . . . I tell the senator that his predictions about the dread of our people as for loss of blood and treasure provoking them to disloyalty, are false in sentiment, false in fact, and false in loyalty. Five hundred million dollars? What then? Five hundred thousand men? What then? It is not a question of men or of money. All the money, all the men, are, in our judgment, well bestowed in such a cause. . . .

Sir, how can we retreat? Sir, how can we make peace? Who shall treat? What commissioners? Who would go? Upon what terms? Where is to be your boundary line? Where the end of the principles we shall have to give up? What will become of constitutional government? What will become of public liberty? What of past glories? What of future hopes? Shall we sink into the insignificance of the grave — a degraded, defeated, emasculated people, frightened by the results of one battle, and scared at the visions raised upon this floor by the imagination of the senator from Kentucky? No, sir; a thousand times, no, sir! We will rally — if indeed our words be necessary — we will rally the people, the loyal people, of the whole country. We will pour forth their treasure, their money, their men, without stint, without measure. The most peaceable man in this body may stamp his foot upon this Senate chamber floor, as of old a warrior and a senator did, and from that single tramp there will spring forth armed legions!

Shall one battle determine the fate of empire — or a dozen? The loss of one thousand men or twenty thousand, or one hundred million dollars or five hundred million dollars? In a year's peace, in ten years, at most, of peaceful progress, we can restore them all. There will be some graves reeking with blood, watered by the tears of affection. There will be some privation; there will be some loss of luxury; there will be somewhat more need of labor to procure the necessaries of life. When that is said, all is said. If we have the country, the whole country, the Union, the Constitution, free government — with these there will return all the blessings of well-ordered civilization; the path of the country will be a career of greatness and of glory such as in the olden time our fathers saw in the dim visions of years to come, and such as would have been ours now, today, if it had not been for the treason for which the senator too often seeks to apologize!

This speech, and another, by Senator Andrew Johnson of Tennessee, about finished Breckinridge; within a short while he resigned and joined the Confederate army. But they revitalized the fighting spirit of the North, and Baker's put a final check to the seditious schemes of the disaffected on the Pacific coast.

When Gwin read Senator Baker's words, broadcast over California, he understood that the tide had turned definitely, so far as the West was concerned. Had he entertained a design — as he had a decade before — of being on hand to help cradle a new Republic of the Pacific, as he had helped to cradle the state in 1849 — his acumen would have told him that the moment had gone by. But there is no indication that he harbored such a design or entertained such a hope.

So strongly was the Union tide running, in September the Republicans captured California's state government, and the rule of the "Chivalry" was smashed forever. Ironically, it had been Baker, the heir of Broderick, who, by laying bare the treason latent in defeatism, had delivered the lethal thrust that ended Gwin's long dominance of California.

For Baker, too, that speech marked a termination. The challenge to Breckinridge was his last appearance in the Senate. A few weeks later he was shot through the heart while leading his troops, more gallantly than expertly, in a charge at the unimportant battle of Ball's Bluff.

Chapter VII

DR. GWIN HAD been under surveillance by anxious unionists, who were stimulated to make all the more sinister surmises because of his very discretion. The fact that he stayed away from public gatherings and showed preference for neither side seemed suspicious to those who reverenced the memory of Broderick; surely this circumspection imported some secret activity, invisible to the casual eye. The doctor had not acquired a name for subtlety for nothing; his reputation made him dangerous in the eyes of Broderick's mourners. If Senator Baker could say with justice that a word spoken by Senator Breckinridge carried weight, the same might be true of ex-Senator Gwin's silences. What web of intrigue was he spinning? His mere presence at San Francisco was provocative, considering the disturbed public mood, and unionist apprehensions were the keener for being vague. Every action of "Old Gwin" was watched and guesses were made to fathom his intentions.

At Washington, meanwhile, the Secretary of State had taken upon himself the chief responsibility for combatting sedition, and on his orders, active or potential disloyalists were being arrested and confined in Fort Lafayette, a moldering fortress overlooking the Narrows in New York Harbor. A roundup of suspected Confederate agents in the capital had been launched after Bull Run, and among those netted was Rose Greenhow. Her Southern sympathies had never been concealed, yet she had remained on good terms with leading members of the Lincoln government — including Seward himself — who found her tea table attractive. Evidence was adduced to indicate that on the eve of Bull Run, Mrs. Greenhow had smuggled the battle plans of General Irwin McDowell, the Union commander, to the Confederate General Beauregard. She and her daughter were locked up in the Old Capitol prison, while the dragnet was spread for other likely "secesh" agents.

The New York *Herald*, which never, if it could avoid it, erred on the side of moderation, coupled news of Mrs. Greenhow's detention with a sensational report that Mrs. Gwin also had been arrested and was being held prisoner in her own fine mansion at Nineteenth and I streets, not far from the White House. This was startling news, if true. On August 26 the *Herald* published a circumstantially detailed dispatch from its Washington representative, averring that "a proper military guard" had been posted "to prevent any communication between her and rebel spies, who, it is supposed, have been in the habit of frequenting the house."

The cause of the arrest was recounted with thrilling effect:

> A trunk was seized at the depot . . . addressed to Mrs. Gwin. It was opened and found to contain a lot of gentlemen's shirts. Some of them were sewed together, in one of which was found a map of all our fortifications on the Virginia side of the river. This . . . resulted in the immediate arrest of Mrs. Gwin. Altogether about six persons who have called upon Mrs. Greenhough [sic], Mrs. Gwin, and the wife and daughter of Mrs. Philip Phillips have been arrested and held. They are Southerners, and from circumstantial and positive evidence against them are spies.

In the same issue, the *Herald* racily commented upon "rebels in crinoline" and "fascinating female secessionists," blaming them not only for the Bull Run disaster, but for bringing on the whole war. The government, said the *Herald* juicily, was making "astounding discoveries":

Most important are those in reference to certain distinguished female spies who have been suddenly checked in their inglorious career. Mrs. Dr. Gwin, the wife of ex-Senator Gwin of California, Mrs. Phillips, the wife of the ex-Member of Congress Phillips of Alabama, and Mrs. Greenhough, another accomplished high life secessionist, are particularly prominent among the rebels in crinoline who have thus fallen under the special attention of the War Office, and the discoveries . . . throw a flood of light upon the battle of Bull Run.

If yesterday, for example, in a trunk of Madam Gwin, there was found, carefully bestowed among a lot of innocent-looking shirts, some very useful maps and plans of all the fortifications in front of Washington, it may be safely inferred that trunk, shirts, and maps were intended for the camp of Beauregard. Nay, more, we have in this little matter a clue to the mystery of those important government maps and plans which the rebels lately left behind them in their hasty flight from Fairfax Court House on the approach of our army; and we are at liberty to guess how Beauregard was so minutely informed of this advance, and of our plan of attack upon his lines, as to be ready to meet it at every salient with overwhelming numbers. These distinguished feminine rebel Confederates and spies will explain it all.

That was not the worst charge the *Herald* laid against the women reported to be under arrest: they, the paper suggested, had brought on the war.

We are at liberty now to state, too, that these fascinating female secessionists, and others attached to the cabinet and court circles of Mr. Buchanan, were, perhaps, even more instrumental than [Secretaries] Cobb, Floyd, and Thompson [members of Buchanan's cabinet] in bringing down the late administration to the dogs, and our country to this terrible intestine war. Mrs. Gwin, Mrs. Slidell, Mrs. Cobb, Mrs. Thompson and other accomplished and charming ladies of this dominant Southern social circle, during the imbecile administration of Mr. Buchanan, held him, the government, and the destinies of the country in their delicate little hands. Nor did the first French Revolution and reign of terror

produce a circle of feminine politicians more accomplished, sa-
gacious, and industrious than those who led the poor old man of
Wheatland, bound in garlands of roses, through visions of Para-
dise, down the broad road to destruction.

Of these silken conspirators, Mrs. Gwin was by all odds the
foremost, inferred the *Herald*:

> Every class and phase of society in Washington was so deeply
> affected by the charming soirées, receptions, and fancy balls of
> these irresistible Southern ladies that the sudden transition . . .
> from all these social splendors and fascinations to the rough
> simplicity of "Honest Old Abe" and his hordes of backwoods
> office seekers, made Washington ripe for rebellion. The general
> reader will thus understand the capacities and facilities of such
> an ally as Mrs. Gwin for the work of "giving aid and comfort
> to the enemy" at this crisis. The suspension of the peculiar serv-
> ices which she and her feminine confederates in Washington
> have been rendering the enemy will, we dare say, prove a very
> serious loss to Jeff Davis and a corresponding gain to the cause
> of our government.

The electrifying accusation was picked up by California
newspapers with elaborations of their own, and Gwin was
shocked by headlines that screamed in block type: TREASON OF
MRS. GWIN! The San Francisco press had it that just as the
doctor's wife was leaving Washington, she had been stopped,
under suspicion of attempting to smuggle quinine out of the
city, for the use of the Confederate army. It was said that her
trunks had been ransacked, that no contraband drugs had
been found, but tracings of the plans of fortifications defending
the Chain Bridge and other approaches to the capital.

The frantic doctor posted eastward appeals for enlightenment; but even with the pony express in operation, the lag in
communication was long.

At New York, meanwhile, the *Herald* had been forced to
backtrack; for their account of Mrs. Gwin's arrest contained

not a shred of truth. On August 28, two days after their sensational story appeared, a brief item was published at the foot of the *Herald's* front page, under the heading: "A Note From Mrs. Senator Gwin — Not Yet in Fort Lafayette." It was a letter to the editor from the lady herself, dated, "West Point, Rose Hotel, August 27, 1861." Dignified but icy, it read:

> I was startled yesterday, by reading, as an item of intelligence in your paper, that I had been arrested in Washington City for alleged cooperation with the Southern army. I have had no aspirations, I assure you, for either a crown of martyrdom, or any such laurels as your correspondent would encircle my brow with; but have been residing very quietly, with my family, in the place from which this is dated, for the last two weeks, exclusively engaged with domestic concerns. May I ask you to contradict, etc. Yours, respectfully, Mary M. Gwin.

This much the *Herald* printed, with no apology and no overt retraction, and with the sour malice betrayed by the words "not yet" in its heading. Three days later the paper even returned to the subject, this time without naming names, and published a paragraph from Washington headed "Proofs Against Female Spies," which asserted, giving no authority for the positive statement, that "the War Department has proofs strong and sufficient against the women recently arrested to place the fact of their complicity with and aid to the rebels beyond all doubt." "Women recently arrested" presumably referred to all those previously named, without exception. In a further editorial fling at REBELLIOUS CRINOLINE — THE PETTICOAT ELEMENT IN THE WAR, still without using names, the *Herald* soliloquized:

> These fair creatures . . . evidently reposed the most unbounded confidence in the gallantry of Secretary Seward, but they should have recollected . . . that a polished manner does not always cover sincerity of speech.

The press in San Francisco did not print Mrs. Gwin's letter, but grudgingly conceded that after some delay she had been permitted to leave Washington without further molestation. This news, intensely welcome to Gwin, was confirmed by letters that shortly reached him, recounting the episode with (we may be sure) wrathful reflections upon the shameless mendacity of the Yankee press.

The government was meeting with embarrassments in its attempt to deal with "petticoat rebels." Mrs. Greenhow rattled skeletons alarmingly when she was interrogated by a board of three commissioners — all men who had been guests at her table — in surroundings that played into her hands — the ballroom of the Gwin mansion, where all present had been entertained. The house had been taken over by the provost marshal, and Rose Greenhow remarked acidly upon Yankee slovenliness, what with papers littering the stairs, trash in the fireplaces, filthy spittoons, and dust and signs of neglect everywhere. The Housekeeper of the Old School who had danced in that very ballroom two years before challenged her questioners to find out the truth about her activities. If, as they contended, she had in fact smuggled battle plans to Beauregard, from what source, she asked, could she have gotten those plans, except from somebody highly placed in the government? The commissioners shifted uneasily in their chairs at this; did not all Washington know that up to the very day of the battle, Senator Henry Wilson of Massachusetts had been a devotee of the sprightly widow? And Senator Wilson, as chairman of the Senate Military Affairs Committee, had access to War Department secrets. Taking refuge in discretion, the commissioners sent the unabashed Rose back to prison, and as soon as it could be arranged, shipped her off to the Confederacy.

So rife with rumors was the very air of the capital, Secretary Seward could hardly have been startled by a telegram received from John A. Kennedy, the agitated superintendent of police in New York City, reporting that Mrs. Gwin had moved into the New York Hotel there, and asking whether he should arrest Dr. Gwin, should the ex-senator attempt to join his wife? The New York Hotel was a hotbed of rebel sympathizers. Seward replied that the subject of Dr. Gwin's status "has not yet been decided upon." Since the question seemed to be open, Kennedy kept the hotel and its guests under strict surveillance.

2

Though Gwin's mind had been partially set at rest by assurances that his wife was not in jail, her letters brought news that caused him fresh anxiety. His daughter Lucy, he learned, and his son Willie had gone south, leaving their mother and Carrie Gwin in New York. Lucy, an ardent secessionist, was with friends in Richmond. Willie, with the bravado of a seventeen-year-old, had enlisted in a Tennessee cavalry regiment. This he had done without consulting his father, and Gwin was distressed both because of the lad's youth, and because such family support of the Southern cause might jeopardize them all. He determined to get his children out of the Confederacy, if possible.

Cautiously and discreetly, he went about preparing for departure from the West. Whatever business had brought him there, it was time to leave; but he was not aware how he stood officially. In August the State Department had issued an order that every traveler entering or leaving the country must have a passport, either United States or foreign. Gwin did not know how this rule would affect him, should he, for instance, book passage from San Francisco to New York, proceeding from one American port to another. To make sure of his position, through a friend he addressed a formal inquiry to General Sumner as to whether he would be allowed to leave San Francisco freely. Calhoun Benham, the late United States attorney, who wished to go to Washington on legal business, joined Gwin in the request for information. Sumner returned word that he knew of no reason why they should not depart. Therefore in mid-October the two men sailed aboard the steamship *Orizaba* for Panama. At San Diego, Joseph L. Brent, an old-time friend of Gwin's and prominent Los Angeles Democrat, come aboard, and the three men agreed to occupy quarters together.

By coincidence, General Sumner and his staff were also aboard the *Orizaba,* with a detachment of the Third Infantry Regiment. Sumner was being recalled to the active theater of war in Virginia. Simultaneous with the sailing of the *Orizaba* — and unknown to Gwin — a letter went overland by pony express, addressed to Secretary of State Seward, saying that "those two rank traitors," Gwin and Benham, had sailed for Panama, "with their destination 'South.'" The letter was written by A. T. Palmer, postmaster at San Francisco. A Republican appointee, he was zealous in tracking down real and fancied "sesech" plots. When the *Orizaba* was in the Gulf of Panama, Gwin, Brent, and Benham were suddenly summoned to the captain's cabin. There they faced a very angry General Sumner, who informed them curtly that they must consider themselves under arrest. They asked why, and the general replied that they were active Democrats and enemies of the government. The accused men insisted that he put his order into writing, whereupon he amplified the charge, averring that they "were about to leave the United States to engage in rebellion against the government." The general told them there would be no restriction of their movements aboard ship, but they would have to accompany him to New York.

Sumner had acted upon reports from members of his staff, who said they had been sounded out on the possibility of going over to the Confederate army. A short while after making the arrests, the general was informed by other passengers that they had observed what seemed to be books and papers being tossed into the sea from the porthole of the three men's cabin. Sumner then placed the three under guard.

Then the affair took a grotesque turn at Panama. The arrests had been made inside the territorial waters of New Granada (Colombia), and according to the New Granadan authorities, an officer of the United States Army had no power to make arrests in a foreign jurisdiction. Sumner intended to take his prisoners across the Isthmus under military escort; but this was ruled out by the New Granadans. Gwin was well known at Panama, for he had crossed the Isthmus twenty-four times, and had been received with official honors. General Herran, New Granda's minister to the United States and long-time friend of Gwin's, happened to be at Panama on his way back to Washington. With the American consul, Herran went to the governor, who, promising to defend New Granada's sovereignty, marched two hundred and fifty soldiers with two pieces of artillery to the quay, under orders to liberate Gwin and his companions the minute they set foot on shore.

General Sumner was not the man to knuckle under, and a United States warship, the *Lancaster,* being anchored in the roads, he appealed to the skipper for aid. The *Lancaster*'s captain obligingly brought his broadside to bear on the town and sent word that he would blow it to smithereens if General Sumner were interfered with.

Then Gwin, the pacificator, provided a way out of the impasse. While standing on the illegality of his arrest, he consented to accompany General Sumner across the Isthmus voluntarily, and to go with him to New York. Benham and Brent assented to this solution, and the trip was continued amicably, the honor of New Granada and the United States having been preserved intact.

*

3

In New York, Mary Gwin had grown despondent. She longed to go home to Mississippi. On October 28, while Dr. Gwin was on his way from California, his old friend, Samuel Ward, who was staying at the New York Hotel keeping watch for Seward, wrote to the secretary that Mrs. Gwin "meant to have passed the winter in New York, but finds herself lonely and uncomfortable, and would return to her Mississippi plantation, if she felt confident of reaching it. She has inquired of me whether, in case of need, I would be willing to accompany her, and I, of course, had but one answer, 'Certainly.' " The prospect was not exactly to his liking, he added, and he was broaching the matter privately in order that the secretary might "have his reply ready should I apply for a pass."

The next day Ward wrote again, saying that "Mrs. Gwin proposes going to Washington toward the end of the week" to dispose of the last of her furniture; and on November 14 he relayed word to Mrs. Frederick Seward (wife of the secretary's son) that she might buy Mrs. Gwin's piano, which had cost a thousand dollars, for three hundred. For the secretary's benefit, Ward also suggested that it might be advantageous to let Mrs. Gwin depart, since she had become thoroughly disillusioned about the Confederacy's chances and would positively help the Union cause by her pessimistic reports. Only the day before, he said, she had told a friend that she was satisfied that the condition of the South was desperate. "In such a frame of mind, convinced by her own eyes of the strength and will of the North, what better propagandist could be desired?" asked Ward.

But this plan was discarded when, on November 15, the steamer *Champion* landed Gwin, Brent, and Benham at New York. General Sumner released them on parole until he could file his report at Washington, and that morning the doctor walked in on his wife at breakfast. Sam Ward was summoned from his room in haste, and was astonished to find his friend on hand. He listened to Gwin's story gravely, and lost no time conveying it by letter and in full to Seward, stressing Gwin's assertion that he had obtained General Sumner's safe-conduct before leaving San Francisco. According to the doctor, the general had even stated that "nothing would please him more than the doctor's society, and he would do nothing to impede or molest him."

Ward reported that General Herran was preparing a protest to the State Department against the violation of New Granada's sovereignty, and both Gwin and Benham were going to insist that they be restored to liberty at the point where they had been arrested; Brent, having urgent business in New York, preferred an investigation on the spot. Ward's long letter of expostulation wound up on an intimate note:

> Dr. Gwin expressed the earnest hope that his old friend the secretary would do nothing in haste, and would not act before Gen¹. Herran should have laid before him the details of the case and the public law.

Two days later, Ward wrote to Seward:

> Mr. Kennedy spirited away Doctor Gwin and his friends last P.M. . . . Two judges of the U.S. Supreme Court offered to issue habeas corpus which might have been served before the prisoners were handed over to the marshal. But Mrs. Gwin, though in tears and distress, peremptorily declined. "The doctor," she said, "was innocent and such proceedings would injure his case."

The order to put the three men in Fort Lafayette had been given by Seward.

Chapter VIII

THE ARREST OF ex-Senator Gwin coincided with the sensational capture of two of his former Senate associates — James Mason of Virginia and John Slidell of Louisiana — as they were on their way to Europe, carring credentials as agents of the Confederate States of America. They had run the federal blockade of Southern ports on the raider *Shenandoah* as far as Havana, where they had taken passage on the British mail steamer *Trent* for England. Some distance north of Cuba, the United States ship *Jacinto*, commanded by Captain Charles Wilkes, had halted the *Trent* and had arbitrarily taken off Slidell and Mason. The action, received with cheers in such Northern centers as Boston, raised a furor in London, and a stern protest against Wilkes's high-handed, "piratical" violation of British sovereignty and the British flag was being prepared. The affair seemed about to embroil the United States in a war with Great Britain.

Gwin's arrest at the same time set tongues wagging. Had he, too, been on his way to Europe to represent the secessionists? Had he perhaps been heading secretly for Havana, there to join Slidell and Mason, when General Sumner inadvertently spoiled the game? This was an exciting supposition, but there appears to have been no evidence to support it, or to believe that Gwin was engaged in any concerted plan of cooperation with the leaders of the Confederacy, much as he felt for them as friends. An overall suspicion had become attached to his name, however, as a corollary of the popular tendency in California to associate Broderick's name with the Northern cause. If Broderick would have stood for union and freedom, ran the conclusion, then Gwin obviously must be for slavery and treason.

It certainly was unlikely that Gwin would have willingly joined John Slidell in an equivocal mission abroad, for he mistrusted the Louisianan, and considered him reckless, inept, and a menace to any cause he might embrace.

Sam Ward was not the only person who attempted to procure the release of Gwin and his companions. Calhoun Benham's brother-in-law was George D. Prentice, influential editor of the Louisville, Kentucky, *Journal*, and a "war Democrat." Upon receiving word of Benham's detention, Prentice hurried to Washington and called on Lincoln. The President knew little about the matter, and referred Prentice to Seward, who received the editor affably and invited him to tea four days running, without giving a direct answer to his appeal. On the fourth occasion, turning casually to his son, Seward said, "Fred, hand me that paper I asked you to prepare." The paper was produced. Seward signed it and passed it to Prentice, who indignantly saw it was merely a pass permitting him to interview the prisoners in Fort Lafayette — not an order for their discharge. With considerable heat, he spurned the offer, although Seward urged him to talk with them and "report their sentiments." This, Prentice retorted, he would never do; he would not become "a government spy."

Nevertheless, he did visit the men, and returning to Washington laid their case before Lincoln, including their contention that they had been arrested illegally in a foreign jurisdiction after having received General Sumner's safe-conduct. Prentice said that Gwin was ready to submit his "entire record of loyalty to the government" as proof of his good faith, and Lincoln finally agreed to release them pending a hearing.

"All right, I will set your friends free," said the President.

But he refused to put the order in writing, remarking with a twinkle, "This is a very delicate matter, and Seward will be very mad about it. But tell your friends I shall be glad to see them."

Sam Ward wrote to Seward from New York, shortly after this: "I am glad that Dr. Gwin is to have a hearing. He told me that he had felt for six months on a volcano, and knew too much but to keep clear of gunpowder."

How much Gwin knew, Seward was aware.

Released on parole to appear at Washington, Gwin, Benham, and Brent were accorded a hearing, at which General Sumner confirmed the reassurances he had given before the departure from San Francisco; he maintained, however, that he had not intended a blanket safe-conduct. No positive evidence being produced against them, the prisoners were released unconditionally.

Prentice, the prime mover in procuring their freedom, predicted that Benham, at least ("a damned babbler"), would be locked up again "in less than twenty-four hours, for he cannot hold his tongue." Benham disappointed his brother-in-law; he remained in Washington some time attending to legal business — then went south and joined the rebellion.

2

The California newspapers had followed Gwin's arrest with avid interest, and his release was not approved there. The Washington correspondent of the *Alta California* reported that while Brent's release seemed justified, "everybody believes the lenity towards the other two was misplaced. It will be a happy day when the government shall conclude to secure the persons of men known to be inimical to its existence."

Gwin called on Lincoln to thank him for his intercession,

and was received pleasantly. Apparently he did not meet
Seward face to face, although he expressed no resentment
against his old friend. Returning to New York, the doctor took
counsel with his wife as to their future course.

Willie's presence in the Rebel army worried them, and Gwin
determined to get the boy out of action, if possible. There was
Lucy, also, who must be got away from dangerous associations
at Richmond. But while the public remained inflamed over
the *Trent* affair, Gwin hesitated to head south. He lingered
at New York and watched the crisis over Mason and Slidell
develop. On November 30 Great Britain formally demanded
the release of the men, and an apology for Captain Wilkes's
"act of piracy." On both sides of the ocean chauvinists clamored for war. Lincoln's cabinet was divided on the question.
The tumult kept up alarmingly all through December, and
Gwin had reason to regard his brief sojourn in Fort Lafayette
during the peak of the excitement as providential; Sam Ward
told Seward that it was "perhaps the best luck that could have
befallen him." Two days before Christmas, Seward announced
that Slidell and Mason would be allowed to proceed to Europe,
and the tension eased; but there were other developments that
caused Gwin to move with care. One was the taking of Edwin
M. Stanton to the cabinet as Secretary of War.

This occurred in mid-January, and Sam Ward and Gwin discussed the implications of this action. Both men had known
Stanton in California, and Ward's opinion of him was less
favorable than was Gwin's. In any event, Stanton was one who
would bear watching, and Ward so advised Seward in a letter
relaying Gwin's impressions of the man:

> Doctor Gwin came into my room last night [and] spoke ad-
> miringly of Stanton's power and ability, and seemed to think his
> tenacity of purpose would be materially felt in the cabinet, and
> that he was likely to gain a great ascendancy over the President.

He spoke most kindly of the secretary [Seward], and trusted he was on good terms with the new incumbent, for *Stanton was a dangerous foe* — a sleuthhound sort of man who never lost his scent or slackened in his purpose.

This wink from one Democrat regarding a fellow Democrat was reinforced by a penetrating forecast of what would be Stanton's relations with the rest of the cabinet — "He will tomahawk them all."

By February, Gwin's plans were shaped: he would go south and retrieve his son and Lucy, while Mrs. Gwin and Carrie sailed directly to France. There was no place for the Gwins in an America torn by war, and the doctor felt that — since his country, the nation he had known and served — had been taken from him, he must cast about for some sort of life without a homeland. A temporary retreat abroad seemed the wise course for the entire family.

Apparently Samuel Ward was requisitioned to escort Mrs. Gwin and Carrie abroad, for on February 4 he appended to a message for the State Department: "I think of taking a run over to Europe. In Paris I might be useful." But twelve days later he retracted this, writing: "To my inexpressible delight the lady whom I felt bound to escort to France released me from my engagement yesterday."

In March, Mary and Carrie Gwin sailed for France, and soon thereafter were reported comfortably installed at the Grand Hotel in Paris.

Meanwhile the doctor had slipped into the Confederacy, by what route is not known, and was next heard from at Richmond. It seems likely that he met his friends there, from President Davis down, and found them firm in their cause and confident that they would prevail. There were means by which communication could be kept up with friends at the North, and on April 23 Sam Ward wrote to the State Department:

I saw a letter from Dr. Gwin this A.M. It was without date or place, but I imagine it to have been penned in Richmond last week. It was devoted to the expression of his gratification at being once more free and among friends, and of his regard for the friends he had left in the North. The concluding phrase was, "Farewell. We shall meet again. This war cannot last forever, for this people cannot be conquered, nor will they ever consent to a union with their former associates."

Gwin's views were still confused, the clarity of his political perceptions had become clouded, and misled by his sympathies his judgment was no longer true.

3

Getting his son out of uniform and out of the Confederacy required time, and in the interim Gwin withdrew from the center of the Confederacy to his plantation in Mississippi. Lucy joined him there. As it turned out young Gwin's health had not proved equal to camp life, and he was granted an extended sick leave in Richmond. There Mary Boykin Chesnut, the wife of South Carolina's ex-senator, recorded in her diary the lad's infatuation with a flirtatious Richmond belle — he "ten or twenty years younger than herself, utterly upset by love and consumption. It was pitiful. Poor young soldier!"

All during 1862 Dr. Gwin kept out of sight. His hope was to unite the family in Paris; meanwhile he watched the progress of the war with absorption. How he assessed the South's prospects at the start of 1863 is not known, but his own situation had worsened. General Grant was driving on Vicksburg, and in an attempt to hit the fortress from the rear by a thrust up the Yazoo River, the Union forces burned the Gwin plantation. The doctor and Lucy had got away in time, but Gwin's records and papers, the accumulation of years, were destroyed.

That summer the hopes of the Confederacy declined sharply.

Vicksburg fell in July, just when Lee was hurled back at Gettysburg. But in Richmond there was still determination, and in spite of his professed neutrality, Gwin could not wish ill-success to his own people. But neither could he bring himself to lift a hand against the United States. It was an attitude out of harmony with the times; let either side win, his own position would be untenable, for the North would regard him as a traitor, and Southerners were cool because he would not actively assist their fight.

Willie Gwin's enlistment was due to run out in 1863. Meanwhile, Lucy had consented to accompany her father abroad, and it was decided that they should go first, and that Willie should follow. Gwin might try to reach a steamship at some Northern port, although that would involve great risk; or he might run the blockade maintained by the United States fleet around the Confederacy. By 1863 this blockade was tightening, and running the gantlet of federal cruisers was becoming more and more difficult. But Gwin no longer trusted his vagarious friend Seward; hence he deemed less hazardous an attempt to get away on a blockade runner.

These swift craft plied irregularly between a few Southern ports and Bermuda or the Bahamas. In August Dr. and Lucy Gwin reached Wilmington, North Carolina, a port that was still open. There they took passage on a noted runner, the *R.E. Lee.* Built in Scotland, this side-wheeler had been purchased by the Confederate government, and under the command of Captain John Wilkinson, a Virginian, a former officer in the United States Navy, it had compiled a record of daring. The *R.E. Lee* had proved a good investment for the rebels, carrying cotton and turpentine to Bermuda, bringing back munitions and luxuries.

Besides the Gwins, a Southern physician and his wife had booked passage on the *Lee,* and the four were the only passengers when, on August 13, she slipped through the inlet after dark, crept past the federal warships outside the bar, and headed seaward. She showed no lights and every sound was muffled. By daybreak she was thirty miles offshore. But the danger was not past.

The *R.E. Lee* burned coal, and at Wilmington, Captain Wilkinson had been able to procure only a small quantity of Welsh coal, which gave off very little smoke; he had been obliged to fill his bunkers mainly with low-grade North Carolina coal, a heavy smoke producer. A little after dawn, the changeover to the Carolina coal was made, and two long streamers at once issued from the twin stacks. This quickly drew the attention of lookouts in the Yankee fleet, and the U.S.S. *Iroquois* gave chase, piling on sail to increase her speed. The steam-powered vessels of the blockading fleet were able to add two or three knots to their speed by using their sails also when the wind was favorable. With this advantage, the *Iroquois* began to overhaul the *Lee*, and Captain Wilkinson estimated that the warship would be alongside by noon. This would mean capture and prison for himself, the crew, and probably the passengers.

The *R.E. Lee*'s engineer, an excitable Frenchman, protested that not a pound more steam pressure could be coaxed from the coal he was forced to burn. Wilkinson ordered him to break out some barrels of turpentine, soak cotton in it, and feed that to the fireboxes. The deck cargo of cotton meanwhile was tossed overboard to lighten the ship, and soon a trail of bobbing bales was strung out astern. The turpentine-soaked cotton jumped the ship's speed from nine knots to thirteen and one-half; this Wilkinson ascertained by casting the log himself. But the fierce fire made the deck so hot it became impossible to stand on it, and officers and passengers took refuge on the bridge that stretched from side to side between the paddle boxes.

Still the *Iroquois* gained, although more slowly, until from the bridge of the *Lee* the muzzles of her guns could be seen protruding from the portholes. Wilkinson was carrying a consignment of gold, being sent to London by the Richmond government, and to guard against its seizure as prize money by the *Iroquois,* he had the kegs brought on deck and opened, intending to distribute it among those aboard at the last minute. Noticing that he was making no provision for himself, Lucy Gwin advised the captain to fill a purse and give it to her; she would hide it under her skirts, and hand it back to him later. She knew she would not be searched (an unthinkable indignity in those days of polite warfare) and she spunkily intended that the Yankees should not get everything.

But the *Lee* had not been caught yet, and Wilkinson tried a new trick, in the execution of which he apparently invented the smoke screen that would be used in evasive tactics by navies of the world in future wars.

The engineer reported that the turpentine-cotton fuel was clogging the flues. Wilkinson ordered him to revert to coal and to create as much smoke as possible. At the same time, he altered his course so as to force the *Iroquois* up into the wind, where her sails would become a hindrance rather than a help. A dense, oily cloud soon was billowing from the *R.E. Lee's* stacks, lying upon the water in her wake like a gigantic smudge, while Wilkinson little by little edged his pursuer into the wind. Finally the *Iroquois* was seen to furl sail, and her speed dropped off. Wilkinson thereupon signaled the engineer to close the dampers, cutting off the smoke. Then making a sharp quarter-turn, Wilkinson sent the *R.E. Lee* scuttling away behind the opaque cloud that was strung out for miles. He was lost to sight by the *Iroquois,* and after an hour he jauntily went to his cabin, confident that he had got away. Taking off his shoes, he put his blistered feet out of the porthole to cool. Lucy Gwin, passing by on the arm of her father, could not resist giving them a tickle.

"Ah, captain," she called out, "I see we are all safe. I congratulate you!"

After this excitement the run to Bermuda was uninteresting. At that transfer point the Gwins boarded a steamer which took them to England, whence they would cross to France, and early in September they were reunited with Mary and Carrie in Paris. A short while later Willie Gwin, honorably discharged for reasons of ill-health, successfully ran the blockade, and the family was together again.

PART FOUR

An Empire Lost

Chapter I

WHAT WERE the thoughts, what were the emotions, of ex-Senator Gwin as he stood on the bridge of the *R.E. Lee* and looked back at the pursuing *Iroquois*? Through the glass he could make out the flag that fluttered from the warship's mizzen peak. That was the flag to which he had sworn allegiance when it had been the emblem of all the United States, not a part. He felt that he had kept faith. His loyalty had been to the nation in fact, and now that nation had been dismembered. In Tennessee, in Mississippi, in Texas, and in California, he had helped, and at times had helped mightily, to make the United States great and powerful. He had been proud of the country, and proud of his position in it. Now he was being pursued by a warship flying a flag that no longer stood for what it had symbolized in Jackson's day. The doctor's thoughts may have been somber. His personal fate hung in the balance at the moment, although it is likely that he felt no great ill will because of that, merely sadness. To the end of his life he would harbor lasting bitterness against only two persons — David Broderick, and another, yet to be named.

Let friends reorient their loyalties as they must, he may have ruminated; he wished them well. Henceforth he would order his life along his own lines. An American citizen, he had been rendered stateless for the time being; but he was confident that he would be able to master the altered circumstances. For years he had chalked up successes; why should the story be different now? At fifty-eight he was shrewd, ambitious, and not disposed to contemplate failure. Of one thing he was sure: he had finished with politics forever.

Dr. Gwin found much to engage him in the Paris of the Second Empire. His wife he found despondent, although she kept up a brave front before the group of Confederates that clustered in the capital. Whatever the outcome of the war, she was sure the South would be ruined. Their property had gone up in smoke, or had been confiscated, and if the North should triumph, she predicted they would be stripped of their last cent without fail. Gwin did his best to encourage her, but succeeded only partially. The family was not destitute, for he had money enough to meet their needs for quite a while, and in war as in politics the unexpected often happened; he felt that something would turn up, and with his family out of the storm raging at home, he could look about for opportunities.

His sojourn in France was his first taste of foreign travel, and he enjoyed it. He had always been able to adapt to a new environment, and the contrast of the confined and shrinking Confederacy to the amplitude and opulence of Paris, the world's social and diplomatic center, stimulated him. The empire was at its high noon of splendid frivolity. Napoleon III was transforming the drab cluttered city of his predecessors into the *ville lumière*, opening wide avenues lined with handsome buildings, which blazed with gaslights after dark. Life was pleasant; the cancan of Offenbach throbbed in theaters and cafés; and the fashionable *couturiers* drew the custom of smart women from all over Europe.

There were many Americans in the city who, for one reason or another, were sitting out the troubles at home. These exiles fell into two camps, those who sympathized with the Confederate states and the partisans of the North. The Confederate supporters were more numerous, and officially and socially they were in favor, the court, the parvenu nobility, and the bankers who set the tone of the town finding them more congenial in

respect to manners and chivalrous sentiments. To Northerners, on the other hand, official doors opened reluctantly, and
socially they were avoided.

A gathering place for the transplanted Southerners was the
house of William Corcoran, the Washington banker, and there
Dr. Gwin found a hearty welcome. Corcoran had been banker
to several Democratic administrations, and Gwin often dealt
with him, both directly and through their mutual friend, Robert Walker. It was with Corcoran's help that Walker had been
able to find the money to prosecute the Mexican War, and
since then there had been many private dealings between
them. Gwin may have employed Corcoran to transfer funds
abroad for safekeeping, for the banker had performed that service for the doctor's friends.

Walker was not present at Corcoran's Paris reunions; he had
gone over to the Union side at the start of the war, and at that
very time was in London, propagandizing to undermine the
credit of the Confederacy in the international money market.
Gwin may have smiled somewhat grimly at the source of the
money Walker was spending so liberally in his patriotic mission; the funds had come from the final settlement of a shady,
and possibly fraudulent, claim to ownership of the New Almaden quicksilver mine in California, one of the richest deposits
of mercury ever found. Gwin had been a member of the syndicate of politicians and bankers that had acquired the dubious title, although whether he had retained his shares until the
long-deferred settlement is uncertain. Walker had collected
half a million dollars, which he was now using to injure his
former friends by spectacular plays designed to defeat secession.

In Washington, Corcoran had been a famous host, but the
invasion of the city by uncouth Republicans had so disgusted
him that he had moved to Paris. He did not retire from business, and kept up his connections professionally as well as so-

cially. His hospitable Paris establishment had become the headquarters of the Southern colony composed of cosmopolites and avowed "Confeds." Mason and Slidell were regularly seen there, although they did not hobnob with Gwin. The doctor suspected that Slidell was more intent upon making money out of equipping Confederate privateers than upon patriotic diplomacy.

2

It was at Corcoran's place, one day in September, that the conversation turned to the subject of Mexico. Louis Napoleon had set in motion a gigantic power play there. He proposed to establish an empire in Mexico, nominally ruled by the Archduke Ferdinand Maximilian, brother of the Emperor of Austria, but dominated by France; and from that base the French emperor dreamed of extending his reach north and south, creating a vast sphere of French influence in the heart of the Americas.

Mexico was a subject upon which Gwin was exceptionally well informed. He knew the history and topography of the country, and he had prospected through Sonora, the Mexican state lying just below the Arizona line. He often had canvassed Mexican questions with his friend Sam Houston, and as chairman of the Senate subcommittee that investigated railroad routes to the Pacific he had become deeply versed in Sonora affairs especially. At the time of the Gadsden Purchase he had been so ardent for acquiring that entire state from Mexico that he had withheld his vote from the final treaty.

There were reasons for this interest in Sonora. For years that area had attracted filibustering expeditions, and most of these had been based in California. As California's senator, Gwin had been obliged to keep track of these generally lawless forays made by reckless adventurers. The lure was the immense mineral wealth of Sonora. In colonial times, under the Spaniards, the gold and silver mines of the province had been among the richest in the world. Old records showed that Sonora's gold output had dwarfed everything produced by California — although in 1863 "California" was everywhere a name carrying golden connotations. Since the overthrow of the viceroys, continuous revolutions and the impotence of the central government had caused northern Mexico to lapse into a condition of semibarbarism, depopulated and pillaged by roving bands of hostile Indians — Apaches, Yaquis, and other bloodthirsty tribes — who warred relentlessly upon settlers. As a result, the land was barren and all but deserted, and the mines had long since fallen into disuse. The very location of some of the more famous had been forgotten, though folklore perpetuated the stories of their prodigious richness.

Excited by these tales, during the 1850s several bands of gold hunters had invaded Sonora in hope of rediscovering the fabled mines and working them profitably. Although for the most part illegal, these forays had been sanctioned by public opinion, in the Far West especially; for it was accepted there as inevitable that the United States take over most or all of Mexico, just as it had absorbed the Mexican territories of Texas, Arizona, New Mexico, and California. The only question was when this would take place.

Sentiment of the time was reflected in a typical editorial printed in the *Alta California* of San Francisco on January 14, 1857. This read plainly:

A SONORA EXPEDITION — ACQUISITION OF MEXICAN TERRITORY

It is, we believe, pretty generally understood among the "knowing ones," that an expedition is soon to start from San Francisco, ostensibly with the purpose of setting the new Territory of Arizona, but in reality with the intent of merely making Tucson a rendezvous for making a foray into Sonora. . . . We will not

here discuss the abstract question of filibustering; and we believe that it is the "manifest destiny" of the States forming the
northern tier of the Republic of Mexico, as well as the peninsula
of Lower California, to fall into the hands of the United States;
the "manifest destiny" of the United States to acquire them. . . .
That is the natural course of the progress of the United States,
and with the decadence of Mexico, Chihuahua, Sonora, and
Lower California will follow ere long, we have no doubt. . . .

Two Frenchmen who had been among those attempting to
take over Sonora, had come to grief in the process. The first
was a ruined nobleman, the Marquis Charles de Pindray, who
contracted with the central authorities of Mexico to take a
band of fighters into the desolated land, pacify or expel or ex-
terminate the Indians, and open up the abandoned mines.
Pindray recruited a motley company in San Francisco, and
marched into the interior of Sonora from the port of Guaymas;
but just when things seemed to be going well, he was killed
under mystifying circumstances, and the expedition disinte-
grated.

Another thirster after gold and glory took up the quest. He
was Count Gaston de Raousset-Boulbon, and twice he landed
with a band of followers in Mexico. The second time he paid
for his temerity with his life before a firing squad.

About the same time, an American, William Walker (a Tennessean like Gwin), also made an attempt, based on San Francisco. This, too, failed, and he was forced to return to the city;
but the setback merely hardened his resolution, and later he
would try again, this time against Nicaragua, with spectacular
temporary success.

All these attempts of course had been brought to the attention of Senator Gwin of California. All of them (with the exception of Walker's in Nicaragua) had been promoted by en-
thusiasts who were without experience or much ability, and
all had been poorly equipped and poorly led. When stripped

of the grandiloquent phrases defining their professed aims, they had been nothing but predatory raids in quest of gold, led by desperadoes or dreamers. Northern Mexico, prostrated by decades of anarchy, was still a magnet for men eager to tap its treasure.

3

During the talk around Corcoran's table, Dr. Gwin intimated that there was a way by which Sonora might be reclaimed for civilization; of course immense profit would accrue to those involved in the reopening of its mines and the reestablishment of its agriculture. His words were eagerly taken up, because Paris was most curious about Mexico, in view of the French undertaking there. Louis Napoleon had pushed his schemes to the point where Maximilian, having been offered the throne of Mexico, was wrestling with the decision to accept it. The archduke was handsome, cultured, mild-mannered, and well meaning; unfortunately he was also weak-willed and unstable; nature had not cut him out to be a ruler. Of the land and the people he was being importuned to govern he was abysmally ignorant, and he would never acquire more than a superficial appreciation of Mexico and the Mexicans. It was not this, however, that was holding him back; he was tortured by the thought of forfeiting his right of succession to the Austrian throne, should he embark for Mexico. The dilemma plunged him into an agony of indecision, which Napoleon was trying to cut short by diplomatic nudging and assurances that with the assistance of France, he could not fail in a new and more glorious station. Meanwhile, in Paris the subject was very much in the air: the volatile Parisians were fascinated by everything pertaining to the remote, romantic land — and especially fascinated by the thought that incalculable wealth lay hidden in its recesses. It was at this juncture that

Dr. Gwin appeared, a man furnished with unique knowledge of Mexico. When questioned about the topic of the hour, he spoke readily, drawing upon his copious store of information, and what he said enthralled his listeners.

His prestige as a former senator from California — that other land of gold —lent authority to his words. The French had seen California emerge from a bare wilderness to become a state rich, populous, and powerful, within a mere fifteen years, thanks to its mineral wealth. As senator, Gwin had played a leading part in that almost miraculous development; and now the Parisians heard this distinguished Californian saying that Sonora was richer in gold and silver than California had ever been.

Among Gwin's auditors was an old acquaintance, the Marquis de Montholon. One Montholon had shared the first Napoleon's banishment to St. Helena, and the present marquis had emulated that example by sharing Louis Napoleon's imprisonment in the fortress of Ham, under the reign of Louis Philippe. Napoleon III had many defects, but ingratitude to those who had stood by him in adversity was not one of them, and Montholon had been liberally rewarded. At the outbreak of the Civil War he had been France's consul at New York, where he had met Senator Gwin. The extreme confidence which Napoleon placed in him was attested to by his new assignment — he was to be the emperor's minister to imperial Mexico. Meanwhile, Montholon had the free access to the Tuileries. He was fascinated by Gwin's tales of Sonora.

During the eighteenth century, the doctor explained, the output of the mines of Sonora almost surpassed belief, if it were not confirmed by figures preserved in colonial records. One of the most fabulous producers had been the Tayopa mine ("the mine with the iron door"), which lay somewhere amid the forbidding canyons of the Sierra Madre; old authorities described the Tayopa as the most valuable single deposit of precious metals known to man. Nearby were the Minas Prietas, and their location could be ascertained from old maps and letters. Spanish priests had worked the Minas Prietas until political unrest and the Indians had driven them out.

At Sombrete, the doctor went on, was a whole complex of mines, one vein of which had been termed by the German scientist Alexander von Humboldt "the richest in the world." In one decade the "king's fifth" (the 20 percent royalty on every pound of ore that was collected by the Spanish crown) yielded by this vein had come to $12,000,000, according to the records. Subsequent owners of the property had taken $2,000,000 from another vein in a few months; all told that vein had yielded $11,000,000, mainly in silver. Gwin did not have authorities at hand, but some figures he remembered, and he had notes on others. The lost Naranjal mine, for instance, had been so rich that its proprietor was said to have paved a path from his hacienda to the church with pure silver. And there was the Planchas de Plata, worked by the Jesuits until the expulsion of their order in the late eighteenth century; the mission bells had been cast in silver, and when the fathers left they had buried the bells, together with a hoard of bullion, somewhere just below the Arizona border.*

Gwin recalled that von Humboldt, in his *Essai Politique*, had stated that from the time of Cortez to 1803 the yield of the mines in Mexico had totaled more than two billion dollars ($2,027,952,000 was the exact figure), while the registered coinage of the Mint of Mexico, from 1733 to 1860, had been nearly a billion and three-quarters ($1,741,573,107). And not only Sonora, but the neighboring states of Durango and Chihuahua possessed mines of enormous value. The Santa Eulalia

---

* In 1964 at least one shaft of this group of mines was rediscovered by Wayne Winters, an American mining engineer, just below the Arizona line. Much wrought silver was found, but not the bells, search for which was continued. The authorities at Mexico City confirmed the extraordinary richness of the ore taken out.

in Chihuahua had registered a yield from 1705 to 1737 of nearly
$56,000,000; while from 1737 to 1791 the yield had been about
$44,000,000, making a total of $100,000,000 obtained during
eighty-six years of operation.

Other figures that Gwin recalled were just as impressive.
From the Carmen mine in Chihuahua masses of pure mallea-
ble silver had been taken that weighed more than eight hundred pounds. The "king's fifth" paid by the San Dimas mines,
in northern Durango, between 1787 and 1807, had totaled
some $11,000,000, and in view of the remoteness of those works,
and the difficulties of transportation in that area, the ore must
have been amazingly rich to pay that duty. Sonora's Pavellon
mine had produced $20,000 a day for five years, until a moun-
tain torrent swept away the workings. Reopened, in ten years
it yielded another $60,000,000. Abandoned in 1696, it was
again reopened in 1787 and in eight months produced ore
valued at $11,500,000.

If figures were of interest, Gwin could supply them, and
though his jottings and his recollection might err in details, he
was confident that the records would confirm everything he
said. He had a notation of the following registered yields, as
set down in the state records, from mines all of which were in
Sonora:

Biscaina vein .... $ 16,341,600
Santa Anita vein .... $ 21,347,210
Valencia vein .... $ 31,813,486
Rayas vein .... $ 85,421,014
Veta Madre vein $225,935,736

All the gold and silver mined in California and Nevada together up to that time did not come up to those figures. Montholon's eyes glistened as the doctor described the desolate
steppe which the once flourishing Sonora had become — ha-
ciendas in ruins, the population decimated or expelled, the

once prosperous countryside reverting to wilderness. The
marquis left Corcoran's murmuring that exalted personages
might be interested in Dr. Gwin's amazing tale.

4

A few days later Dr. Gwin received a call from another old
acquaintance, Henri Mercier, who until recently had been
Napoleon's minister at Washington. Mercier and Gwin had
known each other for years; the Frenchman was friendly to
the Confederates and believed that the South would win its
independence. Now Mercier was attached to the Foreign
Office in Paris, and he lost no time in bringing the talk around
to the subject of Sonora.

Gwin went a step beyond what he had told Montholon, and
frankly stated that the key to reopening that area to civilization lay in attracting the right type of settler. All the filibustering attempts had been mismanaged, fly-by-night affairs,
without authority or resources adequate to the task; but under
the right auspices, there was a way by which Sonora might
be repopulated and its mines reopened profitably. He outlined his plan, which was simple, imaginative, and practical,
and Mercier grew more and more excited as Gwin sketched
the immense possibilities his scheme offered — including the
promise of wealth for the promoters beyond the imaginings of
most men. (Privately, Gwin told himself that if he could call
the turn on this development as accurately as he had on the
political situation in California in '49, he would become one
of the world's richest men, with power and position enough to
satisfy any ambition — and Mary Gwin need not worry about
dying poor.)

Mercier departed in high good humor; and shortly afterward a gorgeously liveried lackey delivered a gilt-edged card
inviting Dr. Gwin to a private interview with the man who,

next to the emperor (and some said even more than the dumpy figure on the throne), was the most powerful person in Europe — the Duke de Morny, president of the Legislative Corps. Besides being Talleyrand's illegitimate grandson and Louis Napoleon's illegitimate half-brother, Morny was credited with being the illegitimate brains of the Second Empire.

Morny's interest in Mexico was keen, because he stood to make millions out of French intervention there. During the successive revolutions that had convulsed Mexico since the throwing off of the Spanish yoke in 1821, one of the ephemeral Presidents, General Miguel Miramón, had become desperate for money to pay the troops who were keeping him in power. He negotiated a loan with a firm of Swiss bankers, Jecker Torre & Company, which became the scandal of financial Europe. Through a series of complex transactions, the Jeckers accommodated Miramón with 3,800,000 francs in gold, for which Miramón gave the Jeckers Mexican national bonds to the value of 75,000,000 francs. Shortly after this, Miramón was driven out by the constitutionally elected President, Benito Pablo Juárez, who denounced the loan and repudiated the bonds.

The Jecker brothers, Jean Baptiste and Louis, approached the Duke de Morny with a proposal that France help them realize on their bonds. For a commission of 30 percent (22,500,000 francs), Morny agreed to take on the job. He put through a law naturalizing the Jeckers as French citizens, thereby laying a basis for French intervention to "protect the interests of its nationals." Meanwhile, Louis Napoleon had hatched his scheme of Mexican empire, and Morny succeeded in tying the Jecker debt to his brother's dream of French dominion in the New World. This was accomplished by inserting a special clause in the Treaty of Miramar, which was negotiated between Napoleon and Maximilian to define the extent of France's participation in the archduke's grab for power.

Under the treaty, Maximilian agreed to assume the cost of a French expeditionary force, and of its maintenance in Mexico indefinitely; and he recognized the validity of the Miramón-Jecker bonds. A simple glance at Mexico's national income would have sufficed to show that the entire product of the country could not meet these obligations, so blithely assumed by the prospective emperor; but neither Morny nor the Jeckers nor Maximilian cared for that; the last was already absorbed in drawing up the ponderous book of etiquette that would prevail at his jejune court. The French army by this time had moved inland from Vera Cruz, and under the pretense of "pacifying" the country had repulsed the troops sent against them by Juárez. With the help of French bayonets, it was expected at Paris that the Mexicans could be forced to pay the Jecker debt.

Under the circumstances, it is hardly surprising that John Bigelow, United States consul at Paris, in keeping Secretary of State Seward abreast of the developments, should call the Duke de Morny "the most unscrupulous speculator in Europe." He might have added that as well as being the most cynical, the duke was the most successful.

5

The meeting between Gwin and Morny took place in the library of the duke's town house. The interview was private and confidential, and the two men took to each other at once. Both had quick perception, both were boldly imaginative; both were receptive to progressive ideas; and both in their time had carried off great gambles. When it came to taking chances, they were equally calculating, and if the odds were favorable they were prepared to risk much. Finally, by temperament and habit, both preferred to do business privately and intimately, not in the glare of public scrutiny. In point of cynicism, Morny could overreach Gwin every time.

The duke listened attentively while the doctor unfolded his plan for Sonora. "There is not a white man in it," the ex-senator succinctly described its present desolation. The need, he went on, was to attract the right sort of settlers — hardy, independent pioneers, of the kind who had been drawn to California in the gold rush. Such men had opened up California, and Morny himself knew with what astonishing rapidity that wilderness had been transformed. The same process could be expected in Sonora, if the conditions were right. First would come the miners, many of whom would have no intention of staying; but behind them, in the second wave of immigration, would come the permanent settlers, men who wanted land and businesses of their own — farmers, merchants, mechanics, teachers, professional men. Commerce and agriculture would be established, cities would spring up, and the now wasteland would flourish more richly than it had flourished before. Naturally those who directed this transformation would profit, the largest profits going to the men who would be in charge and on the ground first. It was hardly necessary to emphasize this point to the Duke de Morny.

Gwin marshaled facts effectively, and he spoke of Mexico with genuine knowledge. Getting down to essentials, he said that the prestige of his name would attract thousands of tough, experienced miners from California. Such men would follow the lure of gold anywhere. These firstcomers would require protection against the marauding Indians, though once they became numerous they could defend themselves. But at the start troops would be needed to ward off the savages, and since France already had an army in Mexico, this military shield might be provided at little expense. If the emperor would send a thousand or so troops to cover the movement in its early stages, Gwin said, he would undertake to promote the immigration.

The interview closed with reciprocal expressions of esteem,

and Morny bowed his visitor into the corridor. Then the
duke rang for his carriage, and was driven to the Tuileries,
where he buttonholed his imperial brother.

Gwin suffered an amusing contretemps while trying to ex-
tricate himself from Morny's labyrinthine palace. No lackey
being in sight, he wandered through a maze of passageways
in search of the street door, and wound up in the kitchens.
What struck him most forcefully there was the immense girth
of the asparagus that was being prepared for the ducal dinner. He emerged without loss of dignity or sense of humor,
and shortly thereafter he was not at all surprised to receive
a summons to an audience at the Tuileries.

Chapter II

HE FOUND NAPOLEON poring over geological maps of Mexico. After the first greetings, the emperor and his guest flattered each other by lapsing into English, Napoleon being rather vain of his fluency in that language. The discussion was animated and thorough; the emperor asked many questions, which Gwin answered — at times with more assurance than he felt, he confessed afterward. He was impressed by the emperor's grasp of the subject and situation, and before the interview was concluded Napoleon had become a convert to Gwin's colonization scheme, while the ex-senator came away filled with admiration for the emperor, whom he considered a consummate politician.

Of course Maximilian would have to be consulted, and as he happened to be in Paris, an immediate audience was arranged. The archduke received the American doctor graciously and gave cordial encouragement to his plan, observing that he wished to attract Americans to Mexico, for he admired their hardihood and enterprise.

It was now September, 1863. For Maximilian's further study, Gwin submitted a summary of the proposed operation. This read like a promissory note on the Bank of Golconda. Gwin knew exactly how to appeal to Maximilian's vanity, self-interest, and high-mindedness, all at once. The memorandum spoke of "mines of fabulous richness — especially of silver" — that had been worked in Spanish times. "One mine produced a solid piece of silver of the value of $4,700, which was sent as a present to the King of Spain. I cannot trust my memory to give the full details, and I have only my memory to rely upon, as the authorities and data of my researches were destroyed, with my whole Congressional library of two thousand volumes, at my plantation on the Mississippi River, by the army of General Grant during the siege of Vicksburg." However, he was sure the Mexican archives would bear him out.

Maximilian was duly dazzled, and on January 5, 1864, Gwin was in a position to address a letter of protocol to Napoleon, formally soliciting French military assistance for putting the project into action. This letter also displayed superb salesmanship. Eschewing the prolixity of which monarchs are occupational victims, the doctor went to the heart of the matter tersely: "There is a large section of the country in the States of Sonora and Chihuahua, in the empire of Mexico, believed to be the richest in minerals on the continent of America."

This was calculated to galvanize the most torpid imagination, and without transition Gwin advanced his pivotal request:

> The undersigned solicits from your Imperial Majesty authority to colonize this country with miners and agriculturists . . . principally from the mining districts of the United States of America. . . . Having resided from early 1849 until the close of 1861 in California, in active public life during the whole of that period, the undersigned is known to almost every inhabitant in [those] regions. . . . [This] would greatly aid him in surrounding himself with a colony that would add to the wealth and give strength to the Mexican empire.

Next, the material benefits that would accrue from the colonization were enumerated:

> The advantages to Mexico in a financial and commercial point of view . . . will be immense. . . . The product of the mines paying royalty, and the revenue from customs on supplies of all

kinds required by the new settlers, going into the imperial treasury, will, in an incredibly short time, enable the Emperor of
Mexico to negotiate a loan based upon these revenues, sufficient
to pay not only the debt to your Imperial Majesty's government,
but to consolidate on favorable terms the entire indebtedness of
his empire.

Since Napoleon's first excuse for moving into Mexico had
been to collect a bad debt, the prospect of plentiful reimburse-
ment "in an incredibly short time" made cheerful reading.
But Gwin emphasized also the political gains that might be
looked for:

> The country now held by wild Indians will be inhabited by
> a hardy and vigorous population, useful not only in developing
> the resources of the country, but presenting an impregnable
> barrier to hostile attacks upon that portion of the empire.

Here, in the circumlocutions of diplomacy, Gwin touched
upon an aspect of the venture that was vital to Napoleon;
"hostile attacks" upon Sonora could come only from Texas
or Arizona, over which either the United States or the Confederate flag would fly at the close of the North-South war. Already Washington had made clear that it resented the
French-Austrian intrusion in Mexico, and that Maximilian's
pretensions would not be recognized. Although at the moment the Lincoln government had its hands full trying to suppress the Southern rebellion, after the war, what then? Should
the Yankees emerge victorious, they would possess the most
powerful army in the world, magnificently equipped and
battle-hardened, and that army might easily be turned against
Mexico.

But what if, by luck and with a little help, the Confederates
should carry off their national gamble? The results in that
case would be difficult to gauge. It was true that French and
Confederate agents had discussed a mutual-aid alliance which
would give the Southern states assistance in their fight, and

in return would — once the Confederacy was securely established — place a buffer state between Maximilian's territory and the Yankees. But offsetting this was that persistent dream held by Southern statesmen of extending their hegemony around the Caribbean; in this way a victorious Confederacy might choose to absorb Maximilian's realm, and itself take over those rich mines of Sonora. Napoleon's position would be delicate as long as the outcome of the war in the United States remained in suspense.

At the outset of that conflict, the emperor, acting in concert with Great Britain, had pledged neutrality. Yet he did not bother to conceal his personal sympathy with the South, and was turning a blind eye to the assistance in money and munitions which Confederate agents were obtaining from French sources. All in all, it behooved Napoleon — and of course Maximilian — to take steps to guarantee the integrity of Mexican territory against aggression from the direction of Texas, whether it be Northern or Southern.

Gwin comprehended the risks Napoleon faced, and in effect was offering the emperor an insurance policy against an American invasion of Sonora. Napoleon on his side grasped the meaning of the doctor's cautious phraseology without need of a diagram: a "hardy and vigorous population," firmly planted in Sonora, should be able to hold that exposed flank of the Mexican empire against any possible attack.

Reading further in Gwin's formal application for military support, the emperor was gratified to find that the doctor's requirements would be modest:

> The undersigned asks for but little from your Majesty. A small military force stationed at some central point to protect the first immigrants from Indian depredations is all that is necessary.

Gwin estimated that a thousand men would be sufficient, and Napoleon ruminated that General Bazaine could furnish a force of that size from the expeditionary army without incurring much extra expense.

A treaty, of course, would have to be concluded between France and Mexico placing the enterprise under French sponsorship and control; but in view of Maximilian's expressed encouragement, this seemed to present no problem. Gwin outlined the essentials which such a treaty should contain: Maximilian must give France protectorate rights over Sonora, together with exclusive privileges of exploration and development — in everything but name making that portion of Mexico a French colony. Gwin would be director of colonization and governor of the province.

By nature and habit Louis Napoleon was secretive and dilatory; he exposed his hand only when compelled to, and preferred if possible to move underground. Gwin's proposals he favored, but weeks passed without his giving the formal sanction that would start the project. In the meantime, Gwin, in further conferences with Morny, reached an agreement by which Morny became a secret partner in the Sonora scheme, responsible for handling the matter at the Tuileries, and for providing the capital to set up railroads, steamship lines, and banks — and of course to work those wonderful mines.

2

The frequent visits of ex-Senator Gwin to the Tuileries did not escape the notice of expatriate Americans in Paris. The city fairly crawled with spies for both belligerents at home, and garbled guesses as to the doctor's business at the palace were transmitted to the American press, North and South. In California, where the subtle doctor's talents for successful intrigue were being awesomely magnified by rumor, the reports aroused trepidation, and the *Alta California* published a dispatch relayed by the Paris correspondent of the New York

Herald, with the prefatory warning: "Another sensation is on the *tapis,* concerning the proposal to unite California with the Mexican States on the Pacific, to form a Pacific Republic!" The dispatch then was quoted at length:

> The emperor has taken Doctor Gwin into his counsels. On Monday last, when his Majesty was at the Tuileries, he sent for the doctor, who is stopping at the Grand Hotel, and receiving him in his *cabinet de travail,* remained closeted with him for more than an hour, after which he gave him an autograph letter to Mr. Drouyn de Lhuys [Foreign Minister], whom Doctor Gwin called on at the Ministry for Foreign Affairs the following day. Now, so far as the fact is concerned, I am sure, beyond the shadow of a doubt, that my information is correct. . . .
>
> All those who know the fact of the doctor's interview with his Majesty understand it to have some connection with Mexican affairs, or rather, perhaps, with the affairs of Texas, where Doctor Gwin has resided, and in which he now has large landed interests. May it be that the emperor still hopes to add the Lone Star State to his new Mexican empire? . . .
>
> It cannot be that the emperor desired to congratulate the doctor upon . . . the present dilapidated condition of the Confederacy, unless, indeed, he advised him, and through him all leading rebels, to leave the sinking ship as quickly as possible. . . . It may be possible that the emperor wished to recommend to Doctor Gwin to use his influence with Jeff Davis and the other Southern leaders to carry into practical operation the recent recommendation of the *Herald,* and remove themselves to Mexico, there to establish the nation which there now seems no probability of their building in the Southern States. . . . You may depend upon it, some intrigue of this nature led to the recent interview.

3

In consigning the Southern cause to defeat, the *Herald* was premature. The condition of the Confederacy was indeed desperate, but its leaders had not given up hope. Should France come to its aid — and Napoleon was playing a shifty game without committing himself irrevocably either way —

his army stationed just below the border, together with a fleet of ironclads to smash the blockade, might conceivably turn the tide. Or perhaps (as some Northerners were speculating) Napoleon had in mind creating a refuge in northern Mexico for the defeated Confederates, and was employing Gwin as an intermediary. As a result of such guessing, the ex-senator, who had believed himself quit of politics for good, was edged into the limelight of international political complications, whether he wished it or not.

Gwin himself could have denied with good conscience that his plan for settling Sonora was politically motivated. He disassociated himself in advance from any political consequences that might flow from it, telling Napoleon plainly that he was an American citizen and would do nothing to injure his country. It may safely be assumed that the emperor murmured vague assent to this reservation, without giving it much weight: it was the sort of thing he would expect a cautious politician to say; he would say so himself, under similar circumstances, reserving the right to interpret his actions according to the light of the moment.

Still Napoleon dallied, and Gwin fretted to get his project under way. The news from the battlefields of Virginia was progressively worse: the Confederates were reeling from blow after blow, and although not conquered, their strength was ebbing, they were in grave straits. In March of 1864 the doctor applied the spur to the laggard emperor and submitted another memorandum, stressing the need for immediate action before Sonora should slip from the grasp of both Mexico and France. Defeat of the Confederacy, he pointed out, would start a rush of ex-soldiers, soured and cynical, into northern Mexico, fleeing from the wrath of the Yankees. These men, once fixed in Sonora, could not be displaced, nor, perhaps, would they accept the authority of Mexico. He wrote explicitly:

[Sonora] should be populated by a hardy, daring race of men . . . and special inducements should be held out to those who would prefer to live under the Mexican government to the one they leave. . . . Let the civil war in the United States cease, and thousands of discharged soldiers, inured to hardship and camp life, who will not go back to their former homes to work if they can help it, would overrun the country, subdue the Indians, and hold it against any force Mexico could bring into the field to expel them. This is the more reason why it should be occupied now.

This prospect jarred Napoleon into action, and Gwin's proposals were laid before the cabinet. There, article by article, they were discussed, and article by article, in the emperor's presence, they were endorsed. Not, however, without opposition from the Minister of Finance, Achille Fould, who urged that large monopolies be granted to capitalists for exploitation of the Sonora mines. Gwin's plan, by contrast, was based on giving full play to the initiative of individual prospectors and miners; this was the system that had long prevailed in Mexico, and had been adopted successfully in California. Napoleon favored Gwin's method, and it was approved.

In the meanwhile, Maximilian's scruples had been sufficiently eroded so that he could consent to ascend the throne of Montezuma. At his Adriatic villa, Miramar, he was invested with the imperial dignities, and on April 14, 1864, amid pomp and misgivings, he and his empress, Carlota, embarked for their new world.

4

Two weeks later Dr. Gwin quitted Paris for England, there to take ship for Vera Cruz. With him he carried an autograph letter from Napoleon III to General Bazaine, the French commander in Mexico, ordering the latter to provide all necessary assistance to put Gwin's plan in effect. The outlook could

not have been brighter for California's former senator. At the
Tuileries it was whispered that doubtless Maximilian would
ennoble the handsome American doctor, perhaps make him a
duke — "Duke of Sonora" might be an appropriate title.

The prospect of such an honor preoccupied Gwin very little
as he waited at Southampton to board the steamer. For the
first time in weeks he had leisure to take stock of himself, to
review the road he had traveled, and to peer into the future.
There were questions in that direction. How, he wondered,
would his new role be accepted in his homeland? This gossip
about a title (American newspapers had picked up the rumor
sarcastically) — a Jacksonian Democrat had small patience
with such trumpery, although probably Mary Gwin would
enjoy being called "duchess." On the threshold of a new career, Gwin opened his heart in a letter to a brother who had
never gone far from Tennessee. Carefully he inscribed the
date:

Southampton, June 1st, 1864

My dear brother:

I am this far on my way to Mexico. A generation has almost
passed away since I left the South. I have relatives and friends
left, whom I love and value highly, but I cannot shut my eyes
to the fact that I am not counted as one of the South, although
highly valued because I am with the South in this contest.

You know I am the "Wandering Jew" of the family, and this is
one of my excursions. Much fatigue and labor will result from
this enterprise, but I do not mind that. In fact, it is necessary to
perfect health and usefulness to me. It is a great work which I
propose to do, to populate an important part of the empire, now
held by wild Indians for more than a hundred years. It is the
richest mineral country in the world, and will attract tens of
thousands of enterprising men.

I intend to reverse my action in California. I went there determined not to make money, but to devote all my energies to
obtaining and maintaining political power. Now I go for money,
and shall let power alone. I want no dukedoms, nor any honors

the emperor can bestow upon me. Nothing can be as high as what I have been, a senator in the greatest body of the greatest nation on earth.

I may not succeed, as I have the prejudices of the Mexicans to contend against, who fear we will take the country away from them; but I am backed by the Emperor of France, and carry with me such authority from him that it is impossible for these prejudices to defeat me. Moreover, the Emperor of Mexico favors my plan, and does not share these fears of his subjects. . . . Write to me to the City of Mexico, under cover to the Marquis de Montholon, minister of France. Any letter to me would likely be opened, as the Federals are troubled about my movements.

5

The steamship that carried Gwin from Southampton toward the scene of his grandiose undertaking carried another letter, which would be transmitted by devious routes to its destination. Dated June 2, 1864, this letter had been written by John Slidell, the representative of the Confederacy at Paris, to *his* Secretary of State, Judah P. Benjamin, at Richmond. It was mainly gloomy, reporting the collapse of plans to deliver to the Confederacy four warships being built in French yards; the protests of Washington against this violation of neutrality had become too menacing, and the Prussian government had eased Napoleon's embarrassment by purchasing the vessels.

"The builders of the two corvettes persist in saying that they will deliver them to us at sea," Slidell went on, but he was not hopeful. "I have been so grievously deceived and disappointed before that I am far from placing implicit reliance on their assurance."

Turning to another subject, he had more cheerful news to impart:

Ex-Senator Gwin is on his way to Sonora. His object is to colonize Sonora with persons of Southern birth or proclivities residing in California. He bears an autograph letter from Louis

Napoleon to the French commander-in-chief warmly recommend-
ing his enterprise. His scheme has been fully examined and approved, and offers, I believe, fair chance of success. If carried
out, its consequences will be most beneficial.

So John Slidell, who was notoriously wily, thought that
Gwin's Sonora plan was well conceived; and when he assured
the astute Benjamin that its consequences would be "most beneficial," he meant beneficial to the Confederate cause.

Intend it or not, ex-Senator Gwin was being enmeshed in
the web of politics again.

Chapter III

WHEN DR. GWIN — prospective governor of a realm covering
some eighty thousand square miles and containing riches that
could only be guessed — sailed from England in June, 1864,
the "Federals" were troubled about many things. The war was
in its bloodiest phase. In May the Battle of the Wilderness
had been fought; the slaughter at Cold Harbor almost coincided with Gwin's departure from Europe. The Confederates were being pounded into defeat, but they had not lost
heart, and one hope to which Jefferson Davis clung stubbornly
was recognition by England or France — or if those nations
would not admit the Confederacy's sovereignty, then recognition by some government, somewhere. Could that be obtained, the wherewithal to fight on might flow into Southern
ports, and the North's will to continue the struggle might be
broken.

For nearly three years, Davis had been striving to bring
this about. At the inception of the Confederacy he had sent
Slidell to Mexico to establish diplomatic relations with
Juárez; but Slidell, slick, irascible, and arrogant, had bungled
the mission and had been turned back disdainfully. Maximilian's assumption of the throne, behind a rampart of French
bayonets, opened another possibility. Washington had recalled its minister to Mexico and continued to recognize the
phantom regime of President Juárez; therefore it seemed reasonable to expect that Maximilian would be receptive to a nod

of courtesy and welcome from Richmond. After all, the arch-duke's upstart empire stood as much in need of acceptance into the community of nations as did Davis's upstart republic. Before the emperor's foot touched Mexican soil, therefore, Davis appointed an envoy extraordinary to Maximilian's court. His choice fell upon General William Preston, a Kentuckian who under President Buchanan had represented the United States in Spain. Preston ran the blockade and reached Havana in the middle of June, 1864, planning to catch there the mail steamer for Vera Cruz; two ships a month, one British, one French, plied regularly between Europe and Mexico via Cuba. The British packet arrived first, and brought an old ac-quaintance — Dr. Gwin, on his way to Mexico. The friends discussed matters of mutual interest, and Gwin gave Preston letters from James Mason, Confederate agent at London, for transmittal to Richmond. How Gwin squared this friendly service with his professed aloofness from the strife in America is conjectural, although it is possible that he would have acted as courier for the United States minister at Paris just as will-ingly, had he been asked to do so.

Gwin also brought the latest information about the situa-tion in Paris, and as a result, Preston altered his plan: he de-cided that instead of proceeding at once to Mexico, he would proceed to France. The reasons for this change he embodied in two dispatches — one official, addressed to Secretary of State Benjamin, and the other a private letter to President Davis.

Gwin had brought word about Slidell's latest costly *faux pas;* during a game of cards, his ungovernable temper had betrayed him into making remarks offensive to Napoleon, Morny, and Maximilian, all three, and consequently Slidell was in Cov-entry and for the time being useless at the French court. Gwin's advice to Preston was to refrain from approaching Maximilian until the effects of Slidell's stupid blunder had

worn off; otherwise a diplomatic rebuff was likely. In the meantime, Gwin himself would try to smooth things over at Mexico
City. This was the gist of Preston's letter to Benjamin.

Writing confidentially to President Davis, Preston dwelt
upon Gwin's enterprise and upon the fine position the doctor
occupied for influencing Mexican opinion. He explained
the doctor's mission, saying:

> He has identified himself with the new empire, and has just
> gone to Sonora to undertake its colonization under flattering
> auspices. The country back of Guaymas is reputed to be richer
> in gold and silver than California. Both emperors are aware of
> this fact, and M. Fould proposed large monopolies to great cor-
> porations for their development. Doctor Gwin combatted his
> views, and was consulted by the Emperor Napoleon, who adopted
> his plan [of] founding colonization upon individual hopes and
> enterprise, instead of corporate wealth and privileges.

Alluding to the pro-Southern aspect of Gwin's scheme in
words that required no underlining for the doctor's old friend,
Preston added:

> It is expected that fifteen or twenty thousand colonists thoroughly
> acquainted with mining can be procured from Southern men in
> California.

That the project would go through Preston had no doubt.
Gwin's method of procedure, he wrote,

> was fully approved by Louis Napoleon, to the annoyance of M.
> Fould. The archduke also heartily approved it, and the doctor
> is to be appointed superintendent or governor of the district. The
> Emperor Napoleon gave him an autograph letter to the com-
> mandant of the French forces to insure the military protection
> of the inhabitants, and the expulsion of the Apaches. Under this
> encouragement he is going forward to the capital.

As for Mexican-Confederate recognition, Preston went on:

> I found Doctor Gwin very anxious to secure friendly relations
> between Mexico and the Confederacy, as the success of his
> scheme will depend upon the emigration of Southern men from
> California. He was afraid, from what he had heard at Paris, that
> attempts to establish intercourse would be abandoned. . . .
> Finding the doctor in this state of mind, I thought it would be
> well to employ him to secure an *invitation* for me to go to Mexico.
> This he is confident he can accomplish in a reasonable time. He
> is to urge the general agreement with all the force he can com-
> mand, and secure the opportune delivery of letters I have written
> to the Marquis de Montholon and General Almonte privately.

General Juan Almonte was a leader of the Conservative
party in Mexico which had tendered Maximilian the throne;
he had been named grand chamberlain at the new court, a
post, in view of Maximilian's preoccupation with etiquette,
of great influence.

Preston announced that his intention to withdraw to France
for a while was in order to give Gwin time

> to awaken Maximilian to the rights of the Confederacy and the
> danger of delay. I will return here in time to receive [Gwin's]
> reply, which he hopes to send me by the English steamer on the
> 6th of September or October, with an invitation to visit Mexico.
> . . . I think we can obtain recognition at Mexico as soon or
> sooner than at any other court.

Here again, in spite of Gwin's disavowal of political motives
— denials which may have been sincere — his project in
Sonora was assuming a strongly pro-Confederate complexion.
Smoothing the way for a diplomatic link between Mexico and
Richmond would serve Gwin's interests, of course, because in
the event of a Southern victory it would insure having an ally
next door to Sonora, and he expected that the miners who
would respond to his call would be mainly Southern, either
in sympathy or in open allegiance.

General Preston duly showed up in France, and he would have been less than amused had he been able to read the sarcastic comment upon his about-face made by John Bigelow, Washington's watchful minister at Paris in a dispatch to Seward. The *ville lumière*, Bigelow observed dryly, doubtless offered "many advantages as a residence for Confederate soldiers over the headquarters of the Confederate army, or even the imperial City of Mexico." Bigelow even suggested that perhaps Preston had never really intended to go to Mexico, once he succeeded in getting out of the beleaguered South.

2

Traveling in the opposite direction from Preston, Gwin landed at Vera Cruz on June 28, 1864, three weeks after Maximilian and Carlota had reached that port. He hastened directly to the capital, jolting in rude stagecoaches over abominable roads, and there was welcomed heartily by Montholon. A Virginia friend, Colonel Talcott, insisted that the doctor be his guest in the Casa Amarillo, a mansion in suburban Tacubaya, and it was in his house that Gwin first met General Achille François Bazaine.

The interview with the general opened Gwin's eyes to the morass of jealousy and intrigue into which he had ventured. Bazaine, a fussy, vainglorious little man, had a good record as a guerrilla fighter in Algeria, and in Mexico was engaged in somewhat similar operations — harassing the bands of republicans and brigands who sporadically raided even the outskirts of the capital. He devoted most of the interview to boasting about his successes and airing his truculent dislike of the palace clique surrounding Maximilian.

Bazaine read the letter from Napoleon with satisfaction, and at once placed himself at Gwin's service for carrying out the Sonora project. However, he said, there were diplomatic requirements to be met first. The treaty giving France protectorate rights in Sonora had not been ratified yet, and mention of the treaty gave the general a pretext for a tirade against Maximilian's political advisers; they were poisoning the emperor's mind against everything French, he rattled on, although Maximilian could see that the only real authority in Mexico was the French army, and the military had no intention of taking orders from Austrians, Belgians, or Mexicans, who made up the emperor's entourage. The Mexicans Bazaine dismissed as treacherous and unreliable; the Belgian Legion that had accompanied Carlota, a Belgian princess, he scorned as "mere boys"; and the Hungarians who composed the imperial guard were too high and mighty for his taste. Bazaine ranted on, warning Gwin that he must expect to encounter obstacles; and while he did not wish to seem pessimistic, and might even lead the troops into Sonora himself, still, if the doctor would accept the advice of a well-wisher, he would avoid the palace functionaries, and might even do well not to attempt to see Maximilian at once, because the emperor believed whatever he was told, and probably the Mexicans had already turned him against Gwin's scheme, simply because it bore the endorsement of the Tuileries. The real "master of Mexico," Bazaine wound up, was himself, and he proposed to remain the master.

Gwin was astonished by the flow of puerilities, and he sized up the general as tricky and eaten up with conceit. If intrigues were being hatched against the Sonora project, that made prompt action all the more imperative. Therefore, disregarding Bazaine's prejudice, the doctor applied without delay for an audience with the emperor. Back came a friendly reply to the effect that Maximilian was starting on a trip through the interior, and would receive the doctor upon his return; meanwhile, the latter was referred to the court officials in charge.

The treaty (technically a convention rather than a treaty)

giving France "direct and sovereign" rights in Sonora for fifteen years, in return for payment of a fixed royalty on all minerals mined there, had been accepted by Maximilian in Europe. But he had demurred against signing it there, arguing that it might be misconstrued by his subjects as giving away a large portion of their territory; once he reached his capital and could explain the agreement personally, he was sure there would be no objection.

But he found his Mexican adherents dead set against the entire scheme; they remembered Texas, and 1848, when they had lost more than half their territory to the insatiable "gringoes"; their suspicions of Americans were ineradicable, and they contended that Gwin's colonists from California would simply take over Sonora for themselves as soon as they became numerous enough. These counselors deployed every ruse and stratagem to frustrate Gwin's plans, insinuating that he had some secret design, some undisclosed purpose, behind his colonization proposals; he might, it was suggested, be seeking to embroil Mexico with the United States in the interests of the Confederacy. Maximilian was susceptible to these insinuations; at the same time he could not ignore Napoleon's sponsorship of Gwin. To escape from the dilemma, therefore, he set out on a royal progress through the countryside, inspecting ruins and practicing taxidermy. Meanwhile, until the treaty should be signed, Bazaine professed himself powerless to move.

3

These delays nettled Gwin but did not dishearten him. He placed no trust in Bazaine, certainly; yet without French troops nothing could be attempted. To bring both the general and Maximilian up to the mark, he decided to apply to Morny, his advocate at Paris. Pressure must be brought to bear upon the shifty Bazaine, and speed was imperative, before the American civil war should terminate. Under the date of July 27, Gwin wrote to his son at Paris:

> My dear son: I have had several very satisfactory interviews with General Bazaine. In the last he told me distinctly that he would put me in position, whether the emperor [Maximilian] agreed to my plan or not. Up to this time I had not approached the emperor, as unless I was certain of the military I could do nothing.
>
> There has been some foul play about my papers. They have never reached the emperor. . . . You can form no idea what an excitement my plan is creating here. As I expected, it has been extensively circulated that I am about to introduce a band of Americans, who will soon seize the country and take it from Mexico. I have omitted to tell you that General Bazaine is going to lead the expedition himself. . . . For fear of accidents, I shall write to the Duke de Morny, to see that no orders countermanding the expedition are issued. The general and I shall travel together; he is a fat, chubby little fellow, and I think I can out-travel him. . . .

This portion of the letter was endorsed "morning." Later, under the heading "evening," it continued,

> I have had two important interviews today, one with the emperor's chief of cabinet and favorite, Mr. Éloin, whom I found (though a Belgian) imbued with all the prejudices of the Mexicans against Americans. We were at it over an hour, and I left him pretty convinced.
>
> The more important one was with Bazaine, this evening, in my rooms at Col. Talcott's. He called with one of his aides, a son-in-law of Gen'l. Harney, of St. Louis (who speaks English), to act as interpreter, and spent an hour. He returned all my papers, saying he had copies of them all, and that he approved my plan, except that he thought the department should take in all Sonora. I told him what had occurred in the morning, at my interview with Éloin, and he replied that the man I had seen was unreliable, could be bought, and the less I had to do with him, the better.

He said he intended to reply by this mail to the letter I had brought him from the emperor [Napoleon], and wished to know if I would write to him. I replied, "Not by this mail."

Gwin had penetrated the motive behind Bazaine's apparently innocuous question: the general was preparing a report on Gwin for Napoleon — quite possibly adverse — and was fishing to find out whether the doctor would be writing at the same time; if not, Bazaine might be bolder in his expressions. Gwin was writing to Morny, not Napoleon, and thus answered Bazaine truthfully if with less than complete candor. The letter to young Gwin continued:

Now, you see, I am between two fires, for there is evidently no good feeling between the French and Mexican authorities. Mr. Éloin intimated that I should have applied for an interview with the emperor before I saw Bazaine. But I have determined to stand by the general, as I know without him I can do nothing, and that he can carry me through. Hence it is of vital importance that the Duke de Morny should see Napoleon soon after he reads Bazaine's letter, and confirm him in his policy of taking his troops to Sonora, and executing my plan of colonization. . . .

A letter to Morny was enclosed, and Gwin told his son that it "should be delivered in person, and the duke urged to see the emperor at once, and also to send out his funds and men with the money."

Two days later a postscript underlined the urgency of the matter:

I have changed my letter to the duke by adding a postscript about our business matters, and leaving the main letter in condition to show to the emperor. It should be suggested to him that it is important for the emperor to see it, especially as there is an anti-French party here, and it may become formidable. The notice of Napoleon, called to it by an impartial observer like myself, who wishes to keep harmony between the two parties, and

---

stands well with both, but who deems it vital to the success of the empire that French influence should prevail here, must have due weight with him. The duke should be advised to say this to the emperor.

Whether M—— should take the letter to the duke or not, you, in family council, must decide, and whether he shall go alone or you accompany him.

Letters between Mexico City and Paris required weeks for transmission, and Dr. Gwin's letter reached his son early in September. The family decided that young Gwin should go alone to Morny, and an interview was requested. This drew the following reply:

Corps Législatif,
Présidence.

Mons. Le Duc de Morny présente ses compliments distinguées à Monsieur Gwin, et le prie de venir lui parler lundi, dans la matinée, 17 Septembre.*

Gwin called and gave Morny his father's letter and message, which the duke undertook to convey to the emperor.

4

Meanwhile, the doctor practiced patience in Mexico City. Though Maximilian was away on his imperial gadding, the Empress Carlota remained in the capital, and Gwin turned to her for support. He was encouraged to find her more capable and clear-headed than her airy-minded husband. By the same steamer that carried the appeal to Morny, the doctor also sent

---

* Legislative Corps,
Presidency.

Sir. The Duke de Morny presents his distinguished compliments to Mr. Gwin, and begs him to come to speak with him on Monday, in the forenoon, September 17.

letters to his wife and daughters which betrayed no slackening of confidence, despite the setbacks. The letter to Mrs.
Gwin read:

> The continued absence of the emperor, and the heavy rains
> that have flooded the whole country, have suspended all business
> of state and military movements. The plan I suggested of sub-
> mitting the question of colonizing Sonora to the empress has been
> executed. . . . I prepared the argument in favor of the policy,
> and Montholon the treaty. Mr. Corta [Napoleon's fiscal agent in
> Mexico] read them at large to her Majesty. The work was well
> done. General Bazaine, although approving all, stood aloof, so
> that if the emperor and empress refused to make the treaty, he
> might not be embarrassed. . . .
> The last time I saw him, I said I was "getting sick of inaction,
> and believed if he would furnish me with an outfit and escort,
> I would join the army en route for Sonora between Durango and
> Mazatlán." He agreed to furnish me with everything I wanted
> at once, but advised me to wait, and go with him, as the most
> comfortable and expeditious mode of traveling. . . . In fact the
> roads are now impassable everywhere. There have not been such
> rains for years. . . . I must, therefore, wait on the seasons. If
> the treaty is made I shall be fully repaid for the delay. I am more
> and more satisfied, as I collect information, of the enormous rich-
> ness of the gold and silver mines of Sonora, and that the climate
> is the most healthy and delicious.

Later that day, in jubilant mood, he wrote to his daughter
Lucy:

> Mr. Corta's interview with the empress was very favorable.
> She raised many objections, as I expected she would, being a
> woman, but they all fell on points of the treaty which were not
> material. She is causing a counter-proposal to be made suggest-
> ing the modifications she wishes made. They will be at once con-
> ceded by Montholon, and then our success is complete! That is
> the way it looks now.
> I have written another letter for the emperor [Napoleon], and
> sent it by Mr. Corta. I will send you the rough copy I wrote, to

show you how free and easy I can write to an emperor. It is strange no Frenchman will write to him in this style. The "memorandum" referred to in the letter was prepared by me, and is the ablest document I ever wrote. It covers thirty-three pages of foolscap, and I wrote it in one evening, and in the morning before breakfast, but I wrote nearly all night. Within twenty-four hours after I was asked to prepare it, it was ready, to the astonishment of all, and I defy any man in Mexico to answer it.

The empress read every word of it in the presence of Mr. Corta, and declared when she began that "we" wanted to take all Mexico from them. But as she read she would say, "that's important" — "this is more important" — and "well, if France gets much, Mexico gets more," etc., etc. She ended by agreeing to everything, except some immaterial matters about permitting bullion being exported free of duty.

I am a little boastful, but it is only to my wife and children — my dear ones so far away from me. The emperor will be back next week, and it is intended that I shall have an audience of several hours with him and the empress (who, by the way, is the better business man of the two) to defend the treaty against all objections. Tomorrow I commence the preparation of a complete system of government to be adopted by the emperor, if he agrees to the treaty.

These tidings he signed, "Your devoted father, W. M. Gwin."

The memorandum he had prepared for the empress stressed the necessity for the occupation of the northern regions of Mexico by a French army "to protect the north from the hordes that will soon environ it . . . if the civil strife ceases in North America." Should Juárez, who was keeping up a token resistance in the north, "invite the disbanded soldiers who have been engaged in that war to join his banner, offering as the reward of success the rich mines of the north, it cannot be doubted that he can hold that country against any force which can be sent against him."

The letter to Napoleon sounded a harsher note. "Sire," read

this communication, dated September 12, 1864: "At the audience which was accorded to me before I left Paris for Mexico, your Majesty was pleased to grant me the privilege of presenting to your Majesty my views on the state of political and military affairs in the empire of Mexico." Having asked for it, Napoleon was told, with Jacksonian bluntness. "Deplorable . . . a century of chaos . . . robbery by government officials a national institution . . . tranquillity possible only a generation hence. . . ." The bill of particulars piled up, none of it flattering to Maximilian or the meddlers around him. Everything depended upon holding the northern department against "all enemies of the empire"; the gold to indemnify France would stream out of Sonora only as rapidly as settlers moved in.

Chapter IV

AT LENGTH MAXIMILIAN returned to his capital, and Gwin awaited a call to discuss business; instead, he received an invitation to a wedding. Julia, daughter of the Marquis de Montholon, was to become the bride of Captain Garcin of the French expeditionary force, and although her Paris wedding gown was stuck in the mud somewhere between Mexico City and Vera Cruz, the emperor decreed that the marriage be celebrated forthwith. Julia must make do with Mexican needlework.

Socially Gwin enjoyed the esteem of the palace, and upon this occasion he was one of the innermost circle, treated with the deference due to a man who spoke familiarly with emperors and whose occult influence must be reckoned with. For his daughter he penned a lively description of the festivities, noting that he and the wife of an American engineer employed by Maximilian were the only Americans among the twenty-odd guests. The emperor and empress stood as witnesses for the bride and bridegroom, and Bazaine attended with his staff, brilliantly uniformed.

The civil ceremony, a tedious affair, was performed in the audience chamber of the palace, followed by a nuptial mass in the imperial chapel, celebrated by the emperor's chaplain, the Archbishop of Mexico. Then the witnesses signed the attestations — emperor and empress first, followed by all the others, a formality that consumed an hour. After that came the wedding breakfast, which lasted until afternoon, and at night there was a grand ball. Gwin confessed that he had got to bed at "six o'clock in the morning, just twenty-four hours from the time I got up to dress for the wedding," and had enjoyed himself hugely.

During the mass he had been placed close to the imperial couple, in a position to study them carefully, and his impression had been on the whole favorable, although his comment on Maximilian was tepid: "Very polite, kind, and amiable" — hardly the essential qualities for a ruler. However, for every reason he wished the pair success.

During October the sociable doctor was treated to another picturesque spectacle, an alfresco military mass celebrated in the camp of the French army. In his account to his family, he told of riding into the camp and being greeted by Bazaine, who had just been created a marshal of France and was infatuated with his new honor.

As I walked among the little Frenchmen, they looked at me with curious eyes, as if they thought me a giant [wrote the six-foot doctor]. Upon the arrival of the royal cortège, the emperor and empress were properly received and escorted to their tents. . . . Shortly afterwards they both came out and walked about, admiring the prospect. She ran around with evident delight, like a school girl on a holiday. Presently the emperor mounted a horse, and with an escort rode off. About an hour later he returned, and dinner was soon announced. Three bands of music played at intervals during the repast, which lasted two hours.

The scene was a grand one. At our feet the City of Mexico, at our right the great snow mountains looming up thousands of feet above us. To add to the imposing effect a thunder storm rolled close by, the thunder reverberating through the mountains, and the rain poured down in sight of but not reaching us. Such beautiful rainbows I never witnessed before in my life. . . . When we rose from dinner the fireworks began. The heavens were illuminated with them, while each discharge was accompanied by the music of bands and the shouts of the soldiers. This continued until ten o'clock, at which hour their majesties retired, apparently enchanted with the whole performance. The marshal then came to my tent and invited me into his, where we had a bottle of fine champagne, and a short chat before turning in.

Just as the day broke, the next morning [the letter continued], I was aroused by the most heavenly music I ever listened to. The three bands were playing a solemn anthem, Austrian I think, preparatory to the celebration of mass. When the music ceased everybody was in action, and we all began to wash and dress right out in the open air, emperor and all. It is a principle of the French officers and soldiers always to keep their tents dry, and they never allow a drop of water to fall inside of them. We were soon dressed, and the bugles on all sides of us called the troops into ranks. Officers galloped rapidly about, and in a short time the whole of the army present had assembled around the altar where mass was to be celebrated. The emperor and empress then emerged from their tents escorted by the marshal and staff, and the ceremony began.

It was very imposing, with the bands playing and the troops presenting and grounding arms at given signals. After it was all over, the emperor and empress stepped into their carriage and drove slowly off. . . . We then took a cup of coffee, and mounted our horses for a ride. We traversed mountain paths, visited ruins in the vicinity, and returned to camp, where, at eleven o'clock, we sat down to breakfast with the marshal and his staff and principal officers. It lasted nearly two hours. I sat on the marshal's right, and the theme during the whole meal was Sonora. The marshal, it seemed to me, wished his staff and officers to hear me on the subject, and they were enthusiastic when he said he might take them all there.

All in all, the doctor thought, it was "the most remarkable excursion I have ever made."

2

But scenic outings did nothing to prosper his plans. Socially he found Maximilian affable, but no word of business escaped the imperial lips. Bazaine, swaggering and sly, offered excuse after excuse for not putting the Sonora expedition into motion.

Gwin strove against an atmosphere of hostility, against eva-
sions and subterfuges, while awaiting the response from Paris
to his jogging of Morny. Let a little pressure be exerted by
Napoleon, and he was sure local objections would melt away.

Napoleon was exerting pressure, although Gwin did not
know it. On November 16, the French emperor had written to
his dilatory puppet in Mexico in an effort to allay Maximilian's
expressed fear that Gwin's scheme was a preliminary to the
taking-over of Sonora — probably by Anglo-Saxon, Protestant
North Americans. "I know that Mr. Gwin's projects have not
met with favor in Mexico," Napoleon adjured his brother emperor, "yet he is the man best able to be of service in that country. In order to exploit Sonora, it is necessary to adopt the
Spanish code for the mines, and that of North America for the
colonists." But this need not be destructive of Mexican interests, Napoleon went on:

> It is feared in Mexico that Sonora may become an American
> province, but believe me, even if nothing is done, it will become
> one by force of circumstances. Colonists and adventurers are
> already entering the province, one by one, and as soon as a great
> number of them are there, without government, organization, and
> control, they will declare themselves independent. This will not
> happen if the government places itself at the head of the im-
> migration, plants its flag there, and organizes the country.

Napoleon wanted the treaty to be concluded and Gwin
started on his way, under Bazaine's escort. But Maximilian
hedged, replying to Paris in a letter dated December 27:

> The establishment of a regular government in Sonora under
> the simultaneous protection of the French and Mexican flags is
> the object of all my care, and will, I hope, enable me in a not
> too distant future to enhance the resources of this interesting
> portion of my vast empire. Thanks to the establishment of this
> government, I shall then be charmed to see Mr. Gwin attract

there the many American colonists who appear to be merely awaiting a sign from him to group themselves around him to seek their fortunes.

But despite such kind words, Dr. Gwin continued to be sedulously avoided at the palace by the misfit who uneasily occupied Montezuma's throne.

All the while, the trend of the fighting in the United States grew more and more disquieting. As the year ran out it seemed inevitable that the Confederacy would crumble. In November, Abraham Lincoln had been reelected President, despite frantic opposition by the peace party, who wished to compromise with the rebels. In Georgia, Sherman, and in Virginia, Grant, were battering the South's last defenses. Gwin still hoped for a Southern victory, although the hope was tenuous. Should the North be victorious, Maximilian and his advisers might abandon the Sonora scheme in fear of the Yankees. Time was running out. Morny was the key to the situation; the duke must make Napoleon realize that if he was to survive in Mexico, he must act swiftly and decisively; Maximilian must be compelled to sign the Sonora treaty, and Bazaine must occupy the province with French troops.

Persuaded that no one could present the impending danger as forcefully as himself, early in January of 1865, Dr. Gwin sailed back to France.

Chapter V

Gwin had been adding to Washington's anxieties. His colonization project was grist for the press, and there was speculation, both friendly and hostile, over the "Duke of Sonora" and his chances of succeeding. Regarding most of this concern with his activities — and their probable ultimate aim — the doctor was kept informed by correspondents; but there was one quarter of which he did not know, where his doings were viewed with stern disapproval. Thus, when he set out for Paris, he was unaware of a letter written by a square-jawed, cigar-chewing man with a stubble beard, at City Point, Virginia, on January 8, 1865. The communication was headed "Headquarters Armies of the United States," and was addressed to "Maj. Gen. I. McDowell, Commanding Dept. of the Pacific," at San Francisco. It read:

It is known that Dr. Gwin, former United States Senator from Cal., has gone to Mexico and taken service under the Maxamillian government. The Dr. is a rebel of the most virulent order. His being formerly a resident of California, and now getting to that State in Mexico bordering on the State of his former residence, portends no good to us. May it not be his design to entice into Sonora the dissatisfied spirits of California, and if the opportunity occurs, organize them and invade the State? I write, without having discussed this question with any one, to put you on your guard against what I believe may prove a great danger. Watch this matter closely, and should you find these apprehensions well founded, prepare to meet them. . . .

In an event like the one alluded to, I would not rest satisfied with simply driving the invader onto Mexican soil, but would pursue him until overtaken, and would retain possession of the territory from which the invader started until indemnity for the past, and security for the future, satisfactory to our Government, was insured. . . .

This letter is intended as *private* until the exigency contemplated calls for action on your part, when it will be regarded as instructions for your guidance in the absence of more recent orders.

[Signed] U. S. GRANT, Lt. Gen.

The Union commander was about to launch his final, successful assault upon Petersburg, and then Richmond. The French-Maximilian incursion into Mexico he regarded as inimical to the United States, and he was prepared, as quickly as military forces could be diverted to that sector, to move against it. And he proposed to temporize with no ex-senator.

In California, the activities of Dr. Gwin were also provoking apprehension, which was intensified by the mystery that surrounded them. While Gwin was at sea, accounts of his purportedly sinister designs were published in the California newspapers. The *Alta California,* staunchly unionist, was both puzzled and frightened by the Gwin enigma, and when the paper tried to ascertain the truth it came up with a thoroughly garbled explanation.

On January 23, 1865, the *Alta* published a dispatch from its correspondent at Mazatlán, dated January 11, which stated that in fulfillment of the Treaty of Miramar (which had bound Mexico to pay the costs of the French intervention and occupation), Maximilian had ceded to France "the entire right and ownership of the States of Sonora, Sinaloa, Durango, and Chihuahua. These States are to be consolidated into one province, to be exclusively French, though under the protection of the Mexican flag." Although this was the proposal Gwin had suggested in regard to Sonora, the Mazatlán reporter erred in stating that it had already taken place. The report went on:

The most curious part of the story is that, after having expended this vast amount of money, incurring the risk of a war with the United States, Napoleon should turn the whole thing over to an American traitor. Ex-Senator Gwin, it is positively asserted by his friends here, has the commission of governor-general or viceroy, and will leave Mexico [City] for Arispe, Sonora — the intended capital — in ten days. A code of laws, drawn up by him while in Mexico last year, was submitted to Napoleon and approved by him. Five or six Americans (Southerners) arrived here last night from Mexico [City], to prepare the way for the new viceroy. Among them I notice . . . a brother of General Beauregard. Judge Shattuck, formerly of your city, and a host of secessionists are here in great glee.

If we are to receive the news of Dr. Gwin's accession to great power under French authority and under the protection of French bayonets as a fact, then we may be permitted to assign a reason for such an extraordinary act of abnegation on the part of the usually tenacious emperor. Either he is greatly deceived in the character of his newly pledged favorite, attributing to him and his followers qualities unknown to the Southern character, or he proposes, with some ulterior motives, to aid in the establishment of a government antagonistic to our own, from the debris of the Southern Confederacy.

In a postscript to this dispatch, the importance of Gwin's role in the alarming development was somewhat diminished:

The mail has just arrived from Mexico [City], by which we have more definite intelligence in regard to the movements of our friend Gwin. It now seems that he is simply the representative of large capitalists in France, who have made arrangements for the purchase of all the public lands in the States of Sonora and Sinaloa, with a view to develop the mineral resources and invite immigration. Mr. Gwin is simply the agent, but is guaranteed by the government every protection.

Two days later, the *Alta* established definitely that something important was going on. "Agents of His Highness, 'El Duque de Gwin,' Viceroy, etc., etc.," were in San Francisco, the newspaper said, "making arrangements for emigration to the new possessions of the Emperor Napoleon on the Pacific coast of America." *Alta* greeted this development with ridicule. An editorial headed "Will You Walk into My Parlor, Said the Spider to the Fly," closed with this caustic injunction:

> The wants of three parties in Mexico will be, to some extent, supplied by the gudgeons caught in the nets of these agents — the Franco-Austrian imperialists, who want help to put down the indomitable republicans; the republicans, who want help to drive the ruthless invaders from their soil; and the Apaches, who are in want of scalps and store clothes and don't care a pin which side they take them from. . . . Discontented and unappreciated descendants of the dilapidated Chivalry, go in! Go in!

Notwithstanding this belittling, many Californians were haunted by the thought of the scheming Gwin poised on their border, obviously for no friendly purpose. His abilities were respected, even by those who denounced him most, and all through January the press probed the mystery without allaying the public's uneasiness. There was much banter about "His Serene Highness, Duke de Gwin," and the French language newspaper at San Francisco, *Echo du Pacifique*, strove to bury the whole subject under its scorn, saying:

> The press, for want of wholesome and substantial nourishment, sometimes lives upon bubbles. The Gwin story is in fact only a bubble, which will burst and leave no trace. We shall not waste any more ink upon the subject.

In reply, the San Francisco *Press* (called by unionists a mouthpiece for copperheads) reiterated that it had confirmation of Gwin's role from the French minister to Mexico:

> We believe Count [sic] Montholon a better authority on French affairs in Mexico than the editors of the *Echo*. . . . Dr. Gwin is agent of both Louis Napoleon and Maximilian, without being the

subject of either — a disinterested party in his relations to both sovereignties. He is no duke, nor holds any title or order of nobility from either. . . .

This failed to reassure jittery Californians. The mystery grew worse when letters and newspapers from Paris contained no mention of Gwin, and the consuls of France, Austria, and Mexico all professed ignorance of his intent. No enlightenment came from Mexico City. As the *Alta California* admitted:

> The proximity of the domain set apart for Gwin by rumor, the large interests of our citizens in its mines, the familiar knowledge that we have of the pretended victory — all these facts render us solicitous.

2

The war was in its penultimate stages. Having marched through Georgia, Sherman was hacking his way through the Carolina swamps, while Grant was demolishing the last resistance around Richmond. With defeat imminent, large numbers of Confederates were eying imperialist Mexico as a possible haven. Simultaneously, in Europe, Napoleon III had become disillusioned with his Mexican glory-hunt. France faced formidable problems in Europe, and the public was grumbling about the burden of maintaining an army across the Atlantic for no profitable reason. The emperor began to flirt with the notion of liquidating the whole affair — if it could be done in a way that would save French pride.

Trial balloons were lofted. On February 8, Bigelow read in the government newspaper, the *Moniteur*, a paragraph saying that "all reports circulating in the journals relative to a cession made to France by the Mexican government of certain premises of Sonora, Chihuahua, etc., etc., are absolutely unfounded." Secretary of State Seward had been prodding Bigelow to get to the bottom of Gwin's real purpose in Mexico. Seward knew and respected Gwin's organizing skill; and might it not be, he suggested to Bigelow, that the ex-senator was aiming to establish a sanctuary for defeated Confederates, or even to provide a fresh foothold for the Confederacy, after it had been crushed and its leaders expelled from the Southern states?

Bigelow sent Seward the extract from the *Moniteur*, with this comment:

> The rumors which this paragraph is designed to put at rest have been widely circulated in Europe and had begun to provoke discussion even in France, but in a tone uniformly unfavorable to the cession — the proximity of the new colony to the United States being always enumerated as its chief objection. Last evening at the palace, before the opening of the ball, his Majesty said to me, "I am sorry those rumors got into the journals about Sonora; there is nothing whatever in them." . . . His Majesty then added laughingly, "What I want is to get out of it altogether."

The *Moniteur* disavowal was picked up by the American press, and *Alta California* matched it with an extract from the Paris newspaper *La France*, a periodical that enjoyed semiofficial status: "We do not know the origin of these [Sonora] reports. We have good authority for saying that there is no foundation for them." All the rumors about "Gwin's appointment to a dukedom, viceroyalty, or other high office, as governor of the ceded province," the *Alta* preened itself upon having discredited from the start; nevertheless it deemed it wise to caution its readers that:

> Even though the rumor about Gwin is false, still there may be some truth in the statement that Mexico has, in a secret treaty, given Sonora to France as security for the war debt. . . . Private letters from the City of Mexico state that Gwin applied in vain to the emperor [Maximilian] for authority to invite immigrants from California, and after a long deferment of his hopes, finally went in disgust to France.

✻

3

Such was the confusion when Gwin reached Paris about March 6. He found Morny desperately ill, unable to receive visitors or transact business. On March 10 the duke died.

With the knocking out of this prop, the whole edifice of Gwin's plan threatened to topple, and temporarily he gave up thought of returning to Mexico. Yet Napoleon still might save the project, if he would act promptly. In any event, a report was due him, and Gwin solicited an audience.

Determined that Napoleon should understand the fiasco building up in Mexico, the doctor used language in this interview which emperors seldom hear. He described Maximilian as an honest man, well intentioned, a patron of the arts, a connoisseur of painting — but "of all men living, probably the least qualified to govern Mexico." Outside the narrow zone occupied by the French army he possessed no authority. He squandered his salary of a million and a half pesos on pageantry, while the people perished of famine; he surrounded himself with guards gorgeously caparisoned, while every highway teemed with beggars and brigands; he had produced nothing but blunders, and had brought nothing except more discords to a hopelessly divided country. In sum, said Gwin, Maximilian was a "paper emperor," and must be dealt with as such: he must be told to approve the Sonora treaty, and Bazaine must be ordered to take the field. Further delay would mean disaster.

Napoleon replied that whatever Maximilian's shortcomings, he was an emperor, and must be accorded the respect due to his station. However, the doctor was correct in maintaining that the mineral wealth of Mexico should be tapped; and he requested Gwin to redraft the colonization scheme on a broader, more comprehensive scale, to take in not only Sonora but such contiguous territory as might advantageously be included.

An emperor's request is a command. Gwin submitted the
enlarged plan, and his estimates of the potential gains rekin-
dled Napoleon's enthusiasm. Again pledging all necessary
military assistance, he urged Gwin to hasten back to Mexico
and get the scheme under way. But Gwin was wary as a result
of previous experience, and he insisted on getting agreement
to his terms in writing, so there could be no misunderstanding.
In a letter dated March 25, 1865, he said:

> I am willing to return to Mexico, to put my plan of colonization
> into operation, provided French troops occupy the State and aid
> me in my enterprise.

This was clear and specific. In a separate memorandum
accompanying the letter, the doctor marked out a path to
French-Mexican solvency that led directly through Sonora and
the adjacent territories:

> If an arrangement can be made with the Emperor Maximilian
> to extend this plan of colonization to the States of North Mexico
> (Sonora, Sinaloa, Durango, and Chihuahua), and the revenues
> from the customs and mines within those States are especially set
> apart to pay the interest — and when in excess of the interest,
> then to be applied to the principal of the debt due from Mexico
> to France — your Majesty may then safely make additional ad-
> vances to Mexico, to meet her immediate, pressing pecuniary
> needs. . . .

Such an extension of the treaty area would take in territory
larger than all of France. To fortify Napoleon in his resolve,
Gwin again pointed out that the "right sort" of colonists in
Northern Mexico would form an effective barrier against interference from the United States. He explained the plight in
which Southern sympathizers in the non-seceded states found
themselves under the Lincoln government, and said these
would be sure to respond to a call to settle elsewhere:

The hostility of the supporters of Mr. Lincoln's government to opponents of that government in the North is as fierce as it is against the Confederate States; the only difference in the contest is that it is carried on by arms in the South. The civil war has uprooted society and the social system that formerly existed in the United States. The opponents of Mr. Lincoln's government in the North will have to accept one of three alternatives — resistance, which would be folly; submission; or expatriation. Give them the alternative, and they will eagerly adopt the latter, leaving the United States by thousands to settle in northern Mexico. . . . There will be no hostile intent against any government, but if war comes, they will be able to defend the country against aggression.

Secretary of State Seward would have been interested in this nod passing between promoter and emperor.

What Gwin himself did not know was that Napoleon had instructed Bazaine to begin quietly withdrawing his troops toward the coast, where they could be taken aboard transports, a few at a time, and returned to France. This meant a gradual, concealed evacuation of Mexico and the abandonment of Maximilian. Bazaine was cautioned to disguise his movements and deny that the French intended to depart; but already the garrisons manning the northernmost outposts had been pulled back, and Juárez's reanimated forces were moving into that region as fast as the French retreated.

Despite this, on March 31 Napoleon gave Dr. Gwin a letter of endorsement dictated by himself, written on embossed stationery bearing the imperial "N" and crown, and signed by the emperor's chief of cabinet, Conti. It read:

Monsieur.
L'Empereur me charge de vous envoyer la lettre ci-jointe pour le Maréchal Bazaine. Dans cette lettre Sa Majesté vous recommande à son intérêt, mais en même temps Elle l'invite à ne pas faire d'expédition compromettante pour la sureté de notre occupation

du Mexique. L'Empereur espère que l'Empereur Maximilian en-
gréera vos projets et le Maréchal a l'ordre de les appuyer auprès
de lui.

Agréez, Monsieur, l'assurance de ma considération très dis-
tinguée.

Le Secrétaire de l'Empereur
Chef du Cabinet de S.M.
CONTI*

Armed with this imperial rescript, and ignorant of Napoleon's real intentions in Mexico, Gwin set out again on April 1,
1865. John Bigelow, watching in Paris, immediately alerted
Seward in a "very confidential" dispatch:

> I understand that Gwin has obtained the promise of the em-
> peror to furnish him as many soldiers as he requires to protect
> him and his men in their mining operations. . . . My authority
> for this at second hand is Colonel Duncan of Miss. [a Confederate
> agent], who stated . . . that after what has occurred he cannot
> live in the United States, and he had determined to strike out
> for Mexico.

That Gwin's activity was tied in with some scheme involv-
ing Confederates, Bigelow was certain.

This alert to Seward was written on April 19 — ten days after
General Lee's surrender at Appomattox, and five days after
President Lincoln's assassination. Neither of these events was
yet known in Europe. Nor was Dr. Gwin aware of them when
he sailed back to the scene of his thus far frustrated hopes.

---

* Sir.
The Emperor has instructed me to deliver to you the accompanying
letter to Marshal Bazaine. In that letter his Majesty commends you to
his interest, but at the same time recommends him not to hazard expeditions which might endanger the security of our occupation of Mexico.
The Emperor hopes that the Emperor Maximilian will favor your projects, and the marshal is ordered to support them in that quarter.
Accept, sir, the assurance of my most distinguished consideration.

The Emperor's Secretary
Chief of His Majesty's Cabinet
CONTI

Chapter VI

ON THIS SECOND journey Gwin took along his son, William, who was to share importantly in the Sonora enterprise. When father and son reached Mexico, they found the situation radically changed. The capital was in a turmoil caused by the collapse of the Confederacy and Lincoln's assassination. Washington was raising a hue and cry against every sympathizer with "the side that killed Lincoln," and Mexican officials were treading on eggshells. The outlook for Gwin's plan seemed far from propitious. His personal position was ambiguous, for where, really, in respect to the American conflict, did he stand? His one-time friend Seward was reported (erroneously, it turned out) to have been slain with Lincoln. Another friend, Jefferson Davis, was a prisoner, captured while attempting to flee the country — heading possibly for Mexico. Disbanded rebels were crossing the border from Texas in considerable numbers, and some of these, especially those who had been active in the guerrilla fighting in the western states, were lawless men.

Gwin had lost a powerful advocate at Maximilian's court by the transfer of Montholon to Washington; with the new minister, Dano, who was expected to arrive daily, Gwin had no rapport. Sonora seemed to be the doctor's best chance, both politically and financially. He knew that he was the object of sinister suspicions in the United States: in California the animosity displayed against him was greater than that felt for avowed Confederates; and from the new President, Andrew Johnson, a

Tennessean who hated Gwin's class of Southern aristocrats, the
ex-senator could expect no clemency. Statements of the utmost bloodthirstiness were emanating from the White House.

Shortly after reaching the Mexican capital, Gwin revealed
his anxieties to his wife, although he insisted that all would yet
turn out favorably. This letter was dated May 11, a month
after Lincoln's assassination:

> We arrived here at a fearful crisis in the affairs of this con-
> tinent. Everything is shaken here, as elsewhere, by the surrender
> of Lee, and the death of Lincoln and Seward. This country is
> paralyzed by the news. The Liberals are rejoicing at the prospect
> of the speedy appearance of the Yankees to exterminate the em-
> pire and restore them to power. Poor, miserable fools! What
> kind of deliverance will they find then? If ever they do overrun
> the empire, they will make helots of the whole population, and
> to that extent they will do some good, for a more indolent set
> of devils does not exist.
>
> I cannot hurry until I find out what results these events in the
> United States will produce in adjoining countries. The Yankees
> here say, "conquest of the North American continent." I don't
> think so, but, if France weakens, the empire is gone.
>
> Marshal Bazaine, aged fifty-five, is soon to be married to a
> mature damsel of seventeen. There is much fun made of this
> marriage, but I fear it will not be fun to those who want business
> transacted in the empire; the time spoken of for the marriage is
> just the time the marshal should be on his way to Sonora. With
> the marshal courting, and the emperor wandering through the
> country stuffing birds, public business is at a standstill.

Gwin's reappearance excited speculation in official quarters.
Although he applied at once for an audience at the palace, his
request was ignored. Maximilian again was browsing through
the countryside, and was busy converting a hacienda at
Cuernavaca into a delicious country retreat. There were also
the distractions attending the celebrating of Carlota's birthday
with fireworks and fandangos. Although General Grant had

sent sixty-five thousand troops under General Philip Sheridan
to the Texas border, and at the instance of another general who
believed in positive action — Sherman — was leaving quanti-
ties of arms and matériel unguarded along the frontier, to be
spirited away by Juáristas, Maximilian was not alarmed. But
Louis Napoleon was becoming sensitive to the increasing indignation expressed by Bigelow. Seward's remonstrances were
becoming peremptory, so much so that the Paris press grew bitter over the "presumption" of Washington in daring to tell
France what it must do. Napoleon tried to placate Bigelow by
assuring him that the evacuation of French forces from Mexico
would be speeded up.

Meanwhile many eyes were upon Gwin, watching his actions
and studying the chances of his getting to Sonora in any capacity. One of Bazaine's staff officers felt that the chances of the
"venerable doctor" were slim, and noted "his restlessness, his
disillusions, and his anger when he came into collision with
Maximilian." On the other hand, the Vera Cruz correspondent
of the New Orleans *Times* believed that Gwin was on the verge
of success. In June this observer reported:

> The Confederates continue to flock to Mexico. There is no
> doubt Doctor Gwin will get his project through. It only awaits
> the signature of Maximilian to become law. He goes out as di-
> rector general of emigration for the States of Sonora, Chihuahua,
> Durango, and Tamaulipas, with extraordinary powers and eight
> thousand French troops to back him. The emigration is to be
> strictly Southern, or Confederate. Ten thousand Confederates are
> to be armed and paid by the empire, but kept in the above-
> mentioned States as protection to the emigrants on the frontier.
> Doctor Gwin's son has applied for and will get an exclusive
> privilege for all the railroads in Sonora. The Southerners are
> elated, and golden visions float before them. . . . The latest news
> from the United States has caused a panic [among Maximilian's
> Mexican adherents], and every mail is anxiously expected. The
> Yankee invasion they consider certain, but hug to themselves the

idea that France, Austria, and Belgium will not allow the United States to invade the empire. . . .

The French loudly complain . . . that if they must fight the United States, the prize must be for them. . . . The Confederates seriously proclaim that they only can save the empire by the emigration of Southerners, who will rally by the thousands at the call of Gwin, and raise an impassable barrier against American aggression. This is seriously believed and proclaimed by the French commander-in-chief.

As usual, Bazaine was full of brag. He breathed fire and scorned the American threat, and to Gwin he continued to make promises and avoided fulfilling them with the agility of a lizard. He really had no time or thought for anything except his approaching nuptials. Gwin felt the ground giving way under him even while he persisted in seeking the all-important assent of Maximilian to the protectorate treaty. But the emperor continued to act like an intelligent tourist, rather than the head of a government that was slithering toward dissolution. Then at this point the wheels of intrigue and high-level diplomacy began to intermesh in a way that would be fatal for Gwin.

2

Colonel Don Enrique A. Mejia was a member of the Liberal (Juárista) party in Mexico. He had held aloof from the fighting, however, and had been living in the United States. Inheriting property at home, he obtained a safe-conduct from the Maximilian authorities permitting him to return and settle the estate. When that business was completed, Mejia set out in June on his way back to the United States. Traveling to Vera Cruz in the same coach with him was another Liberal, and the suspicions of the French military were aroused. At Vera Cruz, Colonel Mejia was arrested, his trunk was searched and his papers were confiscated. He was held eight days; then, without explanation, he was released, his papers were handed back, and he was permitted to continue his journey.

Upon checking over the returned papers, the colonel found among them several that had not been there before. These included letters written by Dr. Gwin and his son, addressed to Mrs. Gwin at 55 Boulevard Malesherbes, Paris, under cover of another envelope addressed to "Messrs. Van den Broeck et Compagnie, rue de la Chausée d'Antin" — Gwin's Paris bankers. Also, there was a letter written by Gwin to Colonel John Winthrop, of New York, enclosed in a second envelope addressed to "Royal Phelps, Esquire, 22 East 16th Street, New York City." And there was a letter signed "Massey," addressed to the "Hon. B. Wood," editor of the strongly pro-Southern New York *Daily News* and brother of the copperhead former mayor of New York, Fernando Wood. Enclosed with the last was an open letter to the editor of the *News*, signed "Journalist."

How this correspondence had strayed into Colonel Mejia's hands was a mystery. Was it by accident? Or had the letters, intercepted by either French or Mexican intriguers, been smuggled intentionally into Mejia's papers under cover of his arrest?

Realizing the significance of the documents, Colonel Mejia, a Liberal, immediately turned them over to the Juárista minister in Washington, Mattias Romero, who lost no time in transmitting them to Secretary of State Seward.

The secretary read the correspondence, ordered Ben Wood arrested on suspicion of sedition, and dictated instructions to Bigelow at Paris to lodge a most vigorous protest against Gwin's dealings with the French government. Copies of the intercepted letters were enclosed, for Bigelow's use. As he would see, they fully justified the secretary's sense of urgency in the matter.

❋

3

In the letter written by Gwin's son to his mother, impressions of their arrival at Mexico City had been set down in snatches extending over several days, the first was dated May 16, 1865. The young man echoed the current refrain:

> All business has come to a standstill because of the emperor's absence. When his august Majesty has sufficiently amused himself with rural sports, he may take a notion to return to his sleeping capital.

Two days later Willie added:

> The old man saw the marshal the other day, but nothing resulted from the interview. He renewed his protestations of friendship, and declared he would urge the old man's claims to the utmost. . . . To think of our being kept here holding our hands, when those prodigious mines are inviting us to fortune, and all because the emperor will stuff birds! . . . I am dreadfully blue about the South. Andy Johnson's speeches breathe such a heinous spirit that I can see nothing ahead but extermination. . . . Johnson says . . . all traitors should be hung, and as we are all traitors, there's nothing left for us but hanging. It really makes me sick. . . .

The doctor's letter to his wife, bearing no date but obviously written at about the same time, was emotional also, though for the sake of the family he refused to despair:

> My dearly beloved Wife and Daughters: The startling news from the U.S. has made the blood of every Southern sympathizer run cold with horror. No one will be safe in our native country. How I thank Providence that I have cast my lot elsewhere, and that very soon I will have a home for my wife and children where they will be safe from oppression, and where we have every prospect of immediate and permanent prosperity. My

policy is on every man's lips as the only one that will save the empire. The emperor remains unaccountably away from the capital; but his minister having charge of this matter considers it so pressing that he has gone to him with it, more than a week ago. . . . The delay is unpleasant, but the certainty of success that will follow . . . gives me great consolation, especially when everything is so dark for us everywhere else.

Never have a doubt of my success — I have less now than ever. Willie is getting into heavy business. They are proposing to give him the entire control of the richest gold mine in the world, in Sinaloa, and he is one of the three who have asked for the concession of all the railroads in Sonora. He will succeed in both, and either of them will make a dozen fortunes. . . .

Never a doubt of my success. . . . That thought he clung to, as a buckler against the perils piling up north of the border. That had been the theme also of Gwin's letter of May 18 to Colonel Winthrop, a friend who was planning to invest in Sonora. "The news from the U.S. appalls every one here and paralyzes business," Gwin had written. But Winthrop must not give way to pessimism:

If anything in the future can be certain in this country, at an early date you will see a decree opening North Mexico to the enterprise of the world. What a people we can assemble there if this policy is adopted! . . . Say to Mrs. W[inthrop] that . . . she shall eat her Christmas dinner in the palace to a certainty, and what a time we will have! The day I leave here [for Sonora], I will send to France for a large supply of the best wines in Europe, and they will be mellow to the taste by Christmas. . . . When I write you to come, bring as many millions as you please, and they will turn into tens of millions. . . . I have to write so obscurely, for fear of accidents, that you may not comprehend me; but have faith that I know what I am about.

The intercepted letter to Ben Wood, signed "Massey," was from Dr. Thomas C. Massey, who had opened an agency to recruit emigrants for Mexico. "You see I have been cautious

but positive about Dr. Gwin," this letter read, and they went
on with positive assurances:

> They have all they want from the French emperor. . . . Mar-
> shal Bazaine has certain orders. The thing will be carried out
> and Gwin will go out as "Directeur-Général, etc." . . . There
> are fortunes in it, and a very peculiar kind of colonization per-
> mitted. . . .

The letter appended to this, addressed to the editor of the
News and signed "Journalist," was in Massey's handwriting,
and it contained what Seward considered flagrantly seditious
statements.

4

In obedience to Seward's instructions, Bigelow, at Paris, on
August 1, handed a strongly worded protest to the French Foreign Minister, Edouard Drouyn de Lhuys, accompanied by
copies of the intercepted letters. These, Bigelow pointed out,
clearly showed that "Dr. Wm. M. Gwin and his family, though
citizens of the United States, are disloyal to its government,
[and are] engaged in obtaining from Maximilian, titular Emperor of Mexico, grants of mineral lands . . . adjoining the
United States," where large-scale emigration "from parties in
rebellion against the United States" was contemplated. Gwin
and his associates, Bigelow complained, were assuring Maximilian and Napoleon "that their contemplated proceedings
will tend at once to promote the projects of Maximilian in Mexico and inure to the injury of the United States." They also
were claiming to have Napoleon's promise of military aid.

Bigelow said that he had been instructed "frankly to state
that the sympathies of the American people for the republicans
of Mexico are very lively, and that they are disposed to regard
with impatience the continued intervention of France in that
country; that any favor shown to the speculations of Dr. Gwin

by the titular Emperor of Mexico or by the imperial government of France will . . . be regarded, perhaps justly, as im-
porting danger . . . to the United States." For these reasons,
assurances were sought that "all the pretenses of Dr. Gwin and
of his associates are destitute of any action from the Emperor
of France. It is unnecessary to add," ran the *envoi* to this bal-
lad of remonstrances, "that, having expelled the insurgents
from our own borders, the United States would not look with
satisfaction upon their reorganization as martial or political
enemies on the opposite bank of the Rio Grande. . . ."

All this was extremely embarrassing to the potentate in the
Tuileries, for he had been caught red-handed assisting a conspiracy against the peace and security of the United States —
or what was so regarded by Washington — in violation of his
repeated pledge to observe neutrality in the American war.
Still, a protest of such gravity could not be overlooked, and on
August 7 Drouyn de Lhuys returned a peevishly phrased acknowledgment of the American minister's "mention of some
plans for the colonization of Mexico deemed to have been conceived with intentions hostile to the government of the United
States. It is not for me to enlighten you concerning the speculations of such and such a person who had emigrated to Mexico," Napoleon's spokesman rejoined toploftily. However,
some roundabout assurance was conveyed in the words: "But
what I know of the intentions of the Mexican government en-
ables me to say that it proposes to let the emigrants from the
Southern States enter upon its territory only individually and
without arms. They . . . will be immediately dispersed
throughout the empire and bound to abstain in their conduct
from anything which might awaken the just susceptibilities of
neighboring nations." In other words, no reconstituted Con-
ferate army was contemplated. There was not a word admitting Napoleon's complicity in the movement, but merely an
expression of resentment that the government should have

been "interpellated in a comminiatory tone, about vague allegations, and based upon documents of a dubious character."

The Empress Eugénie, writing to her vis-à-vis Carlota, termed the American protest positively rude.

Convinced that he had touched a sore spot, Bigelow refrained from rubbing it during the rest of that month. Then on August 31 he had a long interview with Drouyn de Lhuys and reported the conversation in a confidential dispatch to Seward.

The French minister, Bigelow said, had explained that the Tuileries had resented not the protest, but the imputation of having somehow been accessory to "conversations between Gwin, the emperor, and General Bazaine which could never have occurred." True, the emperor had seen Dr. Gwin "two or three times, as he sees all persons who are specially acquainted with any subject in which he is interested," and Drouyn de Lhuys himself had seen the doctor twice; but he denied that there were "any engagements whatever of the character referred to with Dr. Gwin," who had impressed him, in fact, as "a rash though energetic man." Bigelow told Seward:

> I replied that my communication [had been based] not on what the French and Mexican governments might do, but what I knew persons in relation to those governments, and animated primarily by hostility towards the United States, and by a desire to embroil the three governments, were trying to do. . . . I said to him that those people were not going to Mexico for any better purpose than to make that country the base of operations against the United States. . . . His excellency assented to what I said about the desire of the rebel emigrants to make their relations with the Mexican government a source of trouble between the United States and France, as if he had more evidence upon that point than I had myself. . . .

Bigelow's conclusion was that the conversation had confirmed that "the relations of Gwin with the emperor were, or had been, such as would not at present bear the light," and that Napoleon had betrayed his sense of guilt by showing "annoyance and irritation at being questioned upon the subject."

Although he did not know it, Bigelow was belaboring an all but defunct issue. His letter to Seward crossed one the secretary had dictated on August 24, but which would not reach Paris until September 12.

In this communication, Seward announced that latest advices from Mexico indicated that "the schemes of Dr. Gwin and other emissaries in Mexico . . . have altogether failed."

Chapter VII

THE DÉNOUEMENT HAD unfolded in an atmosphere of total
unreality. On June 28, Marshal Bazaine had married his pretty
Mexican heiress, Señorita Josefa Peña y Azcárate, with all the
panoply and pomp the capital could muster, and with the emperor and empress attending. (Exchanging court gossip with
Eugénie, Carlota wrote that the marshal was really smitten, for
he had taken up dancing again, and was boasting that he
never missed a *habañera!*) The festivities, prolonged for
weeks, effectively diverted Bazaine from all thought of martial
exploits. Meanwhile, Maximilian let affairs of state glide
while he applied his energies to projects like establishing an
Academy of Sciences, and assembling the portraits of all the
rulers of Mexico back to Montezuma. The Sonora treaty, on
which Gwin's calculations all rested, gathered dust in a palace
pigeonhole.

And the longer the emperor dallied, the bolder grew Gwin's
enemies at court. Soon rumor had it that the doctor was not
backed by Napoleon at all, but was a mere freebooter masking
his real purpose in Sonora, which indubitably was inimical to
Mexican interests. At first only a few inconsequential newspapers carried sporadic attacks, and no official sanction for
them was alleged. Gwin shook them off without undue alarm.

But now Bazaine introduced a fresh complication. Gwin,
the marshal intimated, ought to "work out an arrangement"
with the Jeckers — who since Morny's death had been pressing

a claim to one-third of all the public lands in Sonora. Gwin wrote to his wife regarding this new impediment:

> I did not think much of [Bazaine's suggestion] at the time, and declined to do so. Since then Jecker has called on Mr. Soulé [an associate of Gwin's], and left the impression on his mind that he was sent by the marshal. After full consideration, we decided to see Jecker. The result has been that a contract is almost completed by which I become the owner of the claim, which is to be tendered to the Mexican government on the same terms I have made for my other operations.

This must have struck a chill to Mary Gwin's heart, for the Jeckers had been calamitous to France; if the doctor had been compelled to enter into any deal with them, he must feel his situation to be desperate! Possibly Mary Gwin braced herself for doleful developments, and these came shortly thereafter.

On the very day when Marshal Bazaine went prancing toward the bridal bed — June 28 — an important Mexico City newspaper, *El Pajaro Verde*, reprinted an excerpt from the New York *Express*, which fallaciously reported that Dr. Gwin, escorted by French troops, was already on his way to Arispe by way of Guaymas, to establish an American colony in Sonora.

On that same day Maximilian's ministers broke their silence on Gwin, issued an emphatic denial that Sonora had been ceded to France, and *El Diario del Imperio*, the government newspaper, published a repudiation of Gwin and everything he was trying to accomplish:

> The emperor [Maximilian] has not pledged, much less already aliened, the department of Sonora. Mr. Gwin has not received from his Majesty any mission, nor any of the titles attributed to him. He is not attached to the government in any relation whatsoever. It appears even that he is entirely unknown to members of the administration. His sojourn in Mexico has no political significance whatever, the gates of the empire being open to the whole world.

We are also authorized to say that the magnanimous and intelligent monarch who directs the destinies of France has given official notice to us, by the intermediary of his legation in this capital, that he has no part in the combinations which are being formed, relative to Sonora, our government being free to act as it shall judge most suitable for the national interest.

This was categorical — a double betrayal, by Maximilian and Napoleon. Hastening to Bazaine, Gwin angrily demanded that the marshal exact a retraction from *El Diario*. But the bridegroom had other things on his mind, and he shrugged that the repudiation must have been inspired by Maximilian, or at least was not discountenanced by him; therefore no retraction would be forthcoming. Gwin protested that Bazaine, who knew the facts, could at least vindicate his good faith by publishing them; but the marshal again declined to meddle in a matter that concerned the honor of his sovereign.

Gwin laid the repudiation to the fright taken by Maximilian's entourage at the threatening military movements along the Texas border; he was being sacrificed in hope of appeasing Washington. Reviewing the situation realistically, he perceived that he could not count upon a single friend in Mexico. Maximilian's sycophants would be relieved were he to be blotted out by some "accident"; the Juáristas naturally hated him as an imperialist; Bazaine had written him off; to Napoleon he had become an incubus. His position was full of peril. He could accomplish nothing in Mexico now; that much was clear. And he had lost confidence in the permanence of Maximilian's regime. There remained but one course open: to make peace with the United States, if he could; if not for his own sake, then for his family's.

On June 29 — almost exactly one year from the day he had landed in Mexico — he sat down to announce his decision to his family in Paris:

My dear Wife and Children: It will be as sad for you to read as for me to write this letter. Ever since the appearance of the article I enclose [*El Diario*] I have determined to leave this country. The cause of this action is well known here, but will not be appreciated abroad. In fact, the Minister de Fomento [Interior], with whom Mr. Soulé had a long interview last evening, has no idea I am going away, so little do these people understand ours.

I confess it almost breaks my heart to give this thing up, and altogether on account of the pleasure my success would have given you all. I well knew the labor and trials I would have to go through, but there is nothing I would not endure for my wife and children. But we must look the question sternly in the face.

There is not a doubt that the sudden destruction of the Southern Confederacy has been the only obstacle to my complete success here. Fear of the power of the United States seems to be the prevailing sentiment all over the world. We cannot escape that power; its long arm reaches every country. Then why not submit at once? Abler generals and greater men than I am have been defeated by them, and compelled to lay down their arms. Then why should not we do the same? It is the country of our birth, where all we have is situated, and going to ruin for want of attention. . . .

It is in your household that my thoughts are constantly, night and day. . . . But enough on this score; we must meet our destiny as God has shaped it. He has not brought us here, but forces us to our own good to where He brought us into existence.

I send you a copy of a letter to the editor of the paper which published the enclosed article. I am to have an interview with Marshal Bazaine today at 3 o'clock, to read the same to him, and for him to say whether I must send it, for I shall not use the name of the Emperor Napoleon unless I am forced to do so; but if the marshal does not require the insertion of such an article as will satisfy me, I shall certainly send it.

Good-bye, my dear ones; this is the last letter you will ever receive from me in Mexico.

Gwin saw Bazaine, who refused to approve the letter to *El Diario,* and insisted that it should not be sent, because it might reflect invidiously upon Napoleon. Since a letter which lacked Bazaine's endorsement would be ignored, Gwin abandoned that approach. On July 3 he penned a letter to Napoleon himself, reviewing their association, announcing his withdrawal from Mexico, and appealing to the emperor for vindication of his motives.

This letter being dispatched (Napoleon would ignore it), Gwin paid a last call upon Bazaine and requested an escort to get out of the country. The roads were infested by bandits, and any attempt to leave the capital without military protection would be extremely hazardous.

The marshal was charmed to get rid of the troublesome doctor, and assigned an escort of cavalry. In return, Gwin advised Bazaine to take his own departure while there was still time; for Maximilian and his empire he foresaw only disaster.

Gwin might have traveled directly to Vera Cruz and there boarded the comfortable mail steamer for Europe. Instead, he chose to try to reach Bagdad, a Mexican port on the Gulf at the mouth of the Rio Grande; by taking this riskier northern route, he might be able to deflect the flow of immigrants into Mexico which was already under way, stimulated to no little extent by himself. If he could spread word that the Sonora project has been abandoned, and that he was leaving the country, some of these harried Americans might be spared a bitter disillusionment.

In mid-July, 1865, after a farewell salute from Marshal Bazaine, Gwin and his son rode out of Mexico City with their escort. Gwin's face was turned toward the north, toward Texas.

Chapter VIII

THE GWINS HAD a companion on their sortie from Mexico, one who caused them intense chagrin. John B. Clark was an ex-senator, too, but of the Confederate States. The rump legislature convened by Governor Claiborne Jackson of Missouri at the start of the war had elected Clark to the Senate at Richmond, where he had represented Missouri, a state that did not secede. Upon the collapse of the Confederacy, Clark fled to Mexico; but sensing the catastrophe building up there, he decided to strike out for Europe. Full of pity for himself, he was terrified by the thought of capture by the Yankees, for he had been instrumental in arming the guerrilla bands of Quantrill and Jackman that had ravaged Missouri so savagely. With Bazaine's permission, Clark attached himself to Gwin's escort. The doctor had contempt for the man, but could hardly forbid him to come along.

The party worked their way northward cautiously. There were frequent brushes with bandits, and at Monterrey they were held up several days while the escort cleared the route ahead. The plan was to make for the nearest point on the Rio Grande, and from there proceed downriver by boat. But they were forced farther west than they had expected, and reached the river about opposite Laredo, in Texas. There a skiff was procured to take them two hundred miles downstream to Bagdad. Upon their pushing off, however, they found the skiff leaked badly, and after an hour's bailing they made for the closest bank to avoid drowning. That bank was on the Texas side. The three fugitives landed, in the United States again.

Since the chance had fallen so, the doctor accepted it. But he refused to put up with Clark's company further; he not only detested the coward, but considered him dangerous. Striking out with his son for the nearest United States military base, Gwin left the Missourian to his own devices.

Six weeks after he had left Mexico City, Gwin walked into the headquarters at San Antonio of General Wesley Merritt, commanding the area. He identified himself, and requested permission to continue his journey to New York, there to take ship for France. General Merritt received the ex-senator civilly, assured him that he was free to go where he chose, and provided transportation to New Orleans. There Gwin reported to General Sheridan, commanding the Texas-Louisiana department, and Sheridan confirmed that he was at liberty to travel anywhere. Sheridan did make a routine report to Washington of Gwin's appearance, and back came a peremptory order to arrest the doctor and hold him in close confinement. Young Gwin was not mentioned in the order.

Thus suddenly the doctor found himself in military custody, for what reason and at whose instigation he did not know; his request for information was met with silence. Capping his misfortune was the ill luck of being held in the company of Clark, who had been picked up by a cavalry patrol soon after they had parted. Both were held as prisoners of state, and were taken to Fort Jackson, seventy-five miles down the Mississippi, and placed in a casemate of that damp, dismal fortress.

2

The first day they were at the fort, an army surgeon, a "contract officer" who had nothing of the military about him, visited them and painted a lugubrious picture of their probable fate. The man commanding Forts Jackson and St. Philip, he said, was an officer from Maine, Colonel Samuel G. Hamblen, who hated Southerners. Having been captured by the Confederates and treated badly, he had vowed to retaliate upon any "Confeds" who might fall into his hands.

This information threw Clark into a panic; Gwin himself was seriously alarmed. The surgeon's story was a fabrication; Colonel Hamblen had never been captured, and his supposed malevolence was entirely imaginary. But of this the prisoners were not aware, and Clark foresaw summary execution for himself. "I raised troops for Quantrill and Jackman," he moaned, knowing how the cruelties of those two ruffians had inflamed the loyalists of Missouri. Gwin was disgusted by the man's sniveling, and kept as far apart from him as their cramped quarters allowed.

Colonel Hamblen had not been at the fort when the two men were brought in. He returned a few days later, and found orders waiting of the strictest severity. He was commanded to confine the prisoners closely; to deny them communication with anyone, for any reason whatsoever, except in Hamblen's presence and within his hearing; to permit no visitor to see them who did not bring a pass signed by General Sheridan; and to prohibit the slightest discussion of political topics. Hamblen was in the dark as to the reason for such harshness, but deduced that the men were considered important by somebody, and he carried out his orders literally although with no vindictiveness. He at once inspected the casemate to satisfy himself that they were held securely, inquired whether their food was sufficient, and whether they had any complaints. Beyond these necessary questions, he was taciturn, and he made his inspection brief, feeling that under reversed circumstances he would prefer to be left alone. The colonel's brusqueness seemed to bear out the characterization of the man given by the surgeon, and the prisoners replied to their supposedly embittered jailer in the wariest of monosyllables.

The visit threw Clark into a frenzy. There was a case of

stores in their room, and he broke it open, found a bottle of brandy, and drank himself into a stupor that lasted two days, to Gwin's relief. At the end of that time an order came through to release him, and Gwin was left in sole possession of the casemate. He still knew nothing as to the cause of his arrest, or who had ordered it, and he was tortured by uncertainty.

Colonel Hamblen had heard about ex-Senator Gwin. He would have liked to have opened a little freer converse with him, but the doctor seemed to hold aloof. Hamblen respected this attitude, but remained curious. He found the old man physically impressive, the more so because of the patriarchal white beard which the ex-senator had grown since leaving Mexico City. But to Hamblen's tentative approaches, Gwin returned gruff, curt responses. The colonel realized that he was not the kind of man to talk unless he wished to, and that he obviously possessed great powers of circumspection and self-control.

After several weeks, the orders governing Gwin's confinement were relaxed to the extent of allowing him to roam within the limits of the fort. Gwin took eager advantage of this permission to leave the casemate, and every day Hamblen saw him taking exercise ("charging around," the colonel put it) on the terreplane. One day a passing steamboat tossed out a bundle of newspapers, and glancing through them, the colonel noticed a paragraph in the New York *Herald* stating that "W.M. Gwin, the Duke of Sonora," was a prisoner in Fort Jackson. Sure that Gwin would welcome any news from the outside, the colonel sent the paper to him.

The next day, while making his inspection rounds, Hamblen came upon Gwin taking his exercise. The old man seemed agitated, and accosting the colonel he asked abruptly whether the latter has seen the *Herald* report calling him a duke.

"There is not a word of truth in that statement," he exclaimed indignantly. "No power on earth could make me, a foreigner, a duke, even if I wished it, and it was never thought of until the newspapers started printing those articles! I'll tell you how it was."

Seating himself on the trail of a caisson, he poured out the whole story of his wartime experiences, from the moment of his arrest by General Sumner up to the present. He recounted his interviews with Napoleon, praising the emperor as the "ablest man I ever met," and the gradual failure of the plan for Sonora.

"Too bad, too bad," he repeated several times. "I should have had three hundred thousand miners there in two years."

Hamblen was fascinated by the recital, but retained doubts of the doctor's motivation.

"Where would you get your miners?" the colonel asked.

"Why, from the United States, the best miners in the world," replied Gwin.

"And you were to have three hundred thousand men from the United States?"

"That's right. I had the finest thing ever offered to an American citizen."

"How far is Sonora from what might be called the civilized regions of Mexico — the authority, the capital?" Hamblen went on, seeking to test Gwin's sincerity.

"About six hundred miles."

"You have said Napoleon was the smartest man you ever met. Don't you think you outwitted him in your bargain?"

The doctor looked sharply at his questioner. "Why?" he asked.

"You would have had your miners, enough for a small nation — or a large state — all American citizens, in a region adjoining the United States. What would they have done? Submit to the doubtful chance of Mexican control? Or turn to the United States and add another star to the Stars and Stripes?"

"I had nothing to do with that," Gwin objected. "I intended

to carry out my engagements in good faith, but I couldn't engage to control events outside of that."

"But," Hamblen pressed, "W.M. Gwin would have been the first senator from the state of Sonora, all the same."

The doctor waved aside this inference. "That would have been for the future; I should have done nothing to favor it."

"There would have been no need," Hamblen concluded, "nor could you have prevented it, even if so strongly inclined."

Gwin turned the conversation to the subject that occupied his mind incessantly: why he was held, when men of flagrant culpability — like that wretch Clark, for example — were turned loose? Why he was in prison?

"I don't understand why the government follows me so persistently," he said. "I have been in its service for thirty years, up to 1861, continuously, and in all that time have never said or done anything inconsistent with my duties. I was instrumental in establishing the mail route across the continent, largely for political reasons, to unite in interest the Far West and the East. I succeeded in establishing the pony express, and was careful to see that it had its route by the north, as I foresaw the impending difficulty, and how much exposed to forays it would be from the Southern states in the event of an outbreak. I obtained the establishment of the Mare Island Navy Yard, which would always remain under the control of the United States so long as they commanded the sea. When the question of secession arose, I set my face against it from first to last, and steadily refused, in any way, to become identified with it. My wife, the smartest woman I ever saw, would not countenance it, and when the action was taken, went north and remained. My boy went south, and I followed him and carried him to France. All my acts have been for the government, and I never did, or said, anything against it. When Mr. Lincoln arrived in Washington, after his trip through Baltimore, it was my private carriage, borrowed by Mr. Seward for the purpose, that carried him to his hotel. If I had not been known to be friendly, do you think I would have been entrusted with the information of that intended trip? I could easily have notified Baltimore of it — and then the carriage would not have been needed!"

This last was said grimly. Gwin went on:

"Why, when I was arrested coming from California, I recognized the necessity of all precautions on the part of the government, and submitted willingly, crossing the Isthmus, where, on neutral ground, I could have claimed and obtained my liberty; but I preferred to go on, confident that I could establish my record, clear from any taint of disloyalty. And this I did, and was discharged. Now I am under arrest again, by special orders from Washington. What charges have you against me?"

Hamblen could only reply that he knew nothing except that he had orders to keep the doctor inside the fort.

How far did Hamblen's jurisdiction extend, Gwin asked. For instance, should a writ of habeas corpus be served, would the colonel respect it? Hamblen answered that martial law prevailed at the fort, and the writ would be disobeyed. Then Gwin appealed candidly for help.

"I want to learn what the charges are against me, but I don't know your military forms. Will you assist me?"

"With pleasure," the colonel replied. The colonel had been won over by Gwin's magnetism and candor.

3

In this conversation (here presented as set down by Hamblen), the former senator argued his case well. Overtones were missing, it is true, and entirely absent was any expression of realization on Gwin's part that no partisan likes or trusts a neutral. His actions and motives appeared in one light to himself, and in a different light to others who were deeply involved in the national conflict. Again and again, in further talks with Colonel Hamblen, the doctor emphasized that he had made perfectly clear to Napoleon, before consenting to undertake the Sonora project, that he would do nothing hostile or unfriendly to the United States, and in this he doubtless was and had been sincere. But his understanding of what constituted friendliness, and the views of Secretary of State Seward, for instance, were widely different.

Having enlisted the colonel's assistance, Gwin applied in proper form for a statement of the reason for his arrest. This application, forwarded through channels, brought no response. Hamblen then helped to prepare a request by Gwin for trial before a military commission. This also went unregarded. But there did come an order from General Sheridan to allow Dr. Gwin the limits of the garrison, on condition that he give parole not to try to escape. This Gwin gave readily, and Hamblen thereupon installed him in a room next to his own at headquarters. He was also given permission to send and receive letters without censorship, and under these conditions he grew more companionable.

Throughout all this parleying, Colonel Hamblen felt that Sheridan was trying to procure Gwin's release. The general asked repeatedly for special reports, apparently hoping to elicit some facts on which a strong recommendation for release might be based. But months dragged by, and still no sign was received from Washington.

Trying another tack, Gwin then appealed to George D. Prentice, the editor of the Louisville *Journal*, who had helped him at the time of his arrest in 1861. Although he was in failing health, Prentice journeyed to Washington, and in December, 1865, he reported back that the cabinet favored Gwin's release, but President Johnson was set against it. Seward sent a personal message, Prentice wrote: "Tell Doctor Gwin that I love him and I have his interests constantly in mind, but nothing can be done with the President just now."

This letter Gwin carried to Colonel Hamblen.

"Now," he cried, "I understand the whole case. When we were in the Senate, I spiked a fine little scheme Johnson had in mind. He was and is one of the most vindictive of men, and will keep me here as long as he can. We shall wait."

What Prentice did not know, or at least did not report, was that the disinclination to free Gwin was not centered at the White House, but in Congress, among the radical Republicans there. Some Republican senators had misgivings about the elusive doctor, and on December 19 they approved a resolution calling upon the State Department to furnish all the information it had "in regard to plans to induce the immigration of dissatisfied citizens of the United States into Mexico, and especially in regard to the plans of Doctor William M. Gwin and M.F. Maury, and to action taken by the government of the United States to prevent the success of such schemes."

Matthew F. Maury, naval officer and oceanographer, had served the Confederacy in the war and had fled to Mexico, where, three months after Gwin's departure, Maximilian had appointed him director of colonization to carry out Gwin's scheme almost exactly — but with a frankly Confederate slant. At the same time General Sterling Price, late of the Confederate army, was authorized by Maximilian to raise a cavalry force of thirty thousand ex-Confederates. These appointments had been made after Gwin's withdrawal from Mexico, but they were linked in the minds of many members of Congress with Gwin's widely publicized activities.

In compliance with the Senate request, President Johnson on January 10, 1866, submitted a special message containing the correspondence that had passed between Secretary Seward and the Juárista minister at Washington, regarding plots and counterplots affecting the United States. There was little

to show that Gwin was even remotely connected with any disloyal scheme, real or alleged. For example: one letter, written
by the minister, quoted "a friend" (unnamed) as stating on
November 22, 1865, that conversations "with an ex-general
and an ex-senator of one of the States of the Union" had convinced the anonymous "friend" that there was a serious prospect of a massive movement into Mexico of Northerners sympathetic to the South. "The ex-general and ex-senator said that
the French minister had already concluded negotiations in
respect of Sonora and Baja California," the letter continued.
But how this could incriminate Gwin was hard to see, for at
the time referred to in this letter, written on November 22,
1865, the doctor had been a prisoner in Fort Jackson for
weeks.

The President's message was ordered to be printed and ta-
bled, and that was the last of any Congressional action.

4

In December of 1865, the vivacious sister of Colonel Hamblen's adjutant, Colonel Flint, arrived at Fort Jackson, and the
humdrum of garrison life was enlivened. There were picnics
and trips up the river to gather oranges and oleander blossoms,
and oyster roasts on the beaches of the Gulf. In these excursions Dr. Gwin joined with good spirit. Miss Flint aroused his
admiration, for like most Southern men he preferred dashing
women, and her daring gave her escorts many a scare. Having
been a schoolteacher in Alabama before the war, she had
learned to love the active outdoor life of the Southern planters,
and she rode fearlessly. Hamblen rode a stallion named
Philip, which no one else could control; the animal was considered dangerous by the other officers. Several times Miss
Flint had begged permission to ride Philip, and for her own

safety the colonel had refused. One day, while Hamblen was standing at one side deep in conversation with Gwin, the girl recklessly sprang into Philip's saddle, and was swept away in a furious gallop. Leaping upon his own horse, Gwin set off in pursuit, and after a long chase succeeded in overtaking the runaway. As he handed her to the ground, begging to be assured that she was not hurt, she laughed and teased that he had been more frightened than she, for his face had gone white. After that, now and then Gwin would let the girl try the speed of his own "wild horse," Comfort.

Young Gwin often joined the group from the fort in these outings. He was staying in New Orleans, but spent days as Hamblen's guest; there were old family friends in the city, and relatives nearby. Although unable to accomplish anything in regard to speeding his father's release, Willie was a channel of communication with the rest of the family in Paris, and could relieve the doctor's anxiety for them. Gwin still maintained hope that Napoleon would respond to that final letter of appeal from Mexico City, and make clear that Gwin's role in Mexico had been in no way aimed at injuring the United States. But the emperor was trying to forget Mexico.

One day early in 1866 Dr. Gwin came to Colonel Hamblen in great excitement, and predicted that the order for his release would arrive in the next mail. He gave no reason for his confidence, but seemed almost desperately cheerful. The mail came, but no order. When Hamblen told him, Gwin stood silent a moment, as if overcome, then turned and stalked away. That night was a sleepless one for the colonel: from his room he heard the doctor pacing, and the rhythmic opening and closing snap of a long "Texas knife" that Gwin carried. The steady tramp and click of the blade told of the old man's agitation. Hamblen was tense. But in the morning the doctor seemed his usual cool self; whatever the cause of his excitement, he had regained his self-control, and he gave no explanation. A few days afterward, however, he told Hamblen that he wished to place himself entirely in the colonel's hands, his own overtures having proved ineffectual.

"I have decided to give up," he said. "Whatever you advise, I will do."

Hamblen had not ceased to feel that General Sheridan was anxious to assist the doctor, if a way could be found, and he saw an instance of this when Sheridan's medical director, Dr. Morris Asche, appeared at the fort with instructions to examine the prisoner and "report on his health." Hamblen suspected that Asche's real mission was to draw Gwin out, and perhaps elicit some information on which Sheridan could base a recommendation for release. Hamblen on his part felt that if Gwin could be brought to tell the whole story of his involvement in Mexico, just as he had told it to the colonel, that might serve Sheridan's purpose. But he knew Gwin's aversion to talking before strangers, and therefore he was not surprised when Gwin refused to see Dr. Asche.

"I am a doctor myself and perfectly well," he snapped. "What I want is release."

"But you promised to do anything I advised," Hamblen cajoled, and at length he succeeded in bringing the men together.

He left them alone for an hour. When he returned, he found them sitting on opposite sides of the fireplace, conversing in monosyllables about nothing much; Gwin had declined to be drawn out. Hamblen resorted to a ruse. Asche was a German, and the colonel began to discuss the great changes in Germany that had come about during the recent years. The surgeon joined in, and spoke of the strength and virility of the new Germany.

Hamblen slyly remarked, "If France and Germany ever try conclusions again, the French will learn there is a difference between Napoleon the Great and Napoleon the Little."

This touched Gwin in a sensitive spot — his admiration for Napoleon III — and he broke in:

"Oh, you are mistaken there! I know that man personally, and I'll tell you I never met an abler one!"

With a meaningful glance at Asche, Hamblen continued to run down the French emperor, and Gwin to defend him, giving an animated description of his reception at the Tuileries. This led to the whole Mexican episode — Sonora, Bazaine, Maximilian, everything. It was three o'clock in the morning when Gwin concluded with, "and now here I am in Fort Jackson."

A few days later this interview seemed to bear fruit in the form of a letter addressed to the doctor, brought to the fort by one of Sheridan's aides, Colonel Kip. Gwin took the letter and read it. He was seen to flush. Pulling himself erect, he demanded of the officer:

"Do you know, young man, the nature of the message you have brought me?"

Kip replied that he knew the substance of the letter.

His voice shaking with anger, Gwin went on:

"Well, you are simply the messenger, I make no reflections on you, for you have merely done your duty. You bring me a proposition that I accept my release on condition that I leave the country at once and forever. My country! The country I have served for thirty years and never raised my hand or voice against! My country! Where I was born, where my friends are, where my first wife and children and all my family are buried, and where I shall finally find a home! I was arrested with others, who had been active in the attempt to disrupt this government. They were released, but I was retained. I asked for charges, I applied for a trial, with no response, and now you come to me with this proposition, after I have been held for months with no opportunity to be heard! Go back to those that sent you, tell them what I have said, and add this," he roared.

"I sign no pledges! I either leave this place a free American citizen, or I will rot in Fort Jackson!"

That Gwin, whose mastery of his emotions customarily was exemplary, was capable of great rages his intimates knew, but this outburst came as a revelation to those present. Colonel Kip was relieved to get out of the room.

A few days after that, while Gwin and a party of officers and girls were gathering dewberries a mile above the fort, an officer landed from a small boat and handed Colonel Hamblen an order that had just arrived from New Orleans. It read:

> You will, on receipt of this, at once release Dr. W. M. Gwin and furnish him transportation to New Orleans. Request him to call at my headquarters.
>
> P. H. SHERIDAN
> Maj. Gen. commanding

Dewberries were forgotten. The party hastened back to the fort, and the doctor was put aboard the military tug that was waiting. Shaking hands all around, he thanked them for their consideration and kindness. Toward Colonel Flint's sister he was especially gallant, for he had detected Colonel Hamblen's romantic interest in her.

The tug pulled away, and the watching party saw Gwin standing erect on the afterdeck, waving, until the boat rounded a bend.

A little while after this event, Colonel Hamblen and Miss Flint were married, and the esteem and affection in which they held the colonel's one-time prisoner was shown in the name they gave their first born, a daughter — MayGwin.

Chapter IX

From the land of his birth, which had been transformed by the hand of war into a land of harshness for Gwin, the doctor and his son rejoined the family in Paris without delay. Gwin could perceive no security for himself in the United States, at least not for some time to come. The spirit of repression and vengeance was strong there, and no one who in any way had been associated with the late rebellion was safe from proscription. The enmity that had manifested itself against Gwin when he was shut up in Fort Jackson might show itself again, and he wisely declined to take the risk of remaining within its reach. Rather, he would make the best of exile until the political skies cleared.

In Mexico, the inevitable tragedy had moved to the culmination that Gwin had foretold. After the death of Morny, all Louis Napoleon's plans seemed to go awry. Pressed on one side by the United States, and on the other side facing a growing threat from Prussia, the emperor, in January, 1866, withdrew the last of his army from Mexico. Bereft of this indispensable support, Maximilian was doomed. He started to flee; but, indecisive to the end, changed his mind and took the field against the resurgent Juárez forces. At Querértaro, on May 15. 1867, he was betrayed and captured. There, on June 19, the emperor was shot.

The other principals in the drama would fare little better. Bazaine, after France's defeat in the war of 1870, would be accused of treason, convicted, and sentenced to life imprisonment; escaping to Spain, he would drag out his remaining days there in dishonor, a byword among his countrymen. Louis Napoleon, having lost his throne, would soon give up life itself. And Carlota, who had hurried back from Mexico to beseech assistance from Napoleon, from the Pope, from the European powers — assistance which none cared or dared to give — would lose her reason and linger in demented bleakness in a Belgian château until 1926.

Paris danced on, but beneath the hectic gaiety of the late 1860s there lurked increasing disillusionment and ennui. The Gwins joined in the social swirl. The city swarmed with fugitive Confederates, and for these restless exiles Dr. and Mrs. Gwin provided parties that recalled the sumptuous entertainments of Washington. Constance Cary, a Virginia belle, jotted in her Paris diary for the winter of 1866-67: "Went to a ball at the Gwins — everything beautifully done — all the best ex-Confeds there, with crowds of foreigners."

Meanwhile, Gwin kept scanning the political horizon for definite signs that the storm at home was passing, and in the fall of 1867 he detected one favorable omen. This was the election of H. H. Haight, a Democrat, as governor of California. Haight in no way represented the overthrown "Chivalry," being a former Republican who had broken with Lincoln over wartime policy; but Gwin felt that the Democratic victory betokened an easing of the tensions in the West, at least. He decided to make a trial return to the United States. To minimize the risk, he would go alone; then, should conditions warrant, he would summon his family. So telling them, "I am going to California to make way for all of us to live there," he set out early in 1868.

Gwin still possessed certain assets which he proposed to salvage from the wreckage of the South's economy. In California, he had no difficulty in complying with the requisite forms, subscribing to the obligatory oath of loyalty to the United States with a clear conscience; in his own view he had never departed from that loyalty; instead, portions of the nation, North and South, had departed from him. But within a few months all ambiguity as to his position was obliterated when President Andrew Johnson, as one of his last official actions before he left the White House, extended a universal amnesty to all who had been involved in the Southern cause. With the removal of this final obstacle, no hindrance offered to the return of his family, and Gwin sent for them to join him at San Francisco. Lucy came as a bride, having been married in Paris to Evan J. Coleman, a young Virginian and graduate of Harvard law school. Gwin, unable to return for the wedding, had insisted that it proceed without him. The family settled at 507 Harrison Street, while the doctor went about rehabilitating his fortune.

Gwin had always been an able and shrewd businessman. He still held portions of his once enormous land holdings in the South and Southwest, and his prestige and influence in certain commercial and banking circles were high. Most of his properties he disposed of, although he kept one plantation in Mississippi, and by dint of ingenuity and pressure, he managed to pry loose from the confiscators other assets, so as to assemble a capital. With this he embarked upon a coolly calculated speculation, worthy of his old boldness. And this time fortune smiled on him.

Gwin had never bothered with picayune operations. Now he purchased a neglected gold mine in Calaveras County, in the Mother Lode region of the state. He then set about revitalizing the enterprise. His son and son-in-law gave assistance, and in a short while the mine began to yield handsome returns. It would continue to be one of the largest producers of gold in California for decades to come.

Released from pecuniary anxieties by this revival of pros-

perity, Gwin moved his family from Harrison Street to a large
house in South Park — an island of fashionable exclusiveness
set on the slope of Rincon Hill. South Park was modeled upon
a London square, an enclosed oval of fine homes, with a garden
and trees in the center. The Gwin home in this setting became
celebrated for its open-handed and cheerful hospitality — for
oyster suppers, Christmas eggnog parties, Mary Gwin's "kettle-
drums," and private theatricals.

Mrs. Gwin set a social pace in San Francisco during the sev-
enties comparable to her triumphs at Washington. Age had
not betrayed her: though she had gained *embonpoint,* she was
still a regal figure in her Parisian gowns, with her auburn hair
and vividly expressive eyes. Her name was so frequently encountered in the social news, a saying grew up that the only
woman whose name one read oftener was the Empress Eugénie.*

The doctor was a retiring but liberal host. At large parties,
he was most likely to be found in a corner, tranquilly playing
cribbage with a friend but ready to chat with any guest who
dropped by. His interest in politics remained, although he stu-
diously refrained from appearing in political life again. The
veneration in which the memory of his great opponent, Broderick, was held by thousands of Californians would, he realized,
have precluded success had he allowed his name to be entered
for public office again. He was content that it should be so,
although as elder statesman, one who knew more of the political history of the first half of the century than almost any other
man alive, his advice was much sought by leaders of his party,
and he was always ready to give it. A vicarious vindication of
his old flair came about in 1869, when his son ran for the state

* When Governor and Mrs. Leland Stanford gave the memorable ball for
seven hundred guests in their Sacramento mansion on February 16, 1872,
the ex-senator's wife attracted conspicuous attention in the press reports
— "Mrs. William M. Gwin, a beautiful brunette, wearing gros grain with
overdress of tulle; hair à la Grec; full train and low corsage."

legislature as a Democrat, in a Republican district, and defeated his Republican opponent. Gwin had coached the campaign from the sidelines, and he was proud of his son's success.

2

During the winter of 1870, Gwin was called east on business, and while there he revisited Washington. He found the capital bewilderingly altered from the easygoing, shabby half-village he had known; hardly a trace of the lackadaisical Southern tone or Southern influence remained. He found the city distasteful.

During that trip he called on friends of former days, and was disappointed not to meet Colonel and Mrs. Hamblen, whom he remembered with special affection. He was not even sure of their whereabouts. He was delighted, therefore, shortly after returning home, to receive two letters — one from Colonel Flint, Mrs. Hamblen's brother, whom Gwin had known at Fort Jackson, and the other from Mrs. Hamblen herself. Both were inquiries about the feasibility of coming west to settle permanently. They asked Gwin for advice.

He replied frankly, discouraging them. He urged Flint not to invest in California land, since inflation had pushed prices almost out of sight, and a reaction was bound to come. To the Hamblens he held out no more cheerful counsel. In a long letter to Mrs. Hamblen he explained the economic situation; and as old memories crowded into mind, he impulsively diverged and gave the news of himself and his activities since the war.

"It is a long time since I was so surprised and delighted as this morning [when] on enquiry at the Post Office I was handed your letter," he began, under date of "San Francisco, July 10th, '71." Conscientiously taking up Mrs. Hamblen's question about coming to California, he advised bluntly:

This is not a desirable country to emigrate to — not the fault
of the country, but the people. They are selfish to a degree, none
ever get rich enough, always striving for more, and never turning
a dollar out of their own pockets to aid a newcomer or in any way
hold out a helping hand to him. As to the professions of law and
medicine, they are, I may say, *glutted.* . . . Therefore I can hold
out no nope to the Colonel. . . .

California, like the rest of the nation, was in the midst of the
Grant administration's orgy of venality and get-rich-quick ma-
terialism — the Gilded Age. In California, thanks to its natural wealth, the gilt was sometimes twenty-carat, but it was
tawdry just the same.

Gwin went on to suggest that something might be done in
the lumber industry, which was large in California and about
which Colonel Hamblen, a Maine man, already knew something. Gwin said he would consult a neighbor, "a great saw
mill operator," then absent "at his mills up the coast." But he
cautioned:

It must be certain before I say come. If you come, it must be
for always, as it is too costly a country to emigrate *from.* But it
is worth a great risk to go to such a country and become a fixture
in it. It is, perhaps, in all the earth that I have seen, and that
means the greater portion of it, [the one that has] all the elements
that contribute to human happiness and prosperity.

He could not say as much for the antics of the human elements in power:

There is a joint loose in our governmental and financial systems,
that gives no encouragement to emigration to this State, where we
are, I may say, perishing for want of population.

He was proud of having recouped his fortune:

I have been here nearly four years. During that time my son
and son-in-law have developed one of the most extensive gold
mining estates on this coast, at an expense of a hundred and fifty

8

73

thousand dollars in gold coin. It is now yielding from $15,000 to
$20,000 per month in gold bullion, and during the next year the
yield will be double that amount, more than half of which is clear
profit. So you see we have prospered beyond all human calculation — but look at the risk. It is too long a story to tell why we
took so great a risk; but the risk is past and the success certain,
although the chances were ten to one against us.

How I would like to see you and the Colonel and have a talk
with you! And you have my namesake [MayGwin Hamblen]
in your midst! It will not be my fault if you do not come to this
country, but the danger is great of risking your future to the
tender mercies of so selfish a population. . . .

How far from the great overland railroad is your residence?
I crossed the continent last winter and may go again . . . and
I would go any distance out of the way to visit you. . . . My
health is perfect. I could write to you all day and then not know
where to stop, and so it is noon, but you must write again.

True to his word, the doctor quizzed the lumberman regarding that industry, and nine days later submitted his report. It was adverse. This time Gwin wrote from — "Gwin
Mine, July 19th, '71." He began with Southern stateliness, "My
dear Madam," but soon lapsed into affectionate, polished gallantry:

Before I left the city I made especial enquiry in regard to the
lumber business. The same reply met me as is given in every
vocation, dull times, no profit in the trade. It requires so much
capital to start in anything here, the population is so sparse and
means of transportation so limited, that it seems to me the worst
country to emigrate to on the continent.

Times indeed had changed since the bustling influx of the
gold rush. The doctor went on:

I wish I could say something more favorable, for I wish so
much to see you and have you near where I could see you often.
The idea of your having three children, and my name among

them, and you but a bride when I last saw you! It seems but as
yesterday that we were all in boats on the turbid Mississippi on
our way to the quarantine. How certain it was then that but a
few of us would meet again, and yet how certain [we] were that
the parting was not final!

How I should like to show [you] this great mining camp, and
witness your amazement to think that since we last met it had
been created by our energy and capital. It was a barren waste
when we came here three and a half years ago, and now we run
forty-six stamps, crush eighty tons of quartz daily, are putting
in another twenty-four-stamp mill, employ eighty stalwart men,
and the whole establishment superintended by my son with a
skill and energy that amazes everyone. You ought to recollect
him well, for you were a great favorite of his. Who would have
supposed when we three were wandering on the banks of the
river, or fighting our way through briars around the levee, greatly
to the detriment of your dress, that he would develop into one
of the first miners on the continent and show a business capacity
surpassed by no man?

Rebel as he was, he was elected to the State Senate two years
ago, in a Republican district, and has two more years to serve.

This property is all our own, my son and son-in-law (the latter
keeping all the books and managing the financing) having the
entire management of it. I spend most of my time here, but I
require them to do all the work and assume all of the responsibility, and not to be dependent on me for anything. It was severe
on them at first, but they have proved themselves equal to the
work, and it is known to be the best managed and most econom-
ically worked mine in the State.

This is one of the healthiest spots on the earth. I have never
an ache or pain, and am as vigorous as I was forty years ago,
although too heavy to be active. And what is better than all,
I never was so happy in my life, and my wife and children healthy,
happy, and prosperous around me. . . .

Our mutual acquaintances I never see and I know not even
where they are. Can you give me the whereabouts of some or
all of them of our old mess? How vividly I recollect it, and the
colonel's horse, and you, as you were riding my wild horse, Comfort — who is alive and as handsome as ever, on my Mississippi
plantation, but much tamer.

The closing lines were pensive:

> Strange to say, I feel very sad in writing to you, because I feel
> I shall never meet you again, and I know no one who in so short
> a time became so dear to me. . . . If I could only see a hope of
> prosperity for you here and soon, I would say come. . . .

Gwin and the Hamblens did meet again, in Washington.
Overjoyed at the reunion, Gwin insisted on introducing Colonel
Hamblen to a high-ranking army officer, whose goodwill
might be valuable at promotion time. "If ever you can do anything for this man, consider it as done for me; he saved my life,"
the former senator said, in making the introduction, and Hamblen was impressed by the deference displayed by the general,
and the evident weight that Gwin's word carried. What the
doctor meant by saying that Hamblen had saved his life, the
colonel did not know, but his mind reverted to those suspense-
ful nights at Fort Jackson, when he had lain awake listening
to the steady tramp of the doctor's pacing, and the click and
snap of that long "Texas knife" being opened and shut.

3

Business and friendships occupied Gwin's time during these
postwar years. To the new generation he seemed like a sur-
vivor from an antediluvian period, an age that already had
become legendary. One puzzle which he never solved was the
secret of who had put him in Fort Jackson. As time passed, he
assembled clues which led him to doubt that the person responsible was Andrew Johnson; he became morally certain
that Secretary of State Seward had issued the order. This
treachery by a seeming friend he resented, and he gave expression to his feeling when Seward visited San Francisco, after
leaving office. Observing that Gwin was not in the group
welcoming him at the hotel, Seward told a mutual acquaint-

ance, "I would rather see Doctor Gwin than any man in California."

This message being relayed to Gwin, the ex-senator responded with visibly repressed anger that he "would not shake the hand of a man who had done him so much wrong." Seward received the rebuff in silence.*

Although a leading citizen of San Francisco, Dr. Gwin avoided public gatherings; indeed, he made it a rule to join no association that would require him to take part in public demonstrations or public appearances. He broke this rule once, however — on June 4, 1874, when he presided over a reunion of the passengers on the steamship *Panama* when it arrived at San Francisco just twenty-five years before. Twenty-two survivors of that voyage gathered in the Grand Hotel in San Francisco, and after eating their way through a ten-course

---

* Gwin's surmise regarding Seward's part in his imprisonment may have been well founded. After Gwin's death, his son-in-law, Evan J. Coleman, published the story of Seward's communicating with Jefferson Davis, on the eve of Sumter, through Senator Gwin. This historic secret Gwin himself had written out, with corroborative details, but he had suppressed the manuscript during his lifetime. Shortly after Coleman published the account, he received a letter from a man whom he identified as "an old and reliable Kentucky friend of Doctor Gwin," which read:

I am sorry that you did not know of and mention in your article the kindness of George D. Prentiss [sic] — the famous Louisville journalist — in making two trips to Washington, old and feeble as he then was, to effect Dr. Gwin's release. His first visit secured milder treatment for Dr. Gwin, and the second one effected his release.

On his return after the first visit, Mr. Prentiss said to me: "The President and cabinet are all in favor of Dr. Gwin's release, except Mr. Seward, and orders have been issued to allow him every comfort." After his second visit he told me: "The President and cabinet are still in favor of Dr. Gwin's unconditional release, except Seward, who remarked, I have reasons, which I cannot explain, for Dr. Gwin's continued imprisonment, and cannot consent to his liberation."

Mr. Prentiss continued: "Neither the President nor any member of the cabinet opposed Seward during the meeting; but after it adjourned, I went to the White House, and importuned Johnson until I got him to sign an order for Dr. Gwin's release — Seward to the contrary notwithstanding."

The name of the man who wrote this letter is not known. Prentice had died before it was written.

banquet which few modern pioneers could assimilate, they relaxed in a glow of reminiscences. The list of *Panama* passengers who had attained eminence was impressive: two United States senators, three governors of California, numerous Representatives in Congress, two justices of the United States Supreme Court, an admiral, two generals, and others hardly less noteworthy.

Gwin, in his speech, dwelt upon the startling transformations they all had witnessed since their arrival:

"When we landed here," he recalled, "the permanent population of San Francisco did not exceed one thousand; now it is over two hundred thousand. The ground beneath us was a shapeless mound of sandy desert. Diagonally across from where we are sitting is a strip of ground, covered with almost worthless buildings, that sold the other day, as an investment, for $300,000. The 100-vara lot, of which that strip was a small portion, cost, at the date of our arrival, $16, just the fee for issuing the alcalde's title."

On the table stood an oak keg made from timber taken from the *Panama* when she was scrapped after twenty years of service. Gwin ceremoniously tapped this keg and served the punch it contained ("thirty-one-year-old brandy and the finest Roederer"). A letter was read from General Joseph Hooker, recalling that "the pool we passengers formed on the time of our arrival in the bay of San Francisco was won by Doctor Gwin" — then always lucky. Another message of greeting was read from Jessie Benton Frémont, the wife of Gwin's first colleague in the Senate; she, too, had arrived on the *Panama* on June 4, 1849.

Outside of California, Gwin maintained touch with many friends of the old regime among whom were Southerners who had shared his exile in France. One of these was A. Dudley Mann, the Virginia society man who had represented the Confederacy in Belgium. Mann had remained abroad after Ap-

pomattox, and he frequently wrote to Gwin from Paris; they
had been friends since the Franklin Pierce administration,
when Mann was Assistant Secretary of State and Jefferson
Davis was Secretary of War. With the Confederate ex-President, also, Gwin was in occasional correspondence. In 1874
the Davises passed through Paris and called on Mann, and a
few days afterward the latter wrote to his "ever dearest friend,"
the ex-President, a word of the Gwins:

> A long letter today from ex-Senator Gwin, dated San Francisco,
> April 6. Mrs. G[win] had just received one from Mrs. Davis
> telling her that you were in Europe. He said, "The intelligence
> gave me a sharp pang, for I thought what a time we three would
> have had together. How much to talk about!"

4

Age seemed powerless to extinguish either the imagination
or the energy of the doctor. In 1876 he was a delegate to the
Democratic national convention which nominated for the Presidency Samuel J. Tilden — who won the election, according
to the best evidence, only to be cheated out of it. Again in
1880, at the age of seventy-five, Gwin went to Cincinnati with
the California delegation and helped his fellow Democrats
nominate General Winfield Scott Hancock for the Presidency.
James Garfield won that election. In 1884 the doctor again
went east in the interest of promoting a railroad across Panama
from the Chiriqui Lagoon to the Gulf of Dolce; the project was
backed by Comstock-rich Californians, but the cooperation of
the federal government was needed. Gwin was working on
this project when Grover Cleveland was elected President, the
first Democrat returned to the White House since James Buchanan. Gwin rejoiced to see his party in power once more; he
had spanned the interval. Born during the administration of
Thomas Jefferson, he had lived under twenty Presidents, almost all of whom he had known personally.

On March 4, 1885, Gwin reentered the Senate chamber which he had not seen since 1861. Chatting with one of his successors, he recalled the famous men among whom he had moved as an equal in that room, the historic debates in which he had taken part there. That evening, at the inaugural ball, Mrs. Gwin — herself a legend in the capital — entered the hall on the arm of the new President. The wheel had come full circle.

In April, Gwin returned to San Francisco, but he was summoned east again by the railroad project. This occupied him until August, when he prepared to return to California, stopping off at Hot Springs, Arkansas, to visit his friends, the Hamblens. Just before leaving New York, he attended a review of the cadets at West Point, and on the way back to the city he caught a chill which sent him to bed. The illness developed into pneumonia, and on Thursday, September 3, in the New York Hotel, he died. The telegram informing Mary Gwin said, "He kept his courage until unconscious." A relative by marriage was the only representative of the family with him at the end. His age was one month short of eighty.

5

Of a sudden, the all but forgotten "first senator" of California became of interest to the public, and in California his career was reviewed by the press at length. The debt which the state owed to him was acknowledged. Even the *Alta California*, which in the old days had attacked him bitterly, made amends, and confessed that "it may be said that the early public works were all secured by his efforts." The San Francisco *Examiner* agreed: "By his zeal California gained its impetus. Probably to his actions as the first United States senator the State owes its present firm and wisely constructed foundations." The direct appropriations secured by Gwin from a reluctant Congress were estimated to have totaled more than $17,000,000, an unparalleled sum for that period; but money was admitted to be only one of the benefits he had gained for the state. His "magnetic power in securing and holding friendships" the *Examiner* recalled. "His intellect, as his career amply proved, was simply gigantic. All the struggles of his life had been in great outline; he was made of the stuff which in earlier times founded dynasties and empires."

The San Francisco *Call* commented judicially:

> With all his mistakes, false alliances, and errors, ex-Senator Gwin was a great man in some respects — one whose fame and power would have been far greater and more national but for the secession war, that ruined the prospects of so many Southern men who loved the Union and afterwards fought against it. The disintegration of civil war was beneath the instincts of his nature.

It was observed that at the time of crisis, Senator Gwin, by birth and conviction a Southerner, had allied himself, spiritually if not actually, with the South, and the *Call* continued:

> That was his great mistake. He got on the wrong side. . . . Yet he must be given the credit of acting up to his convictions. He did not believe slavery could be abolished and the Union maintained. He remained out of the country during the war, but for all political purposes might as well have been in the Confederate service.

The country's split put an end to his political career, and from then on all his calculations — regarding the South, regarding France, regarding Maximilian — misfired. Yet his old age had been filled with contentment, "pastoral in its serenity."

The belated tribute would have gratified him, for during a quarter of a century — back to those remote days of "before the war" and the Broderick feud — he had been steadily de-

nigrated by a generation of historians blinded by the oversim-
plified tests of slavery and secession. It had become customary
to decry Gwin's contributions to California, and to paint in the
blackest hues his conduct during the conflict. Chroniclers such
as Hubert Howe Bancroft had damned the senator by dismiss-
ing him as merely a foil to Broderick.

"Gwin possessed to a peculiar degree that smooth self-asser-
tion and readiness at extricating himself from embarrassing
positions without blame, which is known as diplomatic talent,"
sneered Bancroft. "In public affairs he was avaricious, heartless,
and devoted to his own aggrandizement." Yet in the next
breath, this biased judge was constrained to bestow upon Gwin
a title that he never claimed, but in which he would have
taken pride — "the almighty providence of California."

As was meet, the body of California's "first senator" was returned to the state for burial. The funeral in San Francisco's
Grace Cathedral (not the imposing edifice on Nob Hill but
the former church that vanished in the 1906 fire) brought out
the city's notables, and the pallbearers included the state's
highest political figures — the governor and both United States
senators. None of these was as illustrious as the man they
were helping to bury. By request of the family, there was no
eulogy.

Then William McKendree Gwin was borne to Lone Mountain cemetery, to lie not far from James King of William and
David Colbrith Broderick. Soon David S. Terry, who had so
tragically entered the lives of those antagonists, Broderick and
Gwin, would join them there, shot down by a paid gunman in a
wayside railroad station.

Reading List and Bibliography

As was noted at the beginning, the materials for a biography of William McKendree Gwin are meager. Of primary sources, little of significance has survived. His personal papers were destroyed twice — the first time when Federal troops burned his plantation in Mississippi, and the second time when the 1906 San Francisco earthquake and fire destroyed the family home on Sacramento Street.

Gwin's son-in-law, Evan J. Coleman, preserved the text of some of Gwin's letters from Mexico by publishing them after the doctor's death; the originals have disappeared. There are a few scraps of letters in Mississippi and California, but they contribute little to an understanding of the man. Coleman also published Gwin's account of his dealings with Seward just before the war. Gwin told the story again in the fragmentary *Memoirs* which he dictated but suppressed during his lifetime; these *Memoirs* have survived.

Gwin's political activities may be traced in part in the sterile prose of government documents, Congressional reports, etc. But these throw little light either upon the senator himself, or upon an important phase of his public service — his activities off the floor of the Senate, in committee rooms, and in those private contacts which in the long run make or break legislation; however, of such activities there seldom is a record.

One source that throws a light upon the hitherto obscure episode of Gwin's imprisonment at Fort Jackson after the war, is the manuscript *Reminiscences* of Colonel Hamblen, and also Mrs. Hamblen's unpublished memoirs. These were generously made available by Mr. R. Pierson Eaton, of Warren, Pennsylvania, the Hamblens' grandson — the son of the "MayGwin" mentioned in the story. Mr. Eaton also discovered two hitherto unknown letters written by Gwin to Mrs. Hamblen in 1871. These provide a unique glimpse of Gwin's situation in California after the war, and warmest thanks are extended to Mr. Eaton for his permission to draw upon them.

Gratitude also is expressed to the staffs of the following libraries for assistance: Bancroft Library of the University of California at Berkeley; Henry E. Huntington Library, San Marino, California; Library of Congress; San Francisco Public Library; and the California Section of the California State Library, Sacramento.

The following list of authorities and sources consulted is intended to be suggestive rather than exhaustive. Among histories of California, only those having direct bearing upon the subject are named.

MANUSCRIPT SOURCES

S. L. M. Barlow Papers, Huntington Library.
William Henry Seward Papers, University of Rochester Library.
Colonel Samuel G. Hamblen's Reminiscences (unpublished).
Miscellaneous letters, documents, and scrapbooks in California State Library.

NEWSPAPERS AND MAGAZINES

Harper's Weekly
Overland Monthly
Argonaut
California Historical Society Quarterly
Historical Society of Southern California Quarterly
Congressional Globe
Sacramento Union
Contemporary files of principal dailies of San Francisco
Scattered issues of dailies of New York, Washington, Sacramento, and New Orleans

BOOKS

ADAMS, HENRY, *The Great Secession Winter of 1860-1861, and Other Essays.* George Brookfield, ed. New York: Sagamore Press, 1958.
ALTROCCHI, JULIA COOLY, *The Spectacular San Franciscans.* New York: Dutton, 1949.
ASBURY, HERBERT, *The Barbary Coast.* New York: Knopf, 1933.
———, *The Gangs of New York.* New York: Knopf, 1927.

ATHERTON, GERTRUDE, *California: An Intimate History*. New York: Harper, 1914.

——, *My San Francisco*. Indianapolis: Bobbs-Merrill, 1946.

BALES, WILLIAM ALAN, *Tiger in the Streets*. New York: Dodd, Mead, 1962.

BANCROFT, FREDERIC, *The Life of William H. Seward*. 2 vols. New York: Harper, 1900.

BANCROFT, HUBERT HOWE, *History of California*. San Francisco: Bancroft, 1888.

BARI, VALESKA, ed., *The Course of Empire*. New York: Coward-McCann, 1931.

BIGELOW, JOHN, *Retrospections of an Active Life*. 5 vols. New York: Baker & Taylor, 1909-1913.

BLASIO, JOSÉ LUIS, *Maximilian, Emperor of Mexico*. New Haven: Yale University Press, 1934.

BROWNE, J. R., *The Debates of the Convention of California*. Washington, D.C., 1850.

BUTLER, PIERCE, *Judah P. Benjamin*. Philadelphia: Jacobs, 1906.

CARR, ALBERT Z., *The World and William Walker*. New York: Harper & Row, 1963.

CARSON, JAMES PETIGRU, *Life, Letters, and Speeches of James Louis Petigru*. Washington, D.C.: Lowdermilk & Co., 1920.

CHAMBERLAIN, NEWELL D., *The Call of Gold*. Privately printed, Mariposa, California, 1936.

CHAMBERS, WILLIAM NESBIT, *Old Bullion Benton, Senator from the New West*. Boston: Little, Brown, 1956.

CHESNUT, MARY BOYKIN, *A Diary from Dixie*. Boston: Houghton Mifflin, 1949.

CLAIBORNE, J. F. H., *Mississippi, as a Province, Territory, and State*. Jackson, Mississippi, 1880.

CLAY, CLEMENT C., Jr., *Invasion of Harper's Ferry — Dangers and Duties of the South*. Remarks of Senators Clay, of Alabama, Gwin, of California, and Others Delivered in the Senate of the United States. Washington: Congressional Globe Office, 1859.

CLAY, MRS. CLEMENT C., Jr., *A Belle of the Fifties. Narrated by Ada Sterling*. New York: Doubleday Page, 1905.

CLELAND, ROBERT GLASS, *From Wilderness to Empire*. New York: Knopf, 1944.

COBLENTZ, STANTON A., *Villains and Vigilantes*. New York: Wilson-Erickson, 1936.

COCHRAN, HAMILTON, *Blockade Runners of the Confederacy.* Indianapolis: Bobbs-Merrill, 1958.

COIT, MARGARET L., *John C. Calhoun, American Portrait.* Boston: Houghton Mifflin, 1950.

COLE, CORNELIUS, *Memoirs.* New York: McLaughlin Bros., 1908.

COLEMAN, EVAN J., "Dr. Gwin and Judge Black on Buchanan." *Overland Monthly*, January, 1892.

———, "Gwin and Seward — a Secret Chapter of Ante-Bellum History." *Overland Monthly*, November, 1891.

———, "Senator Gwin's Plan for the Colonization of Sonora." *Overland Monthly*, May, 1891.

———, "Senator Gwin's Plan for the Colonization of Sonora: Postscript." *Overland Monthly*, August, 1891.

CORTI, EGON CAESAR, COUNT, *Maximilian and Charlotte of Mexico.* Translated by Catherine Alison Phillips. 2 vols. New York: Knopf, 1928.

COX, W. V., and MILTON HARLOW NORTHRUP, *Life of Samuel Sullivan Cox.* Syracuse, New York, 1899.

CURTIS, GEORGE TICKNOR, *The Life of James Buchanan.* 2 vols. New York: Harper, 1883.

DAVIS, WINFIELD J., *History of Political Conventions in California: 1849-1892.* Sacramento, 1893.

DERBY, J. C., *Fifty Years Among Authors, Artists, and Publishers.* New York: Carlton, 1884.

DE VOTO, BERNARD, *The Year of Decision: 1846.* Boston: Little, Brown, 1942.

DODD, WILLIAM E., *Jefferson Davis.* Philadelphia: Jacobs, 1907.

DONALD, DAVID, *Charles Sumner and the Coming of the Civil War.* New York: Farrar, Straus & Cudahy, 1961.

DYER, BRAINERD, *Zachary Taylor.* Baton Rouge: Louisiana State University, 1946.

ELDREDGE, ZOETH SKINNER, *The Beginnings of San Francisco.* San Francisco, 1912.

———, *History of California.* 5 vols. New York: Century History Company, 1915.

ELLISON, W. H., *California and the Nation 1850-1869.* Berkeley: University of California Publications in History, 1927.

———, *A Self-Governing Dominion: California 1849-1860.* Berkeley: University of California, 1950.

ESKEW, GARNETT LAIDLAW, *Willard's of Washington.* New York: Coward-McCann, 1954.

FAIRCHILD, MARLON D., "Reminiscences of a Forty-Niner." *California Historical Society Quarterly,* March, 1934.

FORNEY, J. W., *Anecdotes of Public Men.* New York: Harper, 1873.

FURNAS, J. C., *The Road to Harper's Ferry.* New York: William Sloan Associates, 1959.

GOBRIGHT, L. A., *Recollections of Men and Things at Washington During a Third of a Century.* Philadelphia, 1869.

GUADELLA, PHILIP, *The Second Empire.* New York: Putnam, 1923.

GWIN, WILLIAM M., "Memoirs of Hon. William M. Gwin." Edited by William Henry Ellison. *California Historical Society Quarterly,* March-December, 1940.

———, Speeches of Mr. Gwin, of California, on the National Railroad Bill — the Homestead Bill — the Civil Fund Bill — California Indian War Debt — Appointment of a Judge for the Northern District of California — and the Bill to Create a Line of Steamships From California via the Sandwich Islands to China. Washington: Congressional Globe Office, 1853.

———, Speeches of Mr. Gwin, of California, in the Senate of the United States, on Private Land Titles in the State of California. Washington: Gideon & Co., 1851.

HAMILTON, HOLMAN, *Zachary Taylor, Soldier in the White House.* 2 vols. Indianapolis: Bobbs-Merrill, 1951.

HARDING, BERTITA, *Phantom Crown.* México: Ediciones Tolteca, 1960.

HARGIS, DONALD E., "The Great Debate in California: 1859." *Historical Society of Southern California Quarterly,* June, 1960.

———, "The Issues in the Broderick-Gwin Debates of 1859." *California Historical Society Quarterly.* December, 1953.

———, "W. M. Gwin: Middleman." *Historical Society of Southern California Quarterly,* March, 1958.

HAVILAND, JOHN VON SONNTAG, "A Metrical Description of a Fancy Ball Given at Washington, 9th April, 1858." *Magazine of History,* Extra No. 23, New York, 1913.

HENDRICK, BURTON J., *Statesmen of the Lost Cause.* New York: Literary Guild, 1939.

HOLDEN, W. H., ed., *Second Empire Medley.* London: British Technical & General Press, 1952.

HUNT, GAILLARD, *John C. Calhoun.* Philadelphia: Jacobs, 1908.

JOHN, EVAN, *Atlantic Impact 1861.* London: Heinemann, 1952.

KEMBLE, JOHN HASKELL, "The Genesis of the Pacific Mail Steamship Company." *California Historical Society Quarterly,* September-December, 1934.

KENNEDY, ELIJAH H., *The Contest for California in 1861.* Boston: Houghton Mifflin, 1912.

KEYES, ERASMUS DARWIN, *Fifty Years Observation of Men and Events.* New York: Scribner, 1884.

LAMON, WARD H., *Recollections of Abraham Lincoln.* Washington, D.C., 1911.

LATHAM, MILTON S., "The Day Journal of Milton Slocum Latham." *California Historical Society Quarterly,* March, 1932.

LEECH, MARGARET, *Reveille in Washington 1860-1865.* New York: Harper, 1941.

LEWIS, OSCAR, *Sea Routes to the Gold Fields.* New York: Knopf, 1949.

LOLIÉ, FRÉDÉRIC, *The Gilded Beauties of the Second Empire.* London: John Long, 1909.

———, *The Romance of a Favourite.* Translated by Wm. Morton Fullerton. New York: Appleton, 1912.

LOW, FREDERICK F., *Reflections of an Early California Governor.* Sacramento: Sacramento Book Collectors Club, 1959.

LYNCH, DENNIS TILDEN, *"Boss" Tweed: The Story of a Grim Generation.* New York: Boni & Liveright, 1927.

LYNCH, JEREMIAH, *A Senator of the Fifties.* San Francisco: A. M. Robertson, 1910.

MCELROY, ROBERT, *Jefferson Davis.* New York: Harper, 1937.

MCPHERSON, HALLIE MAE, "William McKendree Gwin, Expansionist." Doctoral Treatise (typescript). University of California Library, Berkeley, 1931.

MANN, A. DUDLEY, *"Ever My Dearest Friend," Letters to Jefferson Davis, 1869-1889.* Tuscaloosa, Alabama: Confederate Publishing Company, Inc., 1960.

MEADE, ROBERT DOUTHAT, *Judah P. Benjamin, Confederate Statesman.* New York: Oxford University Press, 1943.

Message of the President of the United States in Regard to the Plans of Dr. William M. Gwin and M. F. Maury. Senate Reports, 39th Congress, 1st Session, Ex. Doc. No. 8, January 10, 1866.

MOORE, JOHN WEST, *The American Congress, a History of National Legislation and Political Events, 1774-1895.* New York: Harper, 1895.

NEVINS, ALLAN, *Frémont: the Pathmarker of the West.* New York: Longmans, Green, 1955.

———, *The War for the Union,* Vol. 1: *The Improvised War.* New York: Scribner, 1959.

NICHOLS, ROY FRANKLIN, *The Disruption of American Democracy.* New York: Macmillan, 1948.

O'MEARA, JAMES, *Broderick and Gwin.* San Francisco, 1881.

PEATFIELD, J. J., "Famous Californians of Other Days." *Overland Monthly,* December, 1894.

PHELPS, ALONZO, *Contemporary Biography of California's Representative Men.* San Francisco, 1881.

PLUME, J. V. (attributed), *Re-Union of the Pioneer Panama Passengers, June 4, 1874: the 25th Anniversary of the Arrival of the Steamship* Panama *at San Francisco.* San Francisco, 1874.

POLK, JAMES KNOX, *Polk, the Diary of a President.* Edited by Allan Nevins. New York: Longmans, Green, 1952.

POORE, BEN: PERLEY, *Perley's Reminiscences of Sixty Years in the National Metropolis.* 2 vols. Philadelphia: Hubbard, 1886.

PRYOR, MRS. ROGER A., *My Day: Reminiscences of a Long Life.* New York: Macmillan, 1909.

———, *Reminiscences of Peace and War.* New York: Macmillan, 1924.

RHODES, JAMES FORD, *History of the United States, 1850-1877.* New York: Macmillan, 1906.

ROGERS, JOSEPH M., *Thomas H. Benton.* Philadelphia: Jacobs, 1905.

ROTHSCHILD, SALOMON DE, *A Casual View of America — The Home Letters of Salomon de Rothschild.* Translated and edited by Sigmund Diamond. Stanford, California: Stanford University Press, 1961.

ROYCE, JOSIAH, *California, From the Conquest of 1846 to the Second Vigilance Committee of San Francisco.* Boston: Houghton Mifflin, 1886.

RUSSELL, WILLIAM HOWARD, *My Diary, North and South.* New York: Harper, 1863.

SEWARD, FREDERICK W., *Reminiscences of a War-time Statesman and Diplomat.* New York: Putnam, 1916.

————, *Seward at Washington.* 3 vols. New York, 1891.

SHENTON, JAMES P., *Robert John Walker: A Politician from Jackson to Lincoln.* New York: Columbia University Press, 1961.

SHERMAN, W. T., *Memoirs.* New York: Webster, 1891.

SMITH, ELBERT B., *Magnificent Missourian: The Life of Thomas Hart Benton.* Philadelphia: Lippincott, 1958.

SOULIÉ MAURICE, *The Wolf Cub: The Great Adventure of Count Gaston Raousset-Boulbon in California and Sonora 1850-54.* Translated by Farrel Symons. Indianapolis: Bobbs-Merrill, 1927.

STEWART, GEORGE R., *Revolution in San Francisco.* Boston: Houghton Mifflin, 1964.

STRODE, HUDSON, *Jefferson Davis, American Patriot — 1808-61.* New York: Harcourt Brace, 1955.

STRONG, GEORGE TEMPLETON, *Diary of George Templeton Strong.* Edited by Allan Nevins and Milton Halsey Thomas. New York: Macmillan, 1952.

SWANBERG, W. A., *First Blood — The Story of Fort Sumter.* New York. Scribner, 1957.

THOMAS, BENJAMIN, and HYMAN, HAROLD M., *Stanton: The Life and Times of Lincoln's Secretary of War.* New York: Knopf, 1962.

"A Threatened Invasion of California." *California Historical Society Quarterly,* March, 1934.

TINKHAM, G. H., *California Men and Events.* Stockton, California, 1915.

VILLARD, HENRY, *Memoirs of Henry Villard.* 2 vols. Boston: Houghton Mifflin, 1904.

WAGNER, HARRY RAUP, "The Life of Ferdinand C. Ewer, May 22, 1826 — October 10, 1883." *California Historical Society Quarterly,* December, 1934.

WALLACE, EDWARD S., *Destiny and Glory.* New York: Coward-McCann, 1957.

WARD, SAMUEL (attributed), *Exploits of the Attorney-General in California, by an Early Californian.* Privately printed, New York, 1860.

WATTERSON, HENRY, *"Marse Henry": An Autobiography.* 2 vols. New York: Doran, 1919.

WERNER, M. R., *Tammany Hall.* New York: Doubleday Doran, 1928.

WHITNEY, J. PARKER, *Reminiscences of a Sportsman.* New York: Forest and Stream Publishing Company, 1906.

WILLIAMS, ROGER L., *Gaslight and Shadow: The World of Napoleon III 1851-1870*. New York: Macmillan, 1957.

WILLIS, HENRY PARKER, *Stephen A. Douglas*. Philadelphia: Jacobs, 1910.

WILLSON, BECKLES, *John Slidell and the Confederates in Paris*. New York: Balch, 1932.

YOUNG, JOHN P., *San Francisco, a History of the Pacific Coast Metropolis*. Chicago: Clark, 1912.

Index

Index

397

Mexican War, 22, 93, 315
Mexico: cession of states to France, 328-329; Gadsden Treaty with, 109, 124; gold and silver mines in, 290-291; Indian raids in, 287; Maximilian's "empire" in, 286ff.
Minas Prietas, 291
Miramón, Gen. Miguel, 294
Mississippi: land speculation in, 14-16; politics of, 9-14
Moffat & Company, 94
Moniteur, French newspaper, 331-332
Monterey, Calif., constitutional convention at, 39-41
Montholon, Marquis de, 290, 312, 322, 337
Montholon, Julia de, 322
Morning Call (San Francisco), 187, 380
Morny, Charles Auguste Louis, Duke de, 294-296, 302, 316-318, 326, 333, 367
Mulligan, Billy, 86, 102, 105, 117-118
murders, number of in California, 115

Napier, Lord Francis, 162
Napoleon III (Louis Napoleon), 286, 290, 310, 330, 333, 352, 365; Mexican adventure of, 289ff.; relations with Gwin, 299-305; repudiates Maximilian, 349-350; death, 368
Naranjal mine, Mexico, 291
Native American party, 111
Negroes, rights of, 167
New Almaden mine, California, 285
New Granada (Colombia), incident in, 267
New Orleans *Times,* 339
New York City, politics in, 53-54
New York *Daily News,* 341
New York *Herald,* 260-264, 302-303
Nullification doctrine, 15, 225

Pacific Mail Steamship Co., 208
Palmer, A. T., 266
Palmer, Joseph C., 103-104
Palmer, Cook & Company, 103
Panama, stopovers in, 27, 60
patronage, distribution of, 148, 154, 179-181

Peck, Elisha T., 103-104, 117
Perley, D. W., 185
"petticoat rebels," 264
Phillips, Mrs. Philip, 247, 260-261
Pierce, Franklin, 92-93, 110, 166, 211, 378
Pindray, Charles, Marquis de, 288
Pinkerton, Allan, 236
Poindexter, George, 11-14
politicians, in California's first decade, 80-81
Polk, James Knox, 3, 24, 71
Pope, Alexander, 158
Prentice, George D., 271, 360
Preston, Gen. William, 310, 313
Price, Gen. Sterling, 361
public lands, speculation in, 14
public office, "sale" of, 87; *see also* patronage

Quitman, John A., 14

Randolph, Edmund, 222, 227
Raousset-Boulbon, Gaston, Comte de, 288
R.E. Lee, blockade runner, 276-278, 283
Republican party, 196, 199, 217-218, 230-231
Revolutionary War, 6-7
Riley, Gen. Bennet, 36, 50
Roman, A. B., 240
Romero, Mattias, 341
Royce, Josiah, 43
ruffianism, reign of, 102, 115-118
Russia: Alaska sale by, 110; Atlantic cable and, 155
Ryan, Belle, 116-117

Sacramento, Calif.: Baptist Church fracas in, 105-106; secret meeting between Broderick and Gwin, 140-141
Sacramento *Union,* 182, 202
San Dimas mines, Mexico, 292
San Francisco: ballot-stuffing in, 86; Broderick machine in, 86-88, 115-116; criminal excesses in, 115-118; Gwin's first sight of, 30; murders in, 115; Navy Yard, 73, 109; Tammany type organization in, 86;